Game
OF
Thieves

Game
OF
Thieves

Robert R. Rosberg

Library of Congress Cataloging in Publication Data

Rosberg, Robert R   1930-
  Game of thieves.

    1. Robbery—United States—Case Studies.
2. Burglary—United States—Case Studies. 1. Title.
HV6658.R67   364.1'552'0973   80-18168
ISBN 0-405-13687-0

Manufactured in the United States.

Third Printing — 1985

Cover Design by Gary Glaser

For Kurstan: The littlest cop of all

ACKNOWLEDGEMENT

I wish to thank the more than 100 police officers, sheriffs, special agents of the Federal Bureau of Investigation (in service as well as retired), prosecutors, newspaper reporters, archivists, victims and those currently incarcerated, for their excellent cooperation and recall relating to the cases involved.

I am especially indebted to Mrs. Pauline Vaughn for her patience, understanding and dedication in preparing this manuscript over the past three years, and to my good friend, Bill Gunn, who provided much of the research material and technical advice needed to complete GAME OF THIEVES.

R.R.R.

CONTENTS

PREFACE

Robert Rosberg is a full-time financial and industrial security practitioner who has developed a unique understanding of criminals and criminal technology through years of indepth study and experience. He has hobnobbed with the "Willie" Suttons, spent time behind bars as a volunteer participant in a state prison program, dissected every major innovation in forcible bank crimes of the past 20 years, and lectured at law enforcement academies here and in Canada. In brief, he has *earned* the reputation he holds as a foremost authority in an increasingly important anticrime field—that of bank robberies and burglaries.

By definition, robberies are *personal* crimes. That is, they involve confrontation between criminal and victim and thus, at least, the implied threat of physical harm. Burglaries and larcenies, on the other hand, are *property* crimes.

The latest available federal statistics, those for the 1979 calendar year, show that 7,037 violations of the Federal Bank Robbery and Incidental Crimes Statute were committed during those 12 months. Robberies and attempted robberies comprised 88.7 percent of that total. Burglaries (which numbered 552) and larcenies (337) accounted for the other 11.3 percent. In addition, 192 federal Hobbs Act violations—that is, extortion-type crimes—involving financial institutions also occurred in the year 1979.

A combination of factors underlies the sharp rise in forcible crimes against financial institutions. Prominent among them is the marked increase in the number of potential targets available to those bent on bank burglary or robbery. The second half of the 20th century has witnessed a mushroom growth of bank, savings and loan, and credit union offices in cities and suburban areas across the United States. The result: by early 1979, there were no less than 90,000 such offices from the Alaskan tundra to the Keys of Florida—roughly twice as many as there were in 1960.

FBI computations, however, disclose that in 1977 there was one violation of the Federal Bank Robbery and Incidental Crimes Statute for every 18 financial institution offices covered by that law. The comparable figure for 1960 was one violation for every 53 such offices. Thus, forcible crimes against financial institutions have been growing at a far greater rate than have banking offices.

Basic to the increase is the fact that more people are committing bank robberies now than ever before. Who are these people? They constitute a virtual cross section of the troubled *and* the troublesome members of our society. Some are hardcore professionals—such as the "Mutt and Jeff" duo credited with ransacking more than a score of banks in the New York area in the mid-1970s. Others are financially pressed working people—such as the midwest laborer who robbed nearly a dozen banks in the 1970s, apparently while en route from home to job site. They also include such bizarre characters as the self-professed revolutionaries of the Symbionese Liberation Army who staged a bank robbery in San Francisco in April, 1974, to showcase Patricia Hearst. And their ranks further include mental incompetents and emotionally disturbed people, as well as the intellectually gifted. In fact, a magna cum laude graduate of an elite New England university was charged with taking part in two bank robberies in the early 1970s, including one in which a police officer was killed.

When a veteran member of a metropolitan police department was asked some months ago to describe the "typical bank robber," he provided this profile: male, between 18 and 25 years of age, unemployed, unskilled, and undeterred by a previous arrest record. One such "typical bank robber," a teenager facing multiple charges at the time, philosophically stated to a newspaper reporter in 1978 that "bank robberies ain't no big thing." It was a flippant remark which earned him far more public attention than he bargained for, and while it cannot accurately be said that federal policymakers share this young hoodlum's views, certain parallels which invite examination do exist.

With little public fanfare or notice to the banking community, the Department of Justice embarked on a program in the mid-1970s that has (1) decreased the federal government's role in prosecuting persons arrested for forcible crimes against financial institutions and (2) shifted more responsibility for the investigation and prosecution of such crimes to state and local authorities. Heralding the change was a letter that was sent from Washington to the offices of all United States attorneys in April, 1974. The letter urged them to encourage more prosecution in state courts of crimes which constitute violations of state, as well as federal laws.

Bank robberies are among the best known of these "joint jurisdiction" crimes, and although evidence is lacking to show how effective both ends of the "transfusion" have been, the record clearly shows that federal prosecutions of bank robbery cases have dropped appreciably since 1974. This fact was highlighted by a Justice Department official who told a committee of the United States in 1978:

"I might point out that the number of federal prosecutions for violations of (the) Bank Robbery and Incidental Crimes (Statute) has decreased in each fiscal year since 1975. For example, in 1975 we filed approximately 2,400 such cases; in 1976, the prosecutions totalled approximately 2,100; in 1977, only 1,800 cases. . . . (It) simply is the fact that many, many fewer bank robberies are being prosecuted in the federal system."

Despite this decrease in federal prosecutions, however, on December 31, 1977, convicted bank robbers still comprised more than 23 percent of the federal prison system's 22,557 inmates—a statistic that says much about the traditionally effective manner of the government's handling of these cases over the years.

Additional pressure for a pullback of federal effort has been exerted by the General Accounting Office, an auditing arm of the Congress. After a study of some 230 bank robbery cases by members of its staff, GAO issued a report in 1978 recommending that the Attorney General (1) . . . direct the FBI to establsih and carry out a plan to minimize the federal investigative involvement in bank robberies" and (2) ". . . establish prosecutive guidelines for bank robbery to minimize federal prosecution except in cases where federal procedures facilitate prosecution."

To those most deeply concerned about the possible consequences of a major reduction of federal effort in this criminal area, a highly disturbing paragraph of the 1978 GAO report is one which reads:

"The FBI places a high priority on solving all bank robberies. On the other hand, the local police generally treat bank robberies as just another robbery unless there are injuries or significant losses. Consequently, the FBI and local police differ substantially in the resources they apply to investigating bank robberies. In addition, the FBI's commitment to solving bank robberies enables it to actively pursue investigations longer than local police generally consider justifiable in light of their other investigative priorities.''

An indication of how extensive that FBI commitment has been can be found in the fact that during fiscal 1977, the FBI devoted 980 work years—or 8.5 percent of its investigative resources—to meeting the challenge of forcible crimes against financial institutions. In 1978, however, administration officials slashed roughly 20 percent—the equivalent of about 200 work years—from the same area of a subsequent FBI proposal, and although Congressional watchdogs played a key role in having part of that cutback restored, it has become abundantly clear that Washington policymakers are firmly committed to shifting additional criminal justice responsibility *and* expense to state and local jurisdictions.

The prospect of such a federal retrenchment has been a source of grave concern not only to law enforcement and other criminal justice officials, but to members of the business, industrial, and financial communities as well. Thus, Bob Rosberg adds to our comprehension of modern day crime and criminals—and of bank robbers and burglars, in particular—at a most propitious time.

From his extensive archives of bank robbery and burglary cases, Mr. Rosberg has selected a handful of the most interesting crimes to share with the readers of this book. His accounts of these cases are memorable not only because they provide an insider's view of how the offenses occurred, but because they shed light on the often bizarre and unpredictable nature of the criminals involved.

G. William Gunn
Former Special Agent
Federal Bureau of Investigation

INTRODUCTION

"For as long as man has had a need to protect valuables from his enemies, other men have devised ways to steal them. It has, and probably always will be, a professional game of 'wit and out-wit'."

Unknown

Burglars are my business and have been for the past twenty years. As a professional but legal safecracker, I have taught burglary attack methods and techniques at many of our nation's most prestigious police academies, colleges and criminal justice schools, including the Federal Bureau of Investigation's Training Academy at Quantico, Virginia; National Crime Prevention Institute, Louisville, Kentucky; Bureau of Narcotics and Dangerous Drugs, Washington, D.C., and many colleges and universities offering law enforcement curriculums.

As a teacher of this unusual subject, I have found that the vast majority of my students—police officers, federal agents, insurance executives, crime prevention specialists and industrial security directors—did not fully understand how vulnerable to attack some of the protection devices and systems used in business really are, even by the most amateur criminals. This statement is not intended as an indictment against the education of the security world, but rather a graphic illustration of the almost total lack of communication surrounding the broad subject of burglary risk management.

Few security practitioners have felt it prudent to discuss such proprietary information as safe cracking techniques, burglar alarm "defeats" or deadenings, and other areas of related knowledge, even with law enforcement officers with proper credentials. As members of private industry, and representatives of one of the world's most reputable security organizations—The Mosler Safe Company—my colleagues and I, founders of the Mosler Anti-Crime Bureau, have tried to lessen the gap between sound security practices and knowledge of the criminal who is dedicated to taking what doesn't belong to him. One of the newer methods of instruction to help reduce this threat is an actual demonstration of how the burglar works his trade, the tools he uses and the cunning with which he carries out his objectives.

Robbers and thieves, by and large, are an unusual breed of criminal. They are craftsmen, engineers, often highly intelligent individuals, but by far their greatest assets are their cunning and their disregard for physical harm. As a general rule, burglars are not violent men. Rather, they are a clever lot depending largely on trick, deception, planning, timely execution, guts and often, plain luck. Seldom do they ever harm victims trapped during the execution of their hit. And while no attempt is made here to understand the psychological side of the burglar—why he does what he does, what motivates him to do "his thing"—it is the purpose of this book to unfold, through documented case histories, how the thief hits his mark.

Most of the cases cited happened as they are related. In several of the episodes I have chosen to dramatize scenes and create dialogue in order to put the reader into the action. In each instance, however, every effort has been made to offer an accurate and realistic accounting of the facts. All of the characters are real people and only where right of personal privacy may jeopardize individuals have identities been changed.

Not all burglary or robbery attacks are committed in stereotypic fashion. As a matter of fact, most of the more spectacular jobs perpetrated today are unique, bizarre incidents.

The Game of Thieves is a collection of true stories that clearly illustrates, "If you've got what I want, I'll get it." Each case was selected for its unusual modus operandi (MO) and non-conformity to the run-of-the-mill hit. In no way do the cases reflect actual "how to" methods and all sensitive types of attacks, penetration and defeats have been purposely altered or omitted. In some instances, the actual event might have been avoided if certain security measures had been taken, while in others the people involved became victims of circumstance and fell prey to the mercy of the thieves.

PART I
The Burglars
—"A Game of Wit"

1

INCREDIBLE SCORE AT LAGUNA NIGUEL

"Perhaps the biggest bank score in U.S. history. The men who executed it were among the best in the business. But five major mistakes cost them 5 million dollars and 20 years."

Evan Maxwell
Staff Reporter
Los Angeles Times

1972 was a bad year for Amil Dinsio and his friends. One of the nation's slickest bank burglars, Dinsio thought he had it all—two bank jobs within 45 days netting his gang of thieves between 5 and 8 million dollars—but then the walls came tumbling down.

Evan Maxwell, staff reporter for the *Los Angeles Times,* followed the case at United California Bank's Laguna Niguel branch from the time of the burglary to the successful prosecution and sentencing of the thieves. His insightful newspaper series, along with official court records and in-depth interviews with F.B.I. special agents, and the Orange County, California, sheriff's department, plus others who wish not to be named, provide the basis for this amazing story.

At age 36, Amil Alfred Dinsio had already earned notoriety as a master bank burglar. He was the best by far in his home territory of northeastern Ohio. And while he had never been convicted of any truly significant bank jobs, his name and MO were linked to as many as a dozen "scores" in the 1960's and 1970's—jobs that cost financial institutions more than 30 million dollars.

Amil was a nondescript individual of medium height and build, and it is unlikely he could have been singled out from other patrons in a crowded neighborhood bar. But Amil preferred this anonymity.

It helped keep him out of reach of the law, and if there is anything a professional bank burglar shuns, it's police attention.

Amil Dinsio never worked alone. The jobs he did required fields of expertise that one man or even two could not handle. They required training and experience in such diverse fields as explosives, weapons, electronics, mechanics and even bank security. The people whom Amil recruited were these types—and all but one of them were related by blood or marriage. There was Amil's brother James, as well as his brother-in-law, Charles Mulligan. There were the brothers Ronald and Harry Barber, sons of Amil's older sister. And there was 29-year-old Philip Christopher, a northern Ohio hoodlum who cast his lot with Amil in 1972 and broke the pattern of nepotism that had prevailed.

The Laguna Niguel job started in mid-February, 1972, when Amil, his wife and Charles Mulligan flew to Los Angeles from Cleveland. Amil's older sister lived in suburban South Gate with her husband and their youngest son, Ronald Barber, and it was there that initial strategy and planning began. It was February 18.

Amil's first task in California was to find a place to live, something close enough so that they could meet at his sister's South Gate home. The Jubilee Motor Inn, located a few miles away on Long Beach Boulevard in Lynwood, was perfect. Jack Cherniss, the owner-operator, later remembered the trio as they checked in; Mr. and Mrs. A. Dinsio of Poland, Ohio, were given the keys to Room 104, and Charles Mulligan from the same Ohio town was assigned to Room 144. During the next few weeks, Amil and Charles, with the aid of nephew Ronald and his 1969 Ford, toured the southern reaches of Los Angeles and Orange County in search of a score. Orange County, one of the wealthiest and most affluent in America, teemed with branch banks rich with deposits. It is not clear why Amil picked the Laguna Niguel branch of United California Bank, or how he even knew it existed. There is still some speculation that another bank, one located in San Clemente where former President Nixon had an account, was a primary target. If so, that target was abandoned in favor of Laguna Niguel, which is only 12 miles north on the busy Pacific Coast Highway. And its position may have been the key to Amil's decision to strike there.

Almost everything about the location was perfect. The prosperous branch, located at 6 Monarch Bay, is situated at one end of a neighborhood shopping center. More important, it is positioned high above the coast highway on an embankment. The front of the bank faces away from the main thoroughfare, and the back, exposed to the highway, opens onto a seldom-used service road where delivery trucks unload their commodities to the dozen or so shops and stores in the complex. During the day and evening hours, the Monarch Bay Shopping Plaza bustles with activity. A restaurant-bar about 200 yards to the north operates well into the night, and automobile traffic in and out of the shopping center doesn't settle down until close to midnight.

Dinsio and Mulligan visited the bank and surrounding area often during their midwinter stay in California. They went inside the one-story building and cased it thoroughly. The bank's vault is situated at the front of the customer lobby and to the left of the glass entrance doors. The back of the vault butts up against a common wall, with the Monarch Bay Drug Store on the other side. The drug store's cashier is positioned less than five feet from the adjacent vault wall—close enough to be aware of loud or unusual sounds in the bank, particularly during non-banking hours.

From the outside, the bank looks typically California-modern. Steeply slanting wooden shakes rise above a frontier-style overhang that shades customers along the multiple-store promenade. This imitation mansard roof hides a false ceiling and flat roof and also conceals a large rooftop air conditioner. It was perfect, because that was the point of entry Amil planned to use when they were ready to attack.

At the rear of the bank building, the side that faces the steep embankment and service road, the men noticed a seven-foot high redwood enclosure used to store unsightly refuse containers. They noted that it would make an excellent place to erect their ladder when the time came. Also on the rear wall, and partially hidden from the service road by a jog in the wall, there was an alarm bell about 10 feet above the ground. It would have to be silenced.

Visual measurements were taken of the bank building's exterior, and then written diagrams of the entire layout were carefully prepared.

To the east, and well beyond the shopping center parking lot, the Laguna Hills gradually rise almost 300 feet, revealing a panorama far over the Pacific Ocean. These hills would later provide an excellent observation point from which the bank could be monitored day and night.

While Amil continued his surveillance at Laguna Niguel, brother-in-law Charles Mulligan took time off to look up an old friend— Earl Dawson, whom he had known back in Ohio about 20 years before. Mulligan and Dawson had grown up together in Youngstown, and fresh out of high school the two boys had enlisted in the Air Force. After a four-year hitch Dawson re-enlisted, this time in the Marines, while his friend Chuck went his own way, a path that in later years led to several arrests for receiving stolen property and for bank robbery. In and out of jail, Mulligan, then 38, had turned to barbering as a profession.

On February 20, Mulligan phoned Earl Dawson at his Tustin, California, home and the two chatted, renewing their longtime friendship. Dawson told his old friend of his Marine career, his marriage and his recent retirement in 1971.

They decided to meet in an hour at the Lynwood Motel. There the two men had a few drinks in the motel bar and then a few more back at Dawson's home. That evening the pair returned to the Jubilee and talked in the motel bar, drinking again. It was past midnight when Dawson left to go home. But he did not arrive there until the next day. He fell asleep in his car outside an all-night diner.

The two men saw each other several more times during the course of the following three weeks. It was during this time that Charles Mulligan pursued more serious matters, for Amil had charged him with the responsibility of securing the mountain of tools and equipment the gang would need for the hit.

First Mulligan read the want ads, looking for a good used car. He easily found one he wanted. He made the purchase in cash and registered the 1962 bronze-gold Oldsmobile Super 88 under the name of Jimmy Elden Wright, 1517 Allen Street, Glendale, California. The name and address given were, of course, false. License plates issued to the car bore the numbers JFT-336. Now Mulligan was mobile and would not have to depend on Ronald Barber and his Ford for transportation.

During the next week, Mulligan started to hunt for tools and equipment, some of which he planned to hide in a specially-made false floor of the Oldsmobile's trunk. He acquired such devices as a Microflame cutting torch, forged steel hammer, V.O.M. meter, one-inch hole saw, sundry flashlights, batteries ranging from 1½ volts to 7 volts, assorted Allen wrenches, oxygen regulators, alligator clips and wire, and a Lafayette walkie-talkie 3-channel transceiver with altered frequencies. More equipment and tools would be obtained later.

On March 8, Mr. and Mrs. Dinsio and Charles Mulligan paid their bills at the Jubilee Motel and got ready to return to Ohio.

Two days before the Dinsios and Mulligan checked out of the motel, Ronald Barber and his older brother Harry, who may have come to California with Dinsio, drove to Laguna Niguel with the intention of finding a more suitable base of operations, closer to the United California Bank branch. The Barber brothers contacted Bond Realty Company and inquired about a condominium townhouse that was being offered for rent by the owner. The real estate saleswoman showed the men a "nice apartment" overlooking the El Niguel Golf Course only a mile and a half from the Monarch Bay Shopping Plaza. The rent was $300 per month. Ronald eagerly accepted the terms and paid nearly $1,000 for a three month lease on which he signed his own name and correct address in South Gate.

Between March 9 and 10, after Mulligan checked out of the Jubilee Motel, he drove his '62 Olds to Earl Dawson's and asked if he could leave the car parked there for a few weeks while he returned to Ohio. Dawson assumed that Mulligan wanted to leave it parked at the curb, but Mulligan insisted on keeping it in the garage, out of sight. Dawson finally agreed, still unaware of Mulligan's real motives.

Less than a week after Amil and Mulligan returned to Ohio, a small band of men gathered at Cleveland Hopkins Airport preparing to board United Airlines flight #73 bound for Los Angeles. It was March 15. The group who checked in at the gate included Amil Dinsio, Charles Mulligan, Philip Christopher and Harry Barber, Ronald's brother. Snow was still on the ground as the huge jet lumbered over the concrete apron waiting for flight clearance. The men spoke of better weather ahead, and as soon as the plane was airborne, some ordered the customary two drinks while the others made small talk or dozed.

It was still light when flight #73 touched down at Los Angeles International Airport. Each man gathered his luggage and presented his claim check to the security guard stationed near the baggage exit. One of the men hailed a Yellow Cab. Then they all helped load their luggage into the taxi's trunk and crammed in the front and back seats.

"Where to, gentlemen?" the cabbie asked.

One of the men, probably Harry Barber, responded with his mother's South Gate address. "That's a long way for a group of men to go in such crowded quarters," the driver was to recall later. But he put his hack into gear and drove off in the twilight.

Presumably after the gang checked in at the Barbers' home, young Ronald drove them to their newly rented townhouse in Laguna Niguel. James Dinsio was to join them there when he arrived from Ohio the following week.

During the ensuing days, Mulligan and others bought or scavenged more tools of their trade. Electric drills, a heavy duty motor, explosives and a specially tooled hammer with tapered head were on their list of needed equipment. They were now ready to begin. Amil Dinsio set the target date for the following weekend—March 24–27, 1972.

Their first operation was scheduled five to six days prior to the actual hit. A reconnaissance team including Amil, and probably Mulligan, drove to Monarch Bay late at night. With them they brought a ladder stolen from a Baptist church nearby. To make sure they were undetected, the men drove completely around the shopping center to the service road immediately behind the bank. So far, so good. As a final check, they drove around again, this time stopping behind the bank next to the high-fenced refuse enclosure. Here they unloaded the ladder and other equipment, including a hole saw, jig saw, some heavy duty cable and a can of tar pitch. Then the car disappeared around the corner onto the main shopping center parking lot. It is thought that only Dinsio and Mulligan remained, while the others may have driven east, to the Laguna Hills, where they could watch the entire scene.

Carefully the two prowlers opened the gate leading into the enclosure. Amil felt in his pocket to make sure he had a pouch of red pepper in case there were trained dogs on the premises. If there was anything a hound would succumb to, it was a spray of pepper in the snout.

The two men raised the ladder against the building. Only the top five feet were exposed because of the natural barrier provided by the fence. Slowly Amil climbed, one sure foot at a time. When he reached the top, he stepped onto the flat roof layered with tar paper and pitch. Then he motioned to Mulligan to withdraw the ladder into the safety of the enclosure.

The night was clear. No ocean fog had settled in as yet, and Amil easily made his way to the center of the roof where there was a huge air conditioner. Circling the unit, he searched for the 220 volt line that supplied power to the cooler and the entire building. He found it, just where he thought it would be. The blood started to flow heavily in his neck. It always did at the thought of a score. Hurriedly he retreated to the edge of the building and called down to his partner that he was ready to tap into the power line and connect his drill. Mulligan raised the ladder again and carried up the power cord, the saws and an extension light that Amil would need later after they broke through the roof.

Tapping into the line was an easy task for a man who knew electricity and electronics. In a few minutes, Amil had converted the 220 volt line to standard 110 VAC housepower. Now he was ready to connect the hole saw that would cut into the thin roof like butter. He tested the drill motor—bzzz. Perfect. Then he cut into the roof. In seconds a one-inch plug fell onto the false ceiling below. Next he used a jigsaw to slice through a manhole size opening. He made sure that he retrieved this 24 by 24 piece before it fell, possibly crashing all the way into the bank lobby. That would have put an end to the caper then and there.

With the roof entrance completed, Amil motioned to his partner to join him and to haul the ladder up too. Mulligan struggled with the extension ladder and carried it over to the relative safety of the air conditioner. By this time, Amil had affixed the electric drop light to a long cord and lowered it into the newly cut opening. On his stomach, he leaned in and for the first time saw the inside of the bank. The crawl space would provide adequate working room for the team when they returned the following weekend.

Dinsio and Mulligan then lowered the ladder into the bank, and Amil descended for a better look around. First he walked over to the place where they would make their entry; he figured that the vault ceiling was at least 18 inches of reinforced concrete, laced every 12 inches or so with 1-inch steel rods.

Then he scouted around for the telephone equipment box. It was here that he would later have to circumvent the vault alarm that would send a signal to a remotely located police monitor.

Within an hour, Amil Dinsio knew everything he needed for the real attack, and everything looked good. Climbing back up to the roof, he silently grinned to Mulligan and then thrust his hand forward, forming a circle with his thumb and forefinger, which was the "go" sign. Mulligan understood.

Before leaving the roof, the two men put the makeshift entrance back into place, and with the tar pitch glued the door back in place to conceal the fact that entrance had been made. As a safeguard, the men angled a small piece of broken mirror into the hardening substance in such a manner that it could be seen through binoculars from a lookout point on the Laguna Hills. Each day until the attack was made, a member of the gang would look for the reflecting mirror; if it were moved, they would know that the police or a bank employee had spotted the reconnaissance entry. They needed this extra bit of insurance.

After the men had finished the job, gathered up their tools and retreated down the ladder to the privacy of the refuse enclosure, one of them used the walkie-talkie to summon their car for pickup. Within minutes Amil and Mulligan were back safely with their friends, and they returned to the hillside lookout point. It was too dark to test the mirror trick—they'd have to wait until morning to do that.

During this time, however, the gang may have been frightened off, perhaps by a passerby or a police cruiser. Whatever the reason, the men departed in a hurry, because the next day, two boys, hiking along the hillside that overlooked the shopping center, stumbled on a ¾ horsepower electric motor that had been converted to a drill, a custom sledge hammer, several drill bits and a can of roofing tar. The boys, not knowing what the items were, turned them over to Laguna Beach police, who, in turn, entrusted them to officers of the Orange County Sheriff's Department. It wasn't until weeks after the burglary that officials connected the equipment with the score.

Amil and his friends were now ready for the real test. They had obtained a new drill and other equipment that had been found by the boys, and through spy-glass surveillance, were satisfied that no one had found their man-made rooftop entrance.

Although no know knows exactly how many men actually pulled the job, it is believed at least six and perhaps eight men took part.

It was now Friday night, March 24, 1972. The United California Bank at 6 Monarch Bay was closed for the weekend. The shopping center parking lot was devoid of traffic except for a few cars parked 200 yards to the north belonging to patrons of the bar.

Because of the unusual amount of equipment necessary to carry out the attack, at least two cars were used to transport the men and their tools to the jobsite. Slowly, one at a time, the drivers in their vehicles traversed the shopping plaza, looking for police cruisers, watchmen or others who might blow the whistle on the caper. As before, they entered the service road and drove past the bank, stopping near the embankment that shielded the complex from the Pacific Coast Highway. Quickly the men unloaded their gear, which this time included a quantity of burlap sacks, dynamite, electrical gadgets, sledges and cutting torches. Then the cars drove away, leaving the small gang hiding in heavy brush along the embankment. Again, they hoisted the 20-foot aluminum extension ladder which had been stolen from the Baptist Church. Each man was ready. Each had a specific job or jobs to do, and conversation was kept to a minimum.

Amil, the leader of the group, took a quick inventory of the equipment and a headcount of his men. Everything and everyone was set. Almost immediately one of the gang switched on his police scanner to begin monitoring emergency calls.

Quickly one of the gang raised the extension ladder against the right rear side of the bank—the short side that jutted out from Monarch Bay Drugs. It was partially concealed by the redwood fence and was hidden from highway traffic by the service road and embankment. Another man climbed the ladder to the bell housing, and with a large aerosol-type canister forced a mixture of freon and polyurethane through the bell louvers. Almost immediately the clapper froze, reducing the sound emitted by the bell to a leaden thud. Then, with another shot from the canister, he discharged more of the material into the structure. In several more seconds, the mixture hardened into a solid plastic, permanently disabling the clapper. All that could be heard was the continuous low whining of the bell, trying in vain to signal for help.

As soon as they had silenced the bell, the two men retreated to the embankment to monitor police calls. They waited in silence, hoping that their deadened bell (called a "defeat") hadn't triggered some other device and summoned police. Fifteen minutes passed with no unusual reports heard.

Next, as Amil had done the week before, he and a few of the others erected the ladder inside the refuse enclosure and quickly ascended to the roof. Kicking the glass mirror loose from the tar, the men then cut away the rest of the sealer and unplugged their secret entrance.

While this was being done, Amil reconnected the drop light and the auxiliary power for the drills. Then silently, armed with flashlight, electronics tool box and some fixed lengths of wire, he slid down the ladder and disappeared. One of the most critical elements of the job would come now—defeating the vault alarm which could trigger a signal at police headquarters.

Inside the vault a series of sophisticated alarm sensors guarded the interior against attacks employing cutting torches, explosion or physical movement. The vault door itself was protected by a triple movement timelock, which, when set, would not allow the door's locking bolts to be deactivated until a predetermined time on Monday morning. Amil knew there was nothing he could do to combat the timelocks, but he did feel reasonably certain he could deactivate the alarm. He was counting on it. Within the false ceiling there was a service walkway that led to a trapdoor, much the same as found in a house with an attic. After he had lowered himself to the main banking floor, Amil made his way to a storage room containing a telephone junction box. It was here that he hoped to defeat the alarm signal. With frequent reference to a printed diagram, Amil snapped alligator clips connected to prepared lengths of wire onto the terminal strips he had selected. In this manner he bypassed the real connection, preventing any true alarm from transmitting its signal farther than the equipment room.

As soon as the defeat was made, he left the way he had come, shouting for everyone to clear off the roof and retreat to the embankment. If his defeat techniques had failed, sirens would be audible within minutes. At least they'd have an even chance to split, to try again some other place, another night. The men huddled around the police monitor, but again they heard no dispatch to the darkened bank. To make sure the police were not using a special code unknown to the thieves, the men decided to wait another half hour. When no patrol car appeared, they nodded their approval, patted one another on their backs and resumed their plan.

Because construction at the shopping center had not been completed, the contractor had employed a private security guard to patrol the area at night. The guard's headquarters were in a temporary house-trailer about 150 yards to the east of the bank—in the same direction as the Laguna Hills lookout point. Although the officer made his rounds with regularity, he rarely spent more than a few seconds checking rear entrance doors along the service road. He posed no serious problem to the burglars. Not immediately, anyway.

Now that the bell and vault alarm had been silenced, the gang had a tougher job to do—to blast their way into the money room.

It was well past midnight, and several of the men climbed back up on the roof with drill rig and masonry bits. They lowered the drop light into the false ceiling and made their way over to the roof of the vault. While some of the group prepared to begin drilling, the others, still hidden on the embankment, began filling 20 burlap feed sacks with dirt. It was an arduous task lugging the heavy bags up the ladder and then into the crawl space, and took more than an hour.

Drilling into the vault ceiling proceeded slowly. It was an extremely noisy procedure, and lookouts kept watch from the roof of the bank, watching for the few pedestrians who left the bar only 200 yards away. When sufficient 1-inch holes were drilled into the 18-inch thick vault, explosive charges were packed into the cylindrical cavities. Then 9 of the heavy earth-filled sacks were placed over the holes, and the remaining 11 bags were stacked some distance away to form a protective shield. The explosives expert carefully wired the charges in series, played out his detonating fuse behind the earthen shield and motioned the remaining crew to exit to safety. It was now or never.

The restaurant bar was virtually empty now and the guard, hidden in his security trailer, was probably asleep. No unidentified cars could be seen in the shopping center parking lot, and those gang members not at specific lookout points gathered nervously around the police radio, ready for whatever might come.

The explosives man lay flat on the decking of the false ceiling, inching precariously close to the protective barrier.

Taking a deep breath, he clenched his teeth, shut his eyes tightly, and then triggered the device. KaBoom! In an instant, a fierce explosion ripped into the vault, with most of the blast forced downward because of the heavily weighted dirt bags on top. The initial concussion lifted the explosives man off the floor and seriously impaired his hearing for a short time. The dust produced in such a confined area was intense.

Those on the embankment cringed when they heard the explosion, thinking every resident in Laguna Niguel must have heard it too. If a call were placed to police headquarters, it would take several minutes for a cruiser to respond, and the patrol car, not knowing exactly what happened or where, would probably not approach with siren or flashing lights. Lookouts with walkie-talkies would advise the team if such an approach were observed. Within seconds of the blast, the small gang raced for the ladder, climbed up and headed for the roof opening, which was now spewing dust and smoke.

"You okay down there?" one of the men shouted. At first there was no response. The explosives man was still badly shaken.

Then the bandits heard a faint voice from within the enclosure. "Yeah, I'm okay. Bring me a fan. I can't see a damn thing down here."

An exhaust fan ran for the balance of Friday night, clearing away the stench of sulphur and blast fumes, smoke and dust. The bomb had done its job. Initial investigation, after debris was shoveled away, revealed a gaping two-foot hole that exposed a criss-cross of steel reinforcing rods.

"We'll finish the job tonight," Amil instructed, as the men made preparations to leave the bank until after dark on Saturday.

Weekend traffic at Monarch Bay Shopping Center was normally heavy. The adjoining drug store opened for business as usual, and the bar traffic picked up shortly after noon. The only tell-tale evidence that the bank had had visitors the night before was the outside bell, slightly dripping with hardened plastic, and some freshly-dug dirt deep in the brushy embankment. A few surveillance passes by some of Amil's crew on Saturday revealed no suspicious movement by police. All went well during the day.

As the sun set over the Pacific Ocean, Monarch Bay again took on the look of a deserted town. Shop owners closed their doors and disappeared for a weekend of relaxation. By 11:00 p.m. on Saturday only bar patrons remained. When it seemed safe, Dinsio and his friends again pulled up behind the bank and unloaded their equipment which, for this phase of the operation, included cutting torch, oxygen, sledges and other special tools needed when they finally broke into the money vault.

When the men slipped back into the false ceiling, much of the dust had settled and the air was at least breathable inside.

Torching the reinforcing rods proved easy, and within an hour the ragged hole was ready for final entry. One of the men sat in the opening and with several good kicks broke the acoustical ceiling fragments and dropped into the darkened tomb. The site Amil had selected for the blast was perfect. It was immediately over a group of filing cabinets, and the first man merely stepped on the metal container and then jumped to the floor. Also inside, conveniently, was a small step stool used by customers with rented safe deposit boxes stacked too high to reach comfortably. This was immediately placed on top of the file cabinet to provide easy access for the others.

Eager to see what spoils they were about to retrieve, a second and third man dropped into the vault, using the stool placed on top of the files as a step. The men were ecstatic as they counted rows and rows of shiny steel safe deposit boxes. One hundred, two hundred— a total of five hundred little safes waited to be cracked open with the specially made, tapered sledge hammer. The double key round locks would be no match for such a powerful tool.

It was early Sunday morning, March 26, when the gang started punching the shiny metal boxes open. The men started their work in orderly fashion, first popping open the doors and removing the bond tins, then neatly stacking them on the vault floor. But as their work progressed, the sight of a veritable mountain of cash, jewels, securities and collectors' coins turned the men from cool profes-

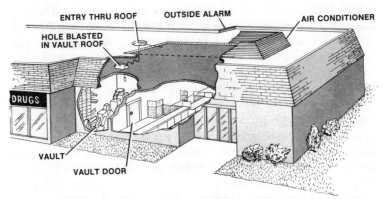

This cut-away drawing of the Laguna Niguel Bank illustrates the burglar's route through the roof and ceiling of the bank vault.

sionals to nearly crazed pirates. As they randomly smashed and sledged with frenzied motion, the small room became a scene of utter destruction. Boxes, locks, tins and a chaotic litter of paper and money were spewn everywhere. Soon there was no more room to work.

Time was also running out. Dawn would soon break over the Laguna Hills, and the men would have to abandon their work until Sunday night—their final chance for the loot and for escape. Amil and his friends couldn't take a chance working inside the vault on Sunday because Monarch Bay Drugs would be open. The drugstore cashier stood only five feet from the bank vault, and it was possible that the noise created by their hammering might be heard. This critical slip would certainly blow the whole caper. Again, the men slipped out of the bank, down the ladder and disappeared in the pre-dawn fog.

Sunday dragged on interminably. The men were edgy. So close, and yet so far from success. Amil knew that Sunday night or early Monday morning the scheme would end, and he wanted to make sure it concluded on the positive side. All during the ordeal, the men had been careful to wear cotton work gloves and to leave behind nothing that would yield a clue to their identity. Time and again they retraced their steps, picking up such seemingly innocent things as cigarette butts, broken drill bits, and other items that might prove helpful to police investigators. Every tool used was wiped clean.

To pass the time and further dispose of some burglar equipment, Amil, Charles Mulligan and young Ronald Barber came out of

15

hiding long enough to visit Mulligan's old friend Earl Dawson again. It was Sunday afternoon when the trio stopped in front of Dawson's Tustin home. As a diversion, Mulligan invited Earl and his wife to have a drink with him at a neighborhood bar. While they were gone, Amil and his nephew transferred the burglar tools to the 1962 Oldsmobile still parked in the Dawson garage. They stashed everything in a false bottom of the trunk and then neatly relaid a shag carpet over the floor, leaving only the spare tire exposed. One of the men also left three articles of loot in the car—three valuable gold coins—an 1886-S Liberty Head $5 gold piece, an 1849-D extra fine Liberty Head $1 gold piece, and an 1849-O Liberty Head $1 gold piece. The value of the coins was later estimated at $500.

An hour or so later, Mulligan and the Dawsons returned home, and the three burglars departed to spend the rest of the day at their rented condominium townhouse.

As Sunday finally gave way to night, the gang returned to Monarch Bay and their final attempt to get the loot. The drugstore was now closed and the shopping center was silent. Upon entering the vault, one of the men smashed the glass-covered triple movement timelock, an act that would prevent bank officials from opening the vault on schedule Monday morning. Then with fevered pitch they continued punching safe deposit locks, extracting what bank and law enforcement officials later believed was at least $5,000,000 in negotiable instruments—cash, coins, diamonds, stock certificates, treasury notes, bonds, and travelers' checks. Altogether, 458 boxes were entered. The sheer bulk of the loot was incredible. After pouring their new-found riches into the feed sacks they had brought, the gang left the way they had come.

They then carefully wiped clean the El Niguel Golf Course condominium, and some of the gang flew back to Ohio. The rest returned on Wednesday, the 29th. Before leaving town, however, Dinsio and Mulligan paid one final visit to Earl Dawson, still the unsuspecting friend. While Amil engaged Earl in conversation on the latter's back porch, Mulligan deposited a few remaining tools in the loaded Oldsmobile trunk. In another five minutes, the two men departed. It was over. Amil Dinsio and his friends were successful. Or so they thought.

It was now Monday morning, March 27. The Laguna Niguel branch of United California Bank was about to open for business. Bank employees arrived one by one, and shortly before opening time, an employee twirled the combination dial as usual. Nothing happened. The door didn't budge. It was tried a second time, then a third. Still nothing. The predicament was reported, and others tried to open the door. Results were the same. In desperation, the branch manager phoned another bank for temporary operating funds. Eventually the lockout was reported to headquarters and a locksmith was summoned. He tried every trick known for such an emergency, but all attempts to open the vault failed. It was midafternoon when the service man finally conceded that repair of the lockout was beyond his capability, or anyone's capability, and that physical entry methods were necessary. The best way to gain entry would be through the roof of the vault, the service representative explained. In this way there would be no mess and unsightly repairs on the banking floor.

The locksmith climbed into the crawl space to check out the situation, but even before he reached the vault area he knew someone had already done the job. Concrete chunks, mutilated feed sacks, bits of metal rods and other debris were all he could see. Peering into the man-made hole, he then saw what he had feared— more rubble, but most disheartening, empty safe deposit box containers. The time was now 3:45 p.m., and immediately police and the F.B.I. were notified.

As the hours and days immediately following the incredible heist passed, more police and special agents of the F.B.I. were assigned to the case. By the end of March, more than 135 law enforcement personnel were digging into the mystery of Laguna Niguel. The search for clues continued around the clock, but little of value was found. The exhaust fan, broken drill bits and stolen church ladder provided little information. At last, after sifting through the damaged feed sacks, agents did find portions of a dynamite cap used to detonate the explosion.

With meticulous care, the investigation crew sorted, matched and inventoried everything in the vault, storing the contents in 55 gallon drums in the basement of the bank. In one of the bond tins they even found the cremated remains of a customer. Then, four days after the burglary, several coupons from stolen treasury bonds were cashed at a bank in New Orleans. But the trail ended there.

As the investigation mounted, customers, employees, deliverymen and others who frequented Monarch Bay shops were questioned. Had they heard or seen any unusual activity that weekend? Patrons at the bar said that in retrospect they thought they had heard something, but had paid little attention.

Box renters were questioned. Some remembered exactly what

they had stored in the bond tins, while others either didn't remember or refused to answer. Officials believed that those not offering specific cash losses might be trying to hide records from Internal Revenue men.

One woman did offer some unusual information. She had made it a practice to record and store the serial numbers of several bills that had significant meaning to her—money that was brought home after memorable vacation trips. Maybe this, she thought, would help if the money was ever recovered.

Then there was the mounting problem of who was liable for the loss. The bank? The vault manufacturer? The alarm company? As this book is being written, some of these questions still are not answered legally.

Then on the night of May 4-5, six weeks after the multimillion-dollar California job, another bank was burglarized by thieves using precisely the same MO. This one was 2000 miles to the east, in Lordstown, Ohio, about 10 miles west of Youngstown and 20 miles from the small town of Poland, Ohio. The victim was the Second National Bank of Warren (Ohio), Lordstown branch. The loss was estimated at $430,000.

F.B.I. investigators immediately recognized the similarity to Laguna Niguel; it was unmistakenly the work of the same gang. But again, there were no clues, no fingerprints, nothing of value left behind.

For Amil Dinsio and his friends, it was here that the walls began to tumble. Frustrated that so few clues had surfaced on either job, F.B.I. special agents at last got a break. In an affidavit later made public, Amil Dinsio admitted he had made a fatal mistake. He had talked about the Ohio job to the wrong people. This information, coupled with the similarity of the MO at Lordstown and Laguna Niguel, set off a tidal wave of investigation that led to three arrests within 60 days.

The string of events leading to those arrests was as dramatic as the burglary itself.

After the Laguna Niguel incident, the F.B.I. had compiled a list of suspects known to be capable of pulling such a complex job. Their list included individuals from Chicago, Kansas City and the Cleveland area. Then when the Lordstown job occurred, they immediately zeroed in on Amil Dinsio. All major airlines were requested to search their computers for passengers who had travelled to Los Angeles several weeks before the burglary. United

Airlines, a major air carrier from Cleveland to the west coast, responded that they had come up with not one but four names on the search list. It was too good to be true. The four had boarded United flight #73 in Cleveland on March 15 bound for Los Angeles. Each had used his own last name and first initial—"A. Dinsio," "C. Mulligan," "P. Christopher," and "H. Barber." That was mistake number one.

UAL's records also disclosed that eight days later, on March 23, one "J. Dinsio" flew from Cleveland to Los Angeles.

Then another bit of luck. At Los Angeles International Airport, agents located a taxi driver who recalled having driven a group of men from the airport to South Gate shortly after UAL flight #73 landed on March 15. The South Gate address furnished by the cabbie proved to be the home of Amil Dinsio's sister and her husband and son Ronald. Furthermore, when a group of "mug shots" was shown to him, the taxi driver tentatively identified pictures of Amil Dinsio and Charles Mulligan as two of the passengers.

Agents didn't want to tip their hand by questioning the family just then. Instead, they started checking all of the motels in the immediate area, hoping to find out where the men had nested during their stay in California. Again their investigation paid off. Jack Cherniss, owner of the Jubilee Motor Inn, had no record of Dinsio and his cohorts on March 15, but he did produce records showing that Mr. and Mrs. A. Dinsio of Poland, Ohio, and Mr. Charles Mulligan, also of Poland, Ohio, had been guests at the motel from mid-February through early March, 1972. Again, their real names gave them away. That was mistake number two.

The motel's records further disclosed that a telephone call had been made from Dinsio's room to a Tustin, California, number. That number belonged to Earl Dawson, who, it was learned, was a former resident of the Youngstown, Ohio, area. Now the noose was drawing tighter around Amil's neck.

Investigation in the Los Angeles area also led agents to the former owner of the 1962 Oldsmobile. He produced evidence that he had sold the car to a Jimmy Elden Wright on March 1. Additional leads uncovered in early June steered officials to Bond Realty Company, where a sales agent produced rental records showing that Ronald Lee Barber, using his real name, paid cash for a townhouse lease running from March 6 to early June. That was mistake number three.

Agents then obtained a search warrant for the golf course

apartment and began combing through it inch by inch, but almost nothing of value surfaced—*almost* nothing. Investigators and fingerprint experts had dusted everything in sight. And then suddenly another break came which produced the gang's fourth mistake. Someone had forgotten to push the button on the dishwasher. Fingerprints of five of the gang members were neatly preserved on the dirty dishes inside.

By late May, sufficient evidence had been gathered to warrant a grand jury investigation, and on May 31st Ronald Barber and his mother were subpoenaed to appear in Los Angeles before a federal grand jury. About the same time, federal agents visited Earl Dawson at his Tustin home. They arrived shortly after 10:00 a.m. on June 1, but found no one home. Not wanting Dawson to slip through their fingers, they questioned neighbors and local police, hoping someone might know his whereabouts. Police suggested they try a nearby bar. Before noon they had located their man. He was drinking beer and shooting pool in the pub that police had mentioned. Cautious, and uncertain whether Dawson was a member of the gang, the agents suggested that he accompany them to his house where they could talk in private.

For the next few hours, two F.B.I. men intensely questioned the suspect concerning Charles Mulligan and the Laguna Niguel burglary. Dawson became visibly shaken by the questioning, repeating over and over that, yes, he did know Mulligan, that his friend had visited him several times during February and March and that Mulligan had left his Oldsmobile parked in the garage. Oldsmobile? The F.B.I. men wondered if that were the key that would spring the lock on the case.

The questions continued at near-combat pace, and it became increasingly clear to Dawson that his friendship and hospitality had been grossly abused by the visitors from Ohio. They had caused him to become a suspect in a major criminal investigation, and he repeatedly assured the agents not only of his innocence, but of his complete willingness to cooperate with them.

Then the phone rang, bringing temporary relief from the inquisition. It was midafternoon. The caller was Charles Mulligan, and he was phoning from Chicago. Perhaps he had been frightened, knowing Ron Barber had been subpoenaed and that the dragnet was out for him. He told Earl that he was on his way to Los Angeles to pick up his car and would be there in a few hours. Mulligan sounded nervous. He told Dawson he thought he was being followed but would try to ditch his pursuers and then come to

Tustin. During the conversation Dawson volunteered his permission for the agents to listen.

"Where should we meet?" Mulligan asked. They agreed that it should be a nearby bar called the Walnut Room.

When Dawson hung up, the agents, feeling a bit more comfortable with their suspect, immediately phoned their office to request permission to search the garaged Oldsmobile. By 8:00 p.m., a federal magistrate had signed the search warrant authorizing the F.B.I. to search the Oldsmobile in Dawson's garage, and a team of special agents was dispatched to open the trunk. They lifted the carpet and false floor door lid. It was all there—burglar tools, two-way radios, shotgun, oxygen regulators, brown cotton work gloves and even a pouch containing red pepper to ward off guard dogs. Also found were three bright gold coins, still wrapped in protective plastic containers. The list of items covered almost four typewritten pages. This information was later presented as evidence in the trial.

When fingerprint experts processed the load of equipment, they found the gang's fifth mistake. Although Amil Dinsio had been so careful to wipe all evidence away, he apparently had forgotten to check the small batteries inside his flashlight, and one clear set of his fingerprints was obtained.

While lab technicians remained at the Dawson home, other agents and a handful of police detectives and deputy sheriffs left for the Walnut Room with Dawson. One agent went to the bar with Earl, while others casually seated themselves in the lounge or positioned themselves strategically outside.

As the time approached for Mulligan to appear, the agent sitting next to Dawson disappeared in the background. Everyone waited. Just before 11 p.m., Charles Mulligan appeared in the doorway accompanied by another man—a cab driver. Sidling up to his friend at the bar, Mulligan asked Dawson if he was alone or if anyone in the place looked suspicious. Then he told Earl about his suspicions of being followed, indicating that the cab driver had brought him there in a roundabout way, which was why it had taken so long.

As the two men talked, Mulligan asked Earl if there was a lake close by where he could dump some tools. At first Dawson played dumb but then took a chance and asked, "Chuck, did you have something to do with that two million dollar burglary at Laguna Niguel?"

"Now, Earl, you know me better than that. Besides it was more like five million."

"What do you do with that kind of money?"

"You don't get as much as you might think," Mulligan continued. "Between thirteen and eighteen percent of the value."

Dawson felt more comfortable talking about it now that he had broken the ice. Then he asked a key question. "How many were involved?"

"Six plus two," came the quick reply. During and after the trial this answer continued to puzzle authorities.

The two men talked until after midnight and then Dawson, pleased with his interrogation, invited Charles to spend the night at his house. They paid the bill and got up to leave. When Mulligan stepped outside, he was greeted by police who quietly took him into custody.

"It was funny," one officer said later. "He didn't say a word."

Charles Mulligan was taken to Los Angeles and booked. Unfortunately, the story of his apprehension leaked out, and the following day newspapers across the nation broadcast that the Laguna Niguel robbery was on the verge of being solved.

Harry Barber immediately fled, and remained a fugitive for eight years. His gold-colored Cadillac was found at Cleveland's Hopkins Airport. The others were not so lucky.

Ronald Barber undoubtedly read the story and left his South Gate home. He remained at large until January 15, 1973, when agents apprehended him in a Rochester, New York, apartment. Philip Christopher and Amil and James Dinsio must have felt there was not enough evidence to convict them and, knowing they were under surveillance, chose to remain in their homes. But they were wrong. Fingerprints on the dirty dishes had clearly shown that Amil Dinsio, Philip Christopher, Charles Mulligan and Ronald Barber had been in the gang's townhouse headquarters.

Christopher had been placed on probation in 1971 following his conviction in federal court in Cleveland involving a theft case. By travelling to California without permission of the parole and probation office, he had violated the conditions of his release, and a federal warrant for his arrest as a probation violator was issued on June 20, 1972. The following morning, F.B.I. agents and Cleveland police officers cautiously approached Christopher's Ruyard Street residence. Knowing the suspect might be armed, the Federal men took every possible precaution. One agent proceeded to a side door while others went to the front door. It was warm that day, and a back door was standing open. There was a young woman in the kitchen, and when the first agent identified himself, she ran into the front room, only to be met by other officers. The woman, purportedly the common-law wife of Christopher, told her visitors that Christopher was not home—that he had taken her son to school. Not believing her, the men started up a flight of stairs near the front door. The first F.B.I. man, who had entered through the kitchen and then had come into the living room, also started up the stairs. When he got to the top, Philip Bruce Christopher had already been apprehended by the first agents. The criminal stood in a bedroom doorway, clad only in short pajama bottoms.

He was told to back into the bedroom and sit on the bed. He obeyed. As one of the F.B.I. men passed an open closet door, Christopher started to get up but was told to remain seated. With pistol drawn, the first agent then began a search of the closet, believing a weapon might have been hidden there. The closet was full, and to the rear, hanging from a clothes rod, a garment bag obscured the dark interior. The agent brushed the bag with his free hand and foot, not sure if someone were hiding there. His foot felt a heavy object at the bottom of the garment bag. He unzipped it and found a tightly wrapped blue and white package; it was the same type of bag found while investigating the California case. Inside the plastic bag were several banded stacks of United States currency, some of which bore the teller's stamp of the Second National Bank of Warren, Lordstown Branch. The agent displayed the money to Christopher and asked how much was there.

"About $30,000," Christopher replied.

Actually there was $32,420 in the garment bag, along with several loose $5 bills. These were later traced back to the woman who had recorded the serial numbers.

The agents read the suspect his rights and asked if he understood the charges. Christopher responded affirmatively. He was given his trousers and other clothing and taken to police headquarters where he was booked.

Five days later—on June 26—a young boy accidentally unearthed a plastic water container on residential property across the street from Amil Dinsio's Boardman, Ohio, home. In it was $98,600. The following day Amil Alfred Dinsio was arrested at his home. On his person he carried $537 in cash. After Amil's arrest, agents armed with a search warrant returned to the Boardman house and turned it upside down, looking for additional evidence and loot. Again they hit pay dirt. Among the items found were a gold-plated silver dollar stolen from a renter's safe deposit box at Laguna Niguel, and a $20 bill that also was positively identified as coming from the California job.

In another search of the Boardman, Ohio, area some months later, F.B.I. agents uncovered a suitcase containing nearly $2.6 million in negotiable United States treasury securities and coupons. This was in addition to approximately $1,000,000 in registered securities found by a California road building crew in rough terrain near Laguna Niguel. Total loot recovered from the Lordstown job and the Laguna Niguel heist was just under four million dollars.

By July, 1972, Amil Dinsio and Philip Christopher were returned to Los Angeles to await trial with Charles Mulligan, who was already incarcerated. Ronald Barber, who was not apprehended until early January, 1973, and James Dinsio, Amil's brother, who was picked up February 5, 1973, would be tried separately later that year.

The first trial could not begin until September because of the veritable ocean of information to be sorted and catalogued. There were literally hundreds of exhibits to prepare: airline tickets, traced phone calls, currency serial numbers, motel records, fingerprints, and a huge cache of burglars' tools found in Mulligan's car trunk. Then there were witnesses: motel clerk, condominium owner and rental agent, cab drivers, airline personnel, bank officials and others. The prosecution worked for 110 days putting the case together, all the while beleaguered by questions from the three counselors defending the suspects.

Then a strange but fortunate series of events unfolded. Amil Dinsio had been assigned to module 2500 of Los Angeles County jail. In that same section of the jail was another previously convicted burglar. His name was Richard Arthur Gabriel—a man who had been sentenced to one year for house burglary. The two men, who were in separate cells, met for the first time in mid-July, exercising on what inmates call the "freeway," a common corridor on the cell block floor. A friendship quickly grew between the two, and it wasn't long before Amil confided in Gabriel, telling him how bank burglaries are committed. He even admitted pulling the Laguna Niguel job. Dinsio said he selected the United California Bank branch "because there were a lot of rich and retired people in the area and there was an obstacle near the bank where you couldn't be seen."

Then he elaborated on how he had silenced the bell, defeated the vault alarm and finally had blown the vault open with explosives. He described in detail how the gang had used radios to monitor police calls, how they had cut the steel reinforcing rods, and how

This collection of ordinary tools constitutes "typical burglar tools." The only suspicious looking piece is the gas mask.

they had hidden the tools in Mulligan's car. In short, he recounted the entire plot to another thief, a man whom he had just met.

One day as the two were talking on the "freeway," Dinsio asked his friend for a favor.

"He stopped me one day," Gabriel later testified, "and asked if I knew anyone who owned or operated an apartment or a motel. He said he wanted to be able to register so he could place himself there during the time of the burglary."

Dinsio asked if Gabriel could arrange for a girl to swear she was with him at the time. In exchange for his assistance, Dinsio offered a sum of cash, or $20,000 in negotiable bonds stolen from the bank.

It was all getting too complicated and involved for Gabriel, and he wanted to wash his hands of the whole thing. Maybe he could use the information for another purpose. Maybe it would help buy him a ticket to freedom!

By August 10, Gabriel had had enough. Through a contact in the Los Angeles County Sheriff's office, he asked to see someone from the F.B.I. Authorities were eager for his information and willingly worked with him. Then the prosecution joined them, and everyone agreed to continue the charade. Officials briefed their spy carefully so as not to tip their hand or become trapped in some legal maneuvers. They instructed Gabriel always to be the recipient of information—never to lead Dinsio into questions.

On August 14 Richard Gabriel was released from jail, but he maintained contact with F.B.I. men and the prosecutor's office. Shortly afterward Amil was released on $250,000 bond, posted by relatives who used personal real estate as collateral.

In the weeks that followed, Gabriel assured Amil that he could, indeed, supply the needed alibi. He handed Amil an area code 702 phone number and told him to call a certain person. Amil called the Las Vegas exchange and spoke with a man at the Frontier Hotel. He told the man what he wanted and the voice at the other end agreed to the scheme. A price was set, and shortly afterward Amil received a hotel receipt to sign, together with photographs of the room (inside and out), names of the entertainers who had performed that night and other pertinent information. If he were ever questioned in court, he would know exactly what his room looked like right down to the shower curtain. What Amil didn't know was that the man he had talked to at the hotel was a special agent of the F.B.I., and the entire conversation had been reported.

One final event of importance took place before the trial began on September 26. Gabriel, through continued contact with Amil

Dinsio, learned of an alleged plot to murder Earl Dawson to keep him from testifying. The trial judge was informed of this possibility, and immediately precautions were taken at the Dawson home to protect Earl and his wife. Fortunately, nothing happened.

The trial began as planned. It proceeded without incident, the prosecution offering more than 250 exhibits and witnesses, including Earl Dawson who was severely attacked by the defense. Then, after nearly three weeks of testimony, the prosecution unexpectedly called on Richard Gabriel. On October 26, exactly one month after the trial began, Gabriel told of his "freeway" meetings and the set-up at the Las Vegas hotel. The defense was visibly stunned but could do little to counter the allegation. Within an hour the prosecution rested its case.

Four days later, it was all over. The defense made its last plea and both sides presented final arguments. A jury of seven men and five women received the case and spent two days locked in secrecy to deliberate the four-and-a-half weeks of direct testimony and cross examination. It was just past 5 p.m. on November 2 when they reassembled in a nearly empty courtroom, the usually packed gallery now occupied only by a few relatives. All three men—Amil Dinsio, Charles Mulligan and Philip Christopher—were found guilty as charged. Sentencing was set for November 20, 1972.

Amil Alfred Dinsio was sentenced to 20 years in the custody of the Attorney General.

Charles Albert Mulligan was sentenced to 20 years in the custody of the Attorney General.

Philip Bruce Christopher was sentenced to 20 years in the custody of the Attorney General.

James Frank Dinsio and Ronald Lee Barber, who were separately tried and convicted of the same crime in May 1973, both received consecutive five-year and ten-year sentences and were remanded to the custody of the Attorney General.

Harry James Barber who had been a fugitive for eight years, was apprehended by F.B.I. agents in Brookville, Pennsylvania, on May 12, 1980.

2

HOW IT STARTED

Today's professional burglar is expert in electronics, demolition, intelligence gathering and even police tactics. He should never be underestimated.

Wilbur Rykert, President
National Crime Prevention Association

Perhaps the single most important reason for this book is to illustrate that no matter what man can build, he can also destroy—providing, of course, he has enough time and the proper tools.

The history of the modern-day safe does not begin until the middle decades of the 19th century. But robbers were plundering hidden wealth as far back as the time of the Egyptian Pharaohs. The pyramids, which were the burial places of the Pharaohs and of the incredible amounts of gold, jewels and other treasure that were to accompany them to the next life, contained clever and often deadly mantraps designed to ward off or destroy intruders. Live snakes and other venomous creatures guarded the tombs, but even these did not prevent many of the pyramids from being sacked.

In later centuries, wood and metal-strapped strong boxes were used to try to protect the fortunes of wealthy merchants. It was not, however, until the westward movement in the United States, when outlaw gangs ravaged and plundered unsuspecting pioneers, rural banks and large city enterprises, that a critical need for improved physical security arose almost overnight.

To provide the reader with a clearer understanding of the intricacies involved in the "defeating"—the technical term for deadening or destroying—of safes, vaults and alarms described in later chapters, it may be helpful to know the chronology and development of these devices, and something about the early burglars whose names are connected with them.

Between 1834 and 1867 no less than seven companies began to manufacture safes in southwestern Ohio alone—an area later to be known as the Safe Capital of the World. Early Cincinnati industrial directories listed such names as Victor Safe Company, Hall Safe Company, MacNeale and Urban, Diebold, Inc. and probably the best known, the Mosler Safe Company.

But almost as fast as these fledgling manufacturers built their "burglar-proof" safes, cracksmen successfully penetrated them.

Competition soon became fierce and the new companies vied for leadership, often trying to seduce buyers with advertisements heralding "absolutely burglar-proof" safes. These heavy cast-iron boxes too soon fell prey to the ingenuity of the burglars.

From 1850 until the mid-1860's most safes were constructed of heavy steel plates, often held together with rivets or bolts. All had square or rectangular doors that provided little protection against explosives. Moreover, all safes of the period stood on wheels, and if the burglar's technology didn't permit him enough time to finish the job in one night, he would simply hitch up a team of horses and drag the heavy iron box out onto the street and pull it away. There were no alarms in those days, and in smaller communities there were often no police to apprehend the thieves.

But burglars were not the only concern of safe manufacturers. Fire was the real dread of businessmen. There is little doubt that the great conflagrations of the century—the Chicago fire in October 1871, Boston in 1889, Cripple Creek, Colorado in 1896, to name a few—were responsible for the loss of more cash and valuables than all of the money stolen by thieves during the entire century. Until the late 1850's most safes provided no fire protection at all for the contents. They were veritable ovens—conductors of heat—that literally cooked paper to ashes. The safe manufacturers answered the call by introducing "fire-proof" safes, great steel boxes heavily filled with a heat-dissipating concrete mixture specially formulated to absorb heat. From the outside, these fortresses looked much the same as their "burglar-proof" counterparts, but in reality they were not. Their massive wall thicknesses and weight were deceiving. Thin wall plates, with a fire-resistant mixture between them, were used instead of traditional, thicker armor plate.

Soon many customers bought fire models to store, not only records, but cash. Many banks and other financial institutions followed suit and, as a result, a whole new era of burglary attacks emerged—the "rip-and-peel" job. Using this method, the cracksman literally peeled away laminations of plate until the fire resistant

This handcrafted pigeon-hole vault (circa 1803) is typical of those used by early nineteenth century New England bankers.

"Gentleman's valuables chest" (circa 1820) is a cast iron box with a hand made key lock.

An overland mail safe constructed of metal plates. Adjustable leg skids and handles allowed for levelling and easy movement. (circa 1835)

concrete became exposed. Then he chopped his way into the interior.

Burglar attacks of the period generally were accomplished employing three basic methods: explosion, using either dynamite or nitroglycerine; sledging with heavy hammers that ultimately cracked iron plate; or peeling away laminations of steel with crow bar, steel wedge and sledge hammer.

Most professional cracksmen, or yeggs as they were often called by the fraternity, usually worked in small groups, not so much for protection or "safety in numbers" but because transportation of heavy equipment necessitated it.

They generally employed a scout or "gay-cat" who never took part in the attack for fear of later being identified and apprehended. He was a front, or advance man, who would case the banking house, counting room, jeweler or other mark selected by the gang's leader.

He often would come into a town posing as a peddler of novelties, a real estate broker or entrepreneur, and would make friends with local business leaders, often gaining their complete confidence. It was his job to ascertain the habits of bank employees, check on local police, the town sheriff and privately-hired watchmen. He learned their routes, noted street illumination and get-away routes, and listed train schedules, blacksmith shops and stables. A good scout was even able to cut telegraph and telephone wires.

Sometimes he would open a small account at the local bank, become interested in the safe or vault, and then strike up a conversation telling the manager how pleased he was to know that his funds were so well protected. Often the unsuspecting banker would show him the money chest, explaining how it worked.

"Look!" the banker would say proudly. "This safe has a new four-tumbler combination that has 100,000,000 possible combination settings. No one could get into this beauty." Then, a week or so later, the forlorn banker would be explaining a $50,000 loss to his board of directors.

As banking houses, particularly those in major cities, grew in size, safe manufacturers introduced vault doors that could be mass-produced. By 1875 these beautiful plate doors with very ornate day-gates graced the finest banking halls in the country. Constructed of one-half-inch solid steel hardplate with exposed boltwork and combination box on the inside, the door, its frame and vestibule were then grouted into reinforced concrete vault walls often measuring 12 or more inches thick. Many had beautiful landscape

This early "burglar-proof" safe had steel plates bolted to a cast iron outer shell. Striking with a heavy sledge hammer opened it.

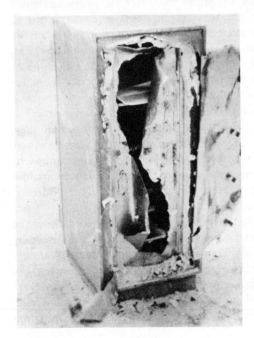

This is an example of an amateur attack on a record safe. The burglar hacked through the back of the safe with a fire axe.

33

scenes hand-painted on the exterior. And, of course, there was always the name of the proud owner lettered in gold leaf across the top of the door or frame.

By 1880 the traditional square door bank safe was rendered all but obsolete. Most could be penetrated in minutes by robbers not even claiming to be expert. Some outlaws were so brazen that to hit only one safe at night wasn't worth their while, and in at least one midwest city, Chicago, an entire business building was raked clean by thieves before dawn. Still, virtually all safe manufacturers continued to proclaim the fact that their equipment was "burglar-proof."

With the industrial age, many new machine tools and construction methods were introduced. Steam-driven grinding wheels, metal lathes and drills gave way to electric-powered machines. Milling machines capable of turning out a cannon breach that had doors measured in thousandths of an inch became common.

It was this technology that enabled the safe industry to develop the screw-type, round-door money chests. They operated like the cannon breach—the door was closed and screwed tightly into place between interlocking lugs that were cast into the body wall. Some models utilized highly desirable manganese as a primary metal. It was almost impervious to drills; moreover, it provided better resistance to explosion. The heavy round doors, often measuring 12 to 14 inches thick, were machined with such precision that when the breach door closed into the body wall, not even water could be forced inside. Experts believed this would eliminate the insertion of nitroglycerine in the cracks, as had been the practice in older, square-door models.

Most manufacturers immediately designed and patented variations of this new and mighty bastion of security. Again their advertising banners broadcast impregnability. This time, however, feeling confident that no explosive power was strong enough to penetrate the reinforced door and body walls, some companies added "completely" or "absolutely" to their standard "burglar-proof" headlines.

It was only a matter of time before these too crumbled under the crackman's hand. The earliest explosives jobs were accomplished by highwaymen or train robbers. Many were not successful simply because the explosive employed was dynamite. Following the westward push, horse-mounted gangs carefully followed east-west railroad timetables and at some point, usually an uphill grade, bandits would board the train, relieve passengers of their valuables

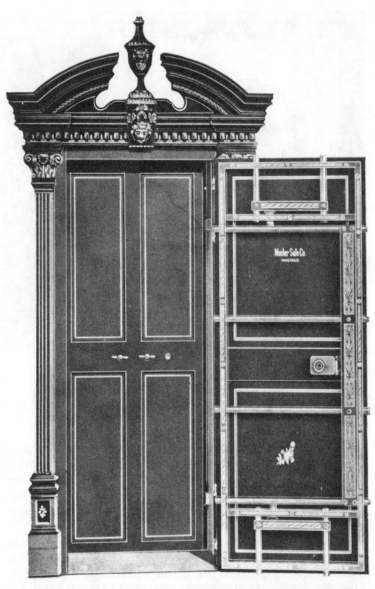

This is an example of an early ''mass produced'' bank vault door manufactured between the years of 1875 and 1890. The doors were beautifully made, often with gold leaf and hand-painted scenes on the front, with all boltwork and combination boxes safely inside.

This picture is of an actual attack on one of the newer cannon-breach money safes. Fissures in the safe body wall were caused by inserting nitro-glycerine in the door seam. Burglar slang in the late 1800s for this type of attack was, "puffing the Peter."

and then break into the baggage car, which was usually locked and guarded by railroad detectives. Here they would strap two or three sticks of dynamite around the safe and detonate the deadly material, using a short burning fuse. In most cases, the uncontrolled explosion would blow the safe, its contents and much of the baggage clear off the tracks.

In later years, nitroglycerine was substituted for dynamite. It was known as the "liquid of professionals." Because it was a very unstable substance, difficult to handle and transport, professional yeggs generally confined use of the high-powered ingredient to quiet rural banks where, after the thunder of explosion, quick getaways could be negotiated.

On a night selected by their scout, the gang would enter a town at the planned hour, usually midnight to three in the morning. A getaway man would hide in an alley with the horses while others took up lookout points in front and to the rear. Telegraph lines were cut at the last possible moment. The nitro expert carried, loosely fastened about his neck, a little rubber flask of "soup" (nitroglycerine) which, at the proper time, he used to "puff the Peter"— burglar slang for cracking a safe. The soup was carried in a rubber balloon to absorb any shock or sudden jar. In his pocket he carried a ball of putty or a bar of soap, well softened and pliable. He also had with him fuses or "puff-string," a box of matches, a candle and a small pocket pump or eyedropper for shooting in the soup. Other articles usually carried to the jobsite included sledge hammer, storage batteries, time clock to attach to the safe or vault, rolls of copper wire and a good supply of bandages—just in case.

Now positioned in front of the safe to be blown, the expert would begin to plaster all four sides of the door, using the putty or soft soap. At the top, he would fashion a small cup that permitted the liquid nitroglycerine to slither down the narrow crevices. Then, with eyedropper in hand, he carefully depressed the rubber ball plunger

On April 25, 1895, security industry consultants, using nitro-glycerine, successfully opened this screw-door-type money safe in just 33 minutes. Note the tool bag, nitro-glycerine vials, detonating wire and sledge hammer on top of the safe.

The Findlay Glycerine Company,

MANUFACTURERS OF AND DEALERS IN
TORPEDOES AND NITRO-GLYCERINE.

WORK DONE THROUGHOUT THE OIL FIELD.   ALL ORDERS PROMPTLY FILLED.
OFFICE, 108 WEST FRONT ST.

BOTH PHONES NO. 12.

Findlay, Ohio, June 19th, 1902.

Messrs. Hibbard, Rodman & Ely, 253 Broadway, N Y.

    Gentlemen: At the request of a banker for my opinion as to the effect
of nitro-glycerine applied to one of your Manganese Safes, and after a careful
examination of the construction of one of your No. 5 Manganese Safes, I feel
warranted in making the following proposition:

    On a wager of One Thousand Dollars ($1,000.00) I will undertake to open
one of your No. 5 Safes in thirty minutes from time of commencement of operation, said safe to be placed in my possession and I alone to operate on it.
Test to be made within thirty days from date hereof. Money to be deposited by
both parties in bank in county in which test is to take place one week prior
to test.   Very respectfully yours,

                            L. H. BROADWATER, Pres. & Gen. Mgr,

                                       Findlay Glycerine Company.

*This is one wager that was not accepted by the Hibbard, Rodman & Ely
Safe Company. In 1903 $1,000 was too much money to wager.*

*Hibbard, Rodman and Ely displayed their famous No. 5 manganese safe at
the Washington State Banker's Assoc. Convention in 1903. With claims
that it was "burglar-proof" they advertised that their safe was "entered for
competitive test with any other safe manufacturers."*

The safe in this photo was opened in 22 minutes — without explosives — debunking the myth of the burglar-proof safe once again.

and forced a few drops into the cup. Then he would repeat the process. The soap by now had hardened against the cold steel and kept the nitro from dripping on the floor. The newer round door models were more difficult to soup. These doors were machined to hairline tolerance, and often a preliminary small explosion was set to provide greater "grip" for a second blast.

When the expert was ready he placed blankets over the safe to help muffle the sound and reduce shrapnel spray. All was ready. The puffing string was inserted into the putty and played out a safe distance. Then ignition. Even with blankets and other coverings, the roar would be deafening, but it didn't matter. If the job were done correctly, the gang was in and out with what they came for in a matter of minutes.

As reports of successful attacks on the screw-door safe began to appear in newspapers, law enforcement officials and security company engineers showed concern for their ultimate weapon. Soon individuals (mostly safe owners) and private consulting groups started a campaign to disprove claims that were fast becoming false representations.

One such group conducted an explosive test on a safe that was legally removed for the purpose from the First National Bank of Effingham, Illinois. The date was April 26, 1895. Sledges and other tools were used to crack a seam in the door jamb wide enough to insert drops of nitroglycerine. An electrical charge then triggered the high explosive, blowing the door away from its crane hinge. A documented report indicated that the total time of the experiment was a mere 33 minutes.

On June 18, 1902, another experiment was initiated at the request of a banker. A telegram was sent to the owners of Hibbard-Rodman, Ely Safe Company of New York. The sender was Mr. L. H. Broadstreet, president and general manager of the Findlay (Ohio) Glycerine Company, manufacturers and dealers of torpedoes and nitroglycerine. The telegram offered a $1000 wager that Mr. Broadstreet could successfully open one of that company's No. 5 manganese models in 30 minutes or less. It is not known whether that bet was ever accepted, but soon afterward Hibbard-Rodman, Ely, through their authorized agent, Norris Safe and Lock Company of Seattle and Portland, Oregon, displayed a unit at the Washington State Bankers' Association convention. A placard on top of the safe read "Champion Burglar-proof Bank Safe of the World." A smaller inscription on the notice said, "Entered here for competitive test with any other safe manufactured." Representatives of Hibbard-Rodman, Ely, in order to prove their claim in front of an intrigued audience, watched technicians pit their expertise against cold steel. To the astonishment of those present, a team of experts opened the safe in a record 22 minutes—*without* use of explosives.

Probably the best-documented experimental attack on the formidable screw-door safe was made on the night of May 5, 1908, by William C. Clark, consulting engineer of Pittsburgh, Pennsylvania. His firm advertised, as its specialty, mob and burglar proof safe deposit vaults and bank safes—expert on high explosives. (Note: It is strange that a consultant who dealt in defeat techniques should announce his specialty as mob and *burglar proof* devices.) On May 20, 1908, Mr. Clark published results of an attack made legally on a bank safe which he successfully opened for his client, The People's National Bank of Economy, Pennsylvania. His public letter addressed, "To Whom It May Concern," read:

I know that you will be interested to learn that I have successfully opened one more of those so-called Manganese

The letter image with letterhead:

WILLIAM C. CLARK
CONSULTING ENGINEER
333 Third Avenue
Pittsburgh, Pa.

May 20, 1908.

To Whom It May Concern:

I know that you will be interested to learn that I have successfully opened one more of those so-called Manganese Steel Bank Safes, made by the Victor Safe & Lock Company, of Cincinnati, Ohio, in the short space of time of forty-eight minutes. This work was done under unusual circumstances.

The People's National Bank, of Economy, Pa., was locked out of their safe, and called me by telephone to come to Economy to help them out of their trouble. The Automatic on their safe could not be made to work. The bank desired to get into the safe in the quickest possible time and were willing for me to blow the door out, which I successfully accomplished by the use of nitro-glycerine, using very little explosive, in the above-named time, without any injury to the vault or the contents of the safe. The Cashier, as soon as the safe was opened, took out the money and securities, which were not injured in the least. Nothing was hurt but the so-called Manganese door, which dropped out on the floor, having been blown apart from the screw-ring which held it in its seat.

The above work was done at night between the hours of one and two o'clock. No one sleeping nearby were awakened; copy of their affidavits I enclose herewith.

Yours very truly,

William C. Clark

The William C. Clark test documented that manufacturer's claims for their product as being "burglarproof" or "absolutely undefeatable" were invalid.

Steel Bank Safes, made by the Victor Safe & Lock Company, of Cincinnati, Ohio, in the short space of forty-eight minutes. This work was done under unusual circumstances. The People's National Bank, of Economy, Pa., was locked out of its safe, and called me by telephone to come to Economy to help them out of their trouble. The Automatic* on their safe could not be made to work. The bank desired to get into the safe in the quickest possible time and were willing for me to blow the door out, which I successfully accomplished by the use of nitro-glycerine, using very little explosive, in the above-named time, without any injury to the vault or the contents of the safe. The Cashier, as soon as the safe was opened, took out the money and securities, which were not injured in the least. Nothing was hurt but the so-called Manganese door, which dropped out on the floor, having been blown apart from the screw-ring which held it in its seat. The above work was done at night between the hours of one and two o'clock. No one sleeping nearby was awakened; copy of their affidavits I enclose herewith.

*Refers to automatic timelocks.

41

A formal statement by the policeman on duty the night of Clark's attack.

State of Pennsylvania (
County of Beaver (**ss**

Before me, a Notary Public in and for said County, personally came Albert J. Carpenter, who being duly sworn according to law did depose and say:- That he lives in the Borough of Economy, Pennsylvania, and his dwelling is within about sixty feet of the building occupied by The People's National Bank, of the same place; that he slept in his said dwelling from before midnight of the 5th day of May, 1908, until his usual breakfast time the next morning, and could and would have heard any extraordinary noise in the way of an explosion that took place in the said bank during the said time. That he did not hear any explosion of any kind during the night referred to by him.

Sworn to and subscribed before
me this 7ᵗʰ day of May, A. D.,
1908.

Albert J Carpenter

Charles F Straub
Notary Public

My Commission Expires

A formal statement by a resident who lived near the bank building.

A lobby view of Peoples National Bank, Economy, Pennsylvania.

Cashier's area of the People's National Bank. William Clark opened the safe seen in the vault on the left.

These experiments were typical of the times, illustrating to those concerned that not only could proven methods "undo" the safes of the day, but that public opinion was a force to be reckoned with.

These boasts were not atypical of the period. Newspaper advertisements promulgated home remedies from life-prolonging elixirs to specially formulated medicines that would "absolutely cure" falling hair. In protest, medical interest groups, societies, associations and individuals published disclaimers against these products as well. Many industries faced the same problem.

But unlike the quick-cure medicine trade, safe-making and security was serious business. By the turn of the 20th century a whole new list of security companies had emerged to deal with a crime wave approaching epidemic proportions. There were concerns like Brink's Incorporated (armored-car money movers), American District Telegraph (ADT, local and central station alarms) and Pinkerton's National Detective Agency. To help law enforcement and private industry apprehend offenders and deter criminal acts, the telephone, electric burglar alarm and a new machine called the automobile considerably narrowed the communications gap.

Still there was more to be done. Truly believing the adage that

The attack on this Victor Safe took only 48 minutes. The triple movement time-locks are still affixed to the back plate of the safe door.

"whatever man can build, man can destroy," the insurance industry, which had banded together in 1894 to form a non-profit testing and product-listing organization, established the Underwriter's Laboratory Incorporated. This small group of engineers, technicians and insurance executives, under the direction of William Henry Merrill, had gathered in Chicago in 1893 at the request of the Chicago Board of Fire Underwriters, to investigate and reduce, if possible, fire losses at the Columbian Exposition.

Merrill was appalled at what he saw. Poor electrical wiring and cheap pavilion construction that included untested wiring techniques made this esteemed electrical investigator shudder. When the exposition was over, Merrill and two assistants set up a small laboratory in a loft above a city fire station and began to gather data and test electrical products. It was there that the now familiar UL™ trademark evolved.

Later, in 1921, the Underwriters Laboratory established the Burglary Protection and Signalling Department, a division dedicated to the evaluation, testing and listing of both physical security and electronic protection devices. Today, the motto of this independent public service organization is "Testing for Public Safety."

Within a very short time those security organizations submitting products to the UL™ for testing changed their advertising strategies and called their safes and alarms "burglary resistant."

The roaring 20's entered like a hungry lion. Barely four weeks into the decade, on January 27, 1920, a gang of thieves successfully entered the Byron branch of the Bank of Tracy, California. With them they brought a device never before used in bank burglary.[1] The new tool was known as an acetylene torch. The yeggs, with the use of rubber connecting hoses, hooked up one tank of oxygen and another of acetylene and then coupled them to a manifold burning wand. Each large metal tank had a regulator to release a gaseous mixture into the lance, which was then ignited by a flint spark. The acetylene acted as fueling agent while the oxygen "pushed" the gas, under great pressure, into the manifold and out into the air.

As a spark caught the mixture a faint pop was heard, and then a burst of bluish flame erupted from the wand. In another second the torch operator adjusted the flame to a bright blue-orange color and then eased the cutting stick into the vault itself.

[1] While the California Bankers' Association listed this as the first torch attack, there is some evidence that torches were employed as early as 1910.

This safe was successfully attacked with a torch and was then filled with water to prevent the money from burning. Wet is better than none.

47

The burglar who attacked this safe with a torch only welded the door closed. He then reverted to peeling the lower compartment — amateur.

Within minutes a small hole appeared just to the left of the combination dial and continued inward toward the master locking bolt. The vault door began to glow an iridescent soft orange, but the operator probed the long rod deeper until a huge gusher of sparks burst through and spilled on the vault floor.

The small group of thieves, surprised that their efforts were rewarded so quickly, began dousing the hot metal door with water. When the first pail of cold liquid struck the near molten slab of steel, steaming droplets bounced back at the men, burning their skin.

When the door cooled enough to resume work, one of the men finished cutting the locking bar; then through the ragged circular opening he reached in and retracted the bolt. In less than an hour from the time of bank entry to extracting the spoils, the first United States bank had been relieved of its cash by the use of a torch.

By the end of the year, dozens of other successful torch attacks were recorded. One interesting case took place in the midwest. It was November 16, 1920, and the selected mark was Farmers National Bank of Rockford, Ohio. The scout had done his homework well. Days, or perhaps weeks, before the gang struck, the advance man came to town to begin his surveillance. Apparently things went so well at the bank that the gay-cat rented a safe deposit box located inside the vault, offering false identification. On the pretext of reviewing some important documents stored in his newly-rented box, he told the custodian that he wished to be left alone. Noting a clipboard hanging on the wall that listed other renters and their box numbers, the scout copied down names and numbers of prominent and wealthy Rockford citizens, hoping their bond-tins would contain the most valuable items. As an added incentive for him to return, he also noted a stack of unregistered Liberty Bonds lying unprotected on steel shelves. If all went well, he and his associates soon would be rich.

All did go well and the gang did get rich. Just over $100,000 in cash, jewels and Liberty Bonds were looted, and when investigators saw the almost perfect square hole torched in the vault door they knew this job would not be the last they would see. The officers of the bank were dumfounded at the sizeable loss, but, in part, it was their fault. They never should have displayed such confidential information on the clipboard. Photographs of the burglarized vault interior clearly showed that those selected boxes were the ones pried open, while others that were either not rented or were thought to contain little of value were left untouched.

The roaring 20's continued to roar right on into the Gangland

This neat hole in a safe deposit vault was cut by a professional gang using a more modern method of attack — a core drill.

30's. Explosive jobs, torch jobs and the new high speed drill jobs all took an incredible toll on U.S. business.

It was midsummer 1934. Headlines of our nation's newspapers were still telling of John Dillinger's demise at Chicago's Biograph Theatre—he had been gunned down by police and F.B.I. agents. Across town, on the city's south side, two safe burglars sat cross-legged in front of a new model, round door money safe—one that bore Underwriter's Laboratory labels for drill and torch resistance. The new safe also had affixed to its locking mechanism a relocking device—a recently introduced innovation that would deadseat the locking bolts if unusual forced pressure or heat were applied to the door.

The men were expert cracksmen who had carefully studied construction of this model and those of other manufacturers. To guide them through their attack plan, one of the men leafed through intricately-drawn diagrams of most known safes then in use. He stopped his search when he came to model 6E, a large cash safe that contained an inner door used for bulk storage. The manual he referred to had been prepared by underworld figures who, during months and years of research, trial and error, had blueprinted from actual burglarized safes the exact dimensions of doors, body walls, locking bolts and combinations.

With the precision of an architect, and with frequent reference to the plans before him, the expert carefully scribed with calipers the precise distance between lock and master bolt. He took several more measurements to cross-check his work. Then with the aplomb of a certified engineer, he affixed a carbide bit to his high-speed electric drill and motioned to his accomplice to plug in the power cord. The motor whined at a high pitch as the drill knurled thin slivers of high grade metal out of the safe door, dropping them in neat curlycues on the floor. More than once the operator stopped to change drill bits that had become dull from the hard surface armor. Time was not a factor. It was Saturday afternoon and the truck storage warehouse would be closed until Monday morning. There were no guards or known police patrols in this area of town. In little more than an hour, with the operator's arms aching from continued applied body pressure, the drill motor suddenly increased in speed—the bit had finally penetrated 3½ inches of hard plate at exactly the right point to sheer off the ¾-inch locking bolt. And even though the relocking mechanism had triggered long before, the yegg had beaten the trap. With a surgeon's skill, he inserted a probe in the tiny hole, pinched the disconnected but still positioned bolt, and withdrew it from the socket. In another instant, with a turn of the door handle, he swung the 15-inch circular door open. The caper was finished. All the money and checks were taken, and the two men picked up their tool bag and left the way they had come—through the front door.

During the 50 years between 1890 and 1940, professional burglar gangs flourished, with little to stand in their way except for a newly developed protection device called the burglar alarm. Most yeggs who cased a bank and saw the strange but formidable cast-iron bell housing protruding from the building exterior realized the menace was more than they could handle. Consequently they were forced to make other plans. Others who dared such an attack were either scared off or apprehended.

In the early days few thieves knew anything about electricity, and what little they heard of its power frightened them. That in itself was a major deterrent.

Well before the year 1900, alarm companies sold their systems to precedent-setting, far-sighted bankers, jewelers and others in high-value industries. Holmes Electric Protection Company (founded 1858) and American District Telegraph (ADT, founded 1872) were two such pioneers. Others which later entered the alarm field included American Bank Protection Company, Minneapolis; Bankers Electric Protection Association, Boston; and Duplex Electric Company, New York. By 1905 electric protection was a mature industry.

The initial concept of bank alarms was very simple yet quite effective. Each used a series of thin metal shields or walls, erected inside the bank's vault, which were then electrically wired in open circuit to a main controlling cabinet (also in the vault) that contained storage batteries for power. If a burglar attempted to drill or bore into the vault, he would be met by failure as soon as the metal shield was penetrated. This would cause both an inside bell and exterior-mounted gong to ring instantly. Testimonials, newspaper reports and editorials bore vivid witness to the effects of the near ear-shattering noise produced by such loud bells.

The president of the Citizens Bank of New Ulm, Minnesota, wrote on August 4, 1902: "I wish to say that the electrical steel lining put in our bank vault two weeks ago seems to work to perfection. After it was completed, we had a test made by boring into the side wall, and the alarm went off. We believe you have headed off the burglar in good shape!"

A reporter for the Redwood Gazette, Redwood Falls, Minnesota

In the successful torch attack on the outside vault door (inset) at the Farmers National Bank, Rockford, Ohio, burglars pilfered safe deposit boxes of the wealthiest depositors—safe was untouched.

wrote on April 10, 1903: "The burglar alarm on the vault of Gold-Stabeck Bank got in its first work at ten o'clock last Wednesday evening, and its effect was wild in its extreme. A crowd commenced to gather as soon as the first bell commenced working, and when the bells got in their work, it was as though the roof was being raised from the building. A telephone message was sent to Will Wallace, who came down on his wheel, and after getting into the bank, he closed the vault door, and the alarm ceased its terrific noise. It appears that E. A. Cross, the Assistant Cashier, left the vault door open when he closed the bank for the evening. The alarm was set for ten o'clock in case anything went wrong. The door being left open, the alarm commenced work on strictly scheduled time."

An editorial of the same period emphasized a different theme. "Citizens here are becoming outraged and deafened by the intolerable noise created by bells and gongs clanging in the middle of the night as a result of devices employed by our local bankers. Livestock, poultry and other creatures cannot do their job of reproducing, laying eggs or giving milk because of the constant noise made by those terrible bells. The constable remained in bed Tuesday after standing guard all night until officials silenced their alarms." Perhaps this could be called an early form of noise pollution.

Despite the conflicting and often-times negative press reports, burglar alarms remained a necessary adjunct to bank security, and the mystery of electricity kept criminals at bay well into the years of World War I. "After all," said one convicted burglar, "what fool would risk life and limb tampering with dangerous electrical circuits? Isn't it electricity that provides the ultimate power for our prison's death chair?"

Today's burglar has learned about electricity, but otherwise he differs little from his brother of past decades. He has the same desire for illegal wealth, the same penchant for danger and the same scheming ideas. Only the tools of his trade have improved and, probably more important, so has his ability to obtain technical training and information. It may be that right now he's waiting, planning, plotting to rip off you—or your bank.

3

THE CANNON SHOT

*"The mark of a professional burglar is not so
much his ability to beat the system but rather his
uncanny penchant for adventure, surprise and
ingenuity."*
Richard Gallagher, Assistant Director (retired),
Federal Bureau of Investigation

Jack Frank and Joel Singer arrived at Washington National on a
flight from New York. The date was March 30, 1965. They rented a
panel truck and drove the short distance from the airport to
Alexandria, Virginia, a point which marked the starting place for
one of the strangest and most spectacular burglaries in United
States history.

The two men slowly cruised down Prince Street to the wharf,
stopping just short of the Potomac River, opposite a two story
wooden building surrounded by a chain-link fence topped with
barbed wire. Weeds and scrub vines grew in abundance around the
property.

On the river side of the building a sign, bolted to a widow's-walk
railing on the roof, can easily be seen by tourists as they pass by on
busy day-cruise liners that plough the waterways. The sign simply
reads "Guns."

The plan had already been made before the two arrived. Frank
would go in to inquire about the purchase of a cannon and some
ammunition. Singer would wait in the van, and if all went well, the
two men would be on their way within an hour.

Jack Frank, the brother of Joel Singer's mother, was an auto
mechanic who lived in a Freeport, Long Island apartment. A
bachelor, he was 33, of medium build, weighed about 180 pounds
and was 5 feet 10 inches tall. On this particular day, he was well
dressed in a conservative business suit.

As he entered the side gate at the Zero Prince Street address, he could see two other signs on the paint-peeled wall. One said "Potomac Arms," the other "Hunter's Haven." The gun shop was within two blocks of Interarmco, one of the largest weapons importers in the nation.

Frank walked up a flight of old wooden stairs to the second floor display room and sales office. Amid the clutter of ammunition boxes, rifles, handguns and automatic weapons stood open crates of Civil War ordnance, along with antique weaponry of all descriptions.

John Richards, the proprietor, waited on Frank, who inquired about the purchase of two World War II vintage Finnish 20mm anti-tank guns, and 200 rounds of armor-piercing ammunition. He had about $800 in cash that Singer had given him for the purchase.

With the sale completed, Richards asked for the buyer's name and address.

"James Finch, 620 Orinoco St., Alexandria," was the nervous reply. "And I'd like the entire order shipped via Railway Express to James Cobb, in care of General Delivery, Plattsburgh, N. Y."

Richards, who had lived in Alexandria all his life, knew the address was false. He stalled the purchaser until the following day by saying that he would clean and crate the equipment. Frank left and returned to his nephew in the waiting van.

Then Richards phoned local police to confirm the fake Orinoco Street address, after which he called the F.B.I. Because there was no federal law covering the purchase or transportation of cannons and ammunition, the F.B.I. had no immediate jurisdiction in the matter. They did, however, notify local police, police in Plattsburgh, customs officials and the Royal Canadian Mounted Police. Plattsburgh is only 25 miles from the Canadian border, and it was feared that the guns might be destined for a political activist group or Latin revolutionaries in Quebec or Central America.

The next day, Singer and Frank returned to the Potomac Arms to pick up their weapons. Richards helped load onto the rented van two grey painted boxes that contained the Finnish Lahti cannons (used in the 1939 border wars with Russia) and one black footlocker that housed the 20mm ammunition. Then the two gun-runners headed in their van for a local shopping center, where they parked and stenciled "Elevator Machinery Parts" on the boxes. Next they drove to the Railway Express office in Alexandria, where they prepaid the shipment and had it loaded on the baggage car. The agent informed Frank the cargo would be delivered in Plattsburgh on April 5.

Potomac Arms Gun Shop at 0 Prince Street, Alexandria, Va. where Jack Frank and Joel Singer purchased two anti-tank guns and ammunition.

This is an exact duplicate of the 20mm Finnish (Lahti) anti-tank gun that Joel Singer used at the Brink's Warehouse in Syracuse, N.Y. When this gun was photographed in 1977 the price tag read $275.00.

With their transactions completed, Jack Frank returned home to his Freeport apartment, while his nephew flew back to his home in Chomedey, Quebec, a suburb of Montreal.

Joel Singer, who was 22, 6 feet 1 inch tall, nearly 200 pounds, and of medium-heavy build with a medium complexion, had brown hair, deep-set blue eyes, and often wore glasses. He spoke fluent French, and after completing his schooling in Canada, he worked as a salesman for various Montreal firms. In 1961 he was convicted of shopbreaking, for which he was given a suspended sentence.

From the time the weapons left Alexandria, bound for the upper New York border town, police kept a watchful eye on the shipment. On April 5, the three crates marked "elevator parts" arrived on schedule at the Plattsburgh express office. There they were unloaded and placed in a locked room. Police officers waited the rest of the day for consignee James Cobb to claim the guns, but he never appeared. April 6 and 7 passed, and still no one arrived to claim them. Then at 5:00 p.m. on the 7th, the express agent closed for the day and went home. At the same time, police withdrew their watch, planning to return the following day at 7:30 a.m.

Early on the morning of April 8, a rented Hertz station wagon bearing Canadian plates drove into the deserted town; Joel Singer and a companion were in the front seat. For nearly an hour the two men cruised around the railroad station and neighboring streets to determine whether police still had the express office staked out. Satisfied that all surveillance had been terminated for the night, Singer drove the wagon alongside the freight entrance and parked.

In a few minutes the two men broke open the latch on the door, cautiously entered the building and stole their own weapons. Nothing further was heard or seen of Joel Singer and his friends until late October, 1965.

Then, during the weekend of October 23–25, Joel Singer surfaced again. He and four other men left Montreal in a late model station wagon and a panel van loaded with one 20mm cannon, more than 100 rounds of armor-piercing shells, high explosives, cutting torch, wrecking bars and other burglar tools.

The two-car caravan headed south across the border into upper New York State, and then down and across the New York Thruway to Syracuse, arriving there late Friday evening. Tired, but well prepared for their pending weekend score, the men checked in at a local motel. They knew full well that the sleep they got that night would probably be their last for more than 48 hours.

Saturday morning the men were up early to make final plans,

Brink's, Inc. garage and depository, located at the corner of Lodi Street and LeMoyne Avenue, Syracuse, N.Y. Personnel door (a) is where initial entry was made. The overhead door (b) is where the gang entered with their van.

A model of the Brink's warehouse. Note the vault at the upper right and the vault room where the cannon was fired at point blank range.

clean their weapons and make one last dry run before the hit.

The Brink's Incorporated office and garage, located on the north side of Syracuse, at the corner of Lodi Street and LeMoyne Avenue, is a small one-story brick building. The neighborhood surrounding the warehouse depository consists of small single and two family homes and a few commercial buildings. A local tavern stands on the corner a short block away.

Brink's is usually vacant from late Saturday afternoon until 8:00 a.m. Monday, when the opening crew and drivers arrive. Police cruisers pass by periodically during the weekend to check the facility.

Joel Singer and his four companions, who had scouted the building on previous occasions, decided to make one more pass in their car before the autumn daylight faded completely. They drove along Lodi Street but slowed down as they passed by the unobtrusive Brink's office. A glass personnel door facing the street opened to a visitor alcove that was protected by a heavy metal bandit barrier. The only other means of entry on that side of the building was three small glass-brick windows about 6 feet off the ground. The men decided that entry on the Lodi Street side would be impractical.

The car then rounded the corner onto LeMoyne and paused. This was the business side of Brink's, where the world-renowned armored trucks entered and left daily, laden with cash receipts from area banks and commercial customers. The entire building facade, including the walls to the rear and the far side, were constructed of brick and cement block. A small parking lot separated the street from the warehouse.

Silently the men sat in the car, knowing exactly what they would do when they returned later that night. There were two overhead doors facing the street, and off to the right side was a metal personnel door that led into the garage. All was quiet that Saturday; only a threat of thunderstorms marred the evening.

Shortly after midnight on Sunday, October 25, the station wagon again appeared on Lodi Street. This time it was followed by a panel van. As the car rounded LeMoyne Avenue, one of the men jumped out and quickly hid in the shadows of the garage.

Immediately the two vehicles continued down LeMoyne past the tavern which had just closed. It was a dark night, and the constant threat of rain kept a heavy cloud cover over the city.

Remaining in the shadows until he got his bearings and his eyes became adjusted to the darkness, the man near the garage reached in his jacket and extracted a flexible piece of plastic about 6 inches long.

He made his way over to the metal personnel door and began to work the plastic strip into the jamb, around the door frame, and then over the locking mechanism. There was no sound as the latch gave way.

Quickly the burglar stepped inside the garage and closed the door behind him. He dared not use his powerful flashlight, fearing the beam might be noticed through two narrow window panels on the overhead doors. Instead, he switched on a pen-light, making sure its beam shone only on the floor. Then he waited.

In another minute the station wagon returned and another figure emerged. This time a ladder and some tarpaper were taken from the roof-top luggage rack. There was little noise and no sudden movement. Everything possible was done to avoid suspicion if anyone happened to be watching.

The second man carried the extension ladder and a roll of paper to the personnel door and quickly entered. Once inside, the two men worked with precision.

First they cut strips of the black paper and taped it over the garage door windows. Next they went to a second overhead door, farthest from the personnel door they had entered, and began to dismantle the automatic opener mechanism.

The stepladder was then moved into position, and the second intruder climbed up to the bracket that controlled a motor-driven chain drive. In less than a minute it came loose and fell to the floor. No words were spoken, and movements were visible only by the beam of the first man's small flashlight.

As the ladder was removed and placed out of the way, the first intruder retied the manual pull-rope so the overhead door would rise to precisely 83 inches—just enough to permit their van to enter—not the full 9 feet it normally would.

Everything was ready. The first man returned to the pedestrian door and looked outside to recheck the area. All was quiet. He then pressed the "send" button on his walkie-talkie and gave the all clear. The van, containing the rest of the equipment and two of the three remaining burglars, returned down LeMoyne Avenue and turned in at the parking lot. As it did, the garage door opened just enough to let the truck in and then immediately closed. Another "all clear" to the station wagon driver signaled him to drive away and remain clear, unless there was an emergency.

Singer and his friends then feverishly unloaded the van: cannon, a

Bandit-barrier door between the garage and check-in room. Burglars smashed the bullet-resistive glass and reached in to open the locked door.

home-made gun mount, ammunition, acetylene torch, circular cutting saw with diamond blade, sledge, wrecking bar, gas masks, mattress and several blankets. Last to be removed was an ammunition canister heavily padded with foam rubber. It contained 4 ounces of nitroglycerine, 4 sticks of 60% dynamite and 12 blasting caps.

The first barrier the gang had to contend with on their way to the money vault was a bullet-resistant door which led from the garage area to the driver's check-in room. The door contained a five-layer laminated glass panel about 2 feet in diameter. It was interlaced with chickenwire to deter splintering if attacked. One of the men from the van began striking the window with the sledge. Small glass chips flew back at the attacker. Again and again he muscled the huge hammer. At last a small hole gave way to a larger opening, big enough for him to reach through and deactivate the lock from the inside. Once inside the check-in room, the men were faced with two more doors of the same construction. One led into the vault ante-room and the other to a money-counting room and utility closet. In both cases these were jimmied open by breaking the lock and then prying open the doors with a wrecking bar and sledge.

Up to this point of the operation, the gang of thieves had operated on sheer guts and razor-sharp nerves, and it was now that their professional training and experience would be tested.

The second van rider was ready to start his exacting work; he was the alarm man. Immediately behind the counting room was a utility closet that housed a telephone company junction box and the alarm system controls. The system used a central station vault alarm that was ultra-sensitive to audible sounds and to heat change. It was monitored through leased telephone lines by operators at a distant location.

The alarm man took several lengths of wire from his case, along with three black boxes containing meters and switches. He carefully made sure that wires didn't cross and that connections were firm. When he was ready, he motioned to the group to prepare for a fast exit if his test failed. The walkie-talkie operator signaled his companion in the station wagon, and in a few moments the wagon turned from Lodi Street onto LeMoyne and parked across the street with lights off in case a fast exit would become necessary.

The sledge operator positioned himself in front of the vault door and waited for another signal. Then the alarm man carefully made his last connection, studied the meters for a moment and directed

These electronic devices were used to defeat the vault alarm system.

the hammer man to give the vault door a few hard blows. Wham! Wham! Another check of the meters was made. So far, so good.

"Try it again," the alarm technician ordered.

Wham! Wham! Wham! Three blows this time. They waited again.

The first two men remained on a silent watch at the outside door, hoping they wouldn't hear sirens. Two minutes passed. Three. Still nothing. The gang had agreed to sweat it out for 15 minutes before they began their actual vault attack. Those remaining minutes seemed to turn into hours, but still there was no police response. When a quarter-hour had passed, the men quietly reassembled in the vault anteroom and with a sigh of relief shook hands, smiling in the dim light.

While their accomplice waited in the car outside, one of the burglars took a small radio, pushed the transmission button and ordered the driver to retreat once more.

They were now ready for the final attack. Their mission that night was to blast their way into the vault with their powerful cannon. It was, perhaps, the first time that such a tactic had been tried. The vault room was an imposing concrete and reinforced-steel monolith with walls a full 18 inches thick. The vault door was solid steel, and the gang knew that to try to penetrate it would be virtually impossible.

If all went as planned, the gang of five would soon be thousands or maybe even millions of dollars richer. The spoils lay only 1½ feet away.

Joel Singer looked at his watch. It was almost 2:00 a.m. Sunday. The men were slightly behind schedule but not enough for concern. They had allowed extra time for mistakes and other contingencies, and if they kept pressing on they could be finished before dawn.

Each gang member had an assigned job for this phase of the operation. Singer remained at the garage door with the walkie-talkie; the alarm expert stayed with his meters to monitor the alarm system. It was up to "sledge-hammer" and the ladder man to retrieve the cannon and set it up for the hit.

There was one problem the burglars hadn't counted on as they lugged the cumbersome 100 pound, 7½-foot gun into the vault anteroom. The total distance from the vault wall to the far side of the anteroom was only 12 feet. That meant that each 20mm shell fired would travel only 4 feet—point blank—before exploding against the concete. The roar of the cannon, explosion of shells bursting, shrapnel and flying debris were sure to be a major hazard for the trigger man.

Within a half hour "sledge" and his accomplice had mounted the gun on a specially constructed angle-iron stanchion and positioned it about 3 feet to the left of the vault door. In order to make room for the cannon, the chairs, tables, automatic coin-counters and other equipment were moved out of the way. Then a water-soaked mattress was hauled in and placed back of the gun. It provided a make-shift shield for the cannon operator. Next, several wet blankets were draped over everything in sight; the wet mattress and blankets would absorb the deafening sound and help contain the dust that was certain to follow each explosion.

The Finnish Lahti was leveled and loaded. Special ski mounts (used during the winter wars of 1939-1940) straddled the angle-iron floor mount and acted as stabilizers.

The trigger man yelled to his accomplices, warning them that he was ready to fire, and each man prepared for the eventual roar and braced himself for the unknown. They all donned the breather masks they had brought along.

Ka-blam! The first shot roared with immense force. It was like being in a bomb shelter during an air attack. The concussion was intense. The first shell burst against the concrete wall with unbelievable force, sending pieces of stone and concrete in every direction at missile speed. When the initial shock had subsided, everyone raced to the target area to inspect the damage. Surprisingly there was very little—perhaps a three inch crater in the vault. The men took their places again—lookout, alarm man, "trigger" and his assistant. This time a burst of three shots rang out.

Singer didn't move from the garage door this time. He was sure that neighbors had heard the shots and were phoning police. Panic began to overcome the young Canadian, but he remained at his post. In the meantime the two gunners edged through the mounting dust again to inspect the damage. This time a bigger cavity was visible. They were definitely making progress. "Sledge Hammer" picked up his weapon and began knocking loose concrete from the hole, which was now about 8 inches deep and 15 inches in diameter. Steel reinforcing rods appeared in the wall, so the men decided to use their cutting saw and torch to clear the way. It was now 2:45 a.m.

The triggerman loaded the Lahti again, this time with a full clip of 12 rounds. Before shooting, however, he aimed the air-cooled barrel slightly to the right to create a larger pattern. Ka-blam! This time a volley of 6 shots pierced the wall, and the hole opened up to nearly 2 feet wide and 15 inches deep. More rods were cut, then more torching and chipping, and another pattern was fired to the left.

The homemade cannon mount on which the 20mm gun was placed. The mattress and spent shells are all tools that were used in the burglary.

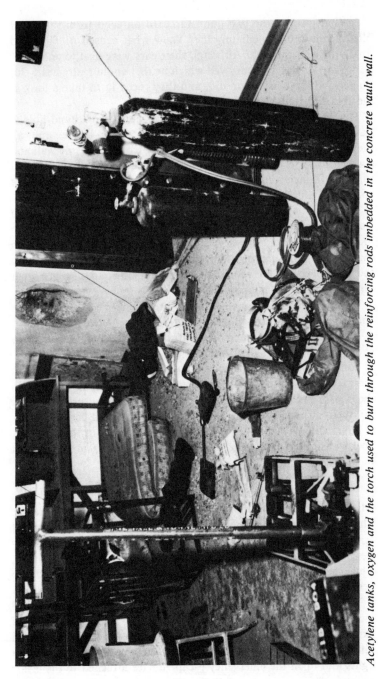

Acetylene tanks, oxygen and the torch used to burn through the reinforcing rods imbedded in the concrete vault wall.

At that instant, the two gunners heard an echo from the cloud filled room and immediately they knew what caused it. They had finally broken through. Although their ears were deaf to conversation, they let out a victory yell which neither could really hear. But Singer and the alarm man did, and they raced in to take a look at the treasure that was almost theirs.

The hole was small, but it was large enough to hand-hold a flashlight inside. As they tried to get a better look in the vault, all they could see was coin bags about 2 feet from the inside wall and stacked 4 to 5 feet high. Their hearts sank. Not only had they blasted through 18 inches of vault; their shells had destroyed thousands of coins and much currency.

The clock kept running, and the men knew they had to finish and leave before daybreak. More digging, sledging and cutting, and then more cannon shot. Twenty, 25, 30 armor-piercing bullets raced through the hole, carving it larger and larger. More coins burst into the four corners of the vault, splattering, sticking and fusing to other objects that stood in the way.

Thirty-one, 32, 33. Finally the gun was silent. The hole was large enough to crawl through.

By this time, ears rang like cathedral bells and throats were choked with cement dust, despite the masks.

The foursome needed a break from the action. They headed for the garage door, opened it into the October night, and breathed in the cool fresh air. Thunder and distant lightning did provide cover for their mission after all, and they were thankful for that.

Eager to let the station wagon accomplice know of their success, Joel transmitted a message that removal of the treasure was about to begin.

The men took one more breath of early morning air and then retreated to the anteroom to inspect their man-made vault entrance. The dust was still thick, but it didn't matter. The burglars knew that at this point, unless they were discovered during the next hour, they were home free. Singer quickly returned to his post in the garage, while the other three picked away at the jagged concrete in order to permit entry.

When they finished, their new door measured about 18 by 30 inches. Since the alarm man was the smallest, he was elected chief explorer. The others helped push him through the opening, handed him a flashlight, and then waited until he could flip on the vault lights and open the emergency escape device attached to the inside

These money bags are part of the $2,000,000 in currency and coin that was left behind in the burglar's haste to leave the Brink's depository.

of the vault door. This was complicated temporarily by the presence of a bank-type grilled day-gate that also had to be opened. Fumbling for a moment, the alarm man finally found an emergency thumb-latch release that permitted the day-gate to open inward. This accomplished, he turned the escape device and the huge door swung open.

Three exhausted figures stood in silence at the vestibule and stared at what appeared to be another Fort Knox. Pallets piled high with bags of coin and currency, many of which had been severely damaged by the continued cannon blasts, lay waiting.

Minutes after the debris had been cleared away the three bandits searched for the most valuable canvas bags—those that contained cold hard cash. The bags that were too badly damaged were left behind, as were thousands of dollars in mutilated coins.

As the truck was being filled with bounty and the cannon removed, Joel Singer heard what he thought was the faint sound of sirens in the distance.

"That's it," he roared as the panic of being caught returned. "Let's split."

In an instant three of the thieves boarded the van, while the fourth

It took 33 firings of the 20mm anti-tank cannon to create this hole in the vault wall. The shells are made to pierce the armor of a tank.

A shot of the vault interior shows thousands of dollars in currency and coin that was destroyed when the cannon shot broke through the vault. Pockmarks on the rear wall are a result of the explosions.

burglar hoisted the garage door. In another few seconds the truck sped out onto the street and screeched to a halt, while the last man lowered the overhead door. In another moment the van disappeared around the corner, and LeMoyne Avenue was once again dark and silent. The sirens heard minutes earlier probably had been those from a fire truck.

The time was now 4:30 a.m. Sunday. Joel Singer, heart still pounding from the tumultuous score, tried to calm himself long enough to transmit a rendezvous message to the station wagon driver. "Meet us at the highway," he half whispered into the crackling radio.

"Gotcha," came the simple but obviously joyous reply.

It was done. The walkie-talkies were silenced for good, and the two-vehicle caravan entered the on-ramp of the New York Thruway and headed east the way it had come. By 8:30 a.m. that morning five men, their cannon, and nearly a half million dollars in cash and negotiables were safely 200 miles away.

Roderick Barber, regional security manager for Brink's, was in a hurry to get to the office Monday morning. A long-standing resident of Syracuse, he maintained his security headquarters in the local Brink's facility rather than in the company's New York City office. He had a flight to catch down to the Big Apple later that morning and wanted to check his mail before leaving.

Rod was a big man, perhaps 6 feet 4 inches tall, and weighed every bit of 250 pounds. He looked like a cop, muscular and well proportioned. He pulled up to his usual spot in the Brink's parking lot at 8:02 a.m. and waited for the opening crew. It was standard procedure to have several guards present before entering the building. As the guards arrived, one by one, they chatted about the NFL games played Sunday afternoon. Then at 8:10 a.m. the lead guard, who had the personnel door key, arrived. He unlocked the door and the men filed in as they always did. Because Rod was not a regular branch employee, he had no reason to enter the men's locker room to change into a uniform. As he waited in the garage for the guards to return and complete their security opening procedures, he noticed a gas mask lying on the floor. Almost immediately his eye then caught the bandit-barrier door that had been smashed early Sunday morning. Instinct told him to go for the handgun that he always kept in his briefcase. As he withdrew it from the leather holster, he waved to the others who had now emerged from the locker room. A few silent motions advised the others of the situation. Carefully they approached the check-in room, not

This view, inside the vault looking out, shows two reinforcing rods still intact in the concrete wall. Money was literally blown away.

knowing what to expect. Guns drawn, they further opened the door which had been left ajar. Finding nothing, two guards cautiously entered the counting room while the other two inched into the vault anteroom. The dust by this time had settled to about eye level, but despite the cloud cover Barber immediately summed up what had happened.

"Don't touch anything," he said in utter disbelief. "You finish checking the place out; I'll phone the police."

By 8:40 a.m., police and the F.B.I. had sealed off the warehouse. Brink's headquarters in Chicago was notified, and by mid-morning the press and camera crews were everywhere.

About noon, Joel Singer phoned his uncle in Long Island. "We did it, Jack," he said. "We knocked off the Brink's office in Syracuse."

By early afternoon, three of the desperados pulled their car up to Frank's apartment and went in to tell him about their escapade. They counted out their share of the money that had been transferred from the van earlier, and split it three ways. Singer gave his uncle less than $200 for his part in buying the cannons earlier in the year. Then Singer's two companions left.

Jack Frank had been married the week before and he, his new bride and Joel went to dinner at his wife's parents house not far away. Singer didn't appear nervous or anxious after the weekend episode, and after a short visit he and his uncle departed.

Later that evening, about 9:30 p.m., the two men left Frank's apartment with the Lahti cannon and the remaining ammunition that they had earlier transferred from the station wagon, and drove out to Jones Beach along the Meadowbrook Parkway. There, in the darkness, they lifted the incriminating evidence over a bridge railing and dropped it into the black tidewater.

It wasn't until Tuesday, October 27, that Frank had second thoughts about the Brink's job. He had now read and reread headlines and detailed stories of the Syracuse cannon shot, and he was desperate. The probability of his being implicated, accused and convicted, especially for so little in return, was too much for the bridegroom, and shortly before noon he telephoned the F.B.I. to confess his part in the conspiracy to commit burglary. Immediately agents went to his apartment and began hours of questioning. Newspapers by this time estimated the loss to be more than $400,000, but Frank was the recipient of only $166.35. He turned the pittance, still neatly wrapped in the Brink's canvas bag, over to the agents.

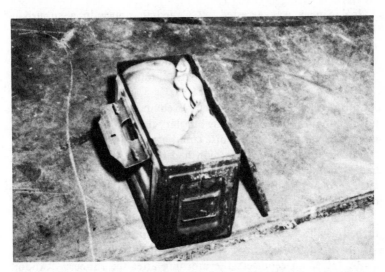

This ammunition canister, stuffed with foam rubber, was found resting on the fender of a Brink's armored car. It contained 4 ounces of nitroglycerine, 4 sticks of 60% dynamite and 12 blasting caps.

During the next several days, Jack Frank retold what he knew of the bizarre incident: how he had bought the guns and then how he and his nephew had disposed of one of them near Jones Beach. On October 30, U.S. Navy and Coast Guard divers searched the waters under the Meadowbrook Parkway for the gun and ammunition. Tides and river currents hampered the operation, but finally, after hours of dragging the bottom, all of the equipment was recovered. F.B.I. laboratory technicians in Washington then compared the expended shells found at the scene with those retrieved from Jones Beach and determined that they were identical. They also examined a wood fragment found in the vault room and learned that it matched the wood on the gun stock of the recovered cannon. The report confirmed that they were once part of the same piece of wood.

On November 19, 1965, the F.B.I. issued a bulletin placing Joel Singer on the Bureau's "Ten-Most-Wanted" list, and a manhunt for the young Canadian was on.

While Singer was the only one charged in the Brink's case, five others were sought in the incident. Jack Frank, who testified for the state, was given immunity for his cooperation and returned to Freeport, Long Island.

Joel Singer was arrested by Canadian police in a suburban Montreal restaurant on December 1, 1965, just 12 days after circulars for his arrest were issued. The apprehension was made quietly and without incident. He was confined in the city's Bordeaux Prison and remained there until extradition to the United States in May, 1966.

During the trial, which lasted seven months, several residents testified that on the night of the burglary they had heard something, but never realized that the noise could have come from a cannon in the Brink's warehouse. One man had thought it was thunder. He had shut the window and gone back to bed. Another had been awakened but he didn't know by what. He, too, had gone back to bed, not suspecting that anything was out of the ordinary.

But most neighbors of the Brink's depository had slept undisturbed as the burglars blasted their way into the vault.

Otto Brauchle, a retired policeman who lived only a few doors away, talked to reporters the morning after the robbery. "About three o'clock, I heard a noise like thunder," he said. "It was a muffled sound, and it could have been the cannon. I remember looking at my watch and it was 12 minutes after 3:00 a.m." Mrs. Brauchle, who worked at a local bar, reported coming home from work at about 2:15 a.m. She had come into the house and locked the door. As she did, she had seen a grey-colored station wagon go east on LeMoyne and park about 300 feet away. As she watched it stop, she said to herself, "Am I glad I'm in the house." She then had gotten a bottle of beer from the refrigerator, turned off the lights and gone upstairs to bed.

On December 17, 1966, Joel Singer was convicted of first degree grand larceny and third degree burglary. Judge Ormand Gale of the Onondaga, N.Y., County Court sentenced the 23-year-old Canadian to 5 to 10 years in Attica State Prison on both counts.

Certain other facts of the case did unfold. The ammunition canister containing the nitroglycerine, dynamite and blasting caps were found by police in the garage area the morning that the burglary was discovered. Apparently the gang had planned to use these devices if the cannon failed. Army engineers called in to dispose of it said there was enough of the explosive to destroy completely not only the vault, but the entire Brink's building and most of the houses on the block.

On February 5, 1966, constables from the Montreal Police Identification and Techniques Department discovered what appeared to be the remaining equipment used by the Brink's gang. On

Two FBI agents inspect the cannon after it was retrieved from tidewaters near Jones Beach, Long Island, New York.

the premises of a local Montreal convent they found more dynamite, nitroglycerine, 20 rounds of 20mm ammunition and a semi-automatic weapon, equipped with silencer, that resembled the Brink's weapon.

After Singer had served his time in Attica Prison, he was released in September, 1972 and immediately returned to Canada. Joel Singer never reached his thirtieth birthday. On February 6, 1973, he was found dead in Montreal. The medical examiner reported his death as suicide by cyanide poisoning.

There still remained a mystery concerning the Brink's case which netted the gang, at final count, $433,587. Later tips from the F.B.I. led authorities to theorize that a professional front organization, probably with headquarters in Canada, had supplied money for purchase of weapons and other equipment for the burglary ring. They suspected that there might be several masterminds behind the plot, one of whom lived in Buffalo. Who were the others who had taken part, and where are they today? And what happened to the money? To this day, aside from the $166.35 surrendered by Jack Frank, none of it has ever been recovered.

4

THE ULTIMATE WEAPON

*"If I were a burglar and wanted to do a number on
a bank, I'd use the core drill—it's the ultimate
burglar tool—safe, quick, sure."*

Leslie Nelson
Sheriff, Cowlitz County, WA

The core drill is one of the most sophisticated methods
of entry in bank burglaries, and is usually used only by
experienced professionals. It was originally designed as a
construction tool, and is a large cumbersome device that
must be water cooled. As the name implies, it cleanly
cuts a core of material out of a safe or vault. A hollow
metal tube, ranging from 1 to 6 or more inches in
diameter, it has diamond or carbon chips impregnated in
the tip. The tube is then affixed to an electric drill which
turns at high speed. Because of the physical pressure
necessary to force the diamond-tipped pipe into the
cutting surface, most core drills cannot be hand held, but
must be fastened to a solid foundation, such as a
concrete floor, by tapping anchor bolts through a base
plate. With all its disadvantages, it is often the tool of
choice when other methods do not prevail.

Early on the morning of Tuesday, May 14, 1974, a late model
station wagon bearing out-of-state plates entered the on-ramp of
Interstate 90 at Opportunity, Washington, near the Idaho border
and headed west. The occupants sat in silence, more because of
restless sleep the night before than lack of topical conversation or
anxiety over their pending score. Almost immediately it began to
rain, the slow, steady, cooling rain of early spring in the Cascades.
As the car, heavy with construction tools, crossed the Columbia

Core drills require some means of applying drilling pressure. One innovative burglar used this air compressor which created a vacuum, thereby fastening the drill tightly to the vault door.

River and began ascending the mountains, a low fog developed that hampered driving. If the three men were to reach their destination by dark, the weather would have to cooperate—and right now it was not.

By early afternoon, they decided to stop and stretch their legs. No gas stations bordered the Cle Elum exit, so they drove north about a mile over a small river bridge and parked. Here they relieved themselves along the roadside. It was a quiet place, with pastures next to the road and a wooded area in the background. Their comfort station, probably chosen by accident, would later prove to be an important clue to Washington State's largest bank heist.

Returning to the Interstate, they continued west, through Snoqualmie Pass and on into Seattle. The rain persisted, but as they descended to lower elevations the fog finally dissipated. After a late afternoon supper, the men were again on their way. This time they drove south on Interstate 5 to Woodland, Washington, a small logging town just north of the Oregon border and Portland. It was now past 6:30 p.m., and most of the local stores were closed, although the streets were still busy with school kids, merchants and businessmen on their way home for dinner.

The men in the station wagon felt it would not be wise for them to be seen roaming around town, especially with an out-of-state license on their car, so they drove down to Ridgefield several miles south and spent a few hours in a bar drinking beer and chatting. They were careful not to discuss their mission. They had laid their plans months earlier, having travelled to Woodland on several occasions to lay out the job, try to check with a knowledgeable local contact, and pay a daytime visit to the bank they were about to burglarize. To risk talking about it now would be foolish, even though the bar they were in was practically deserted.

At 11:30 p.m., the men returned to Woodland and scouted the area around the Bank of the West, a modern glass and brick building situated at one of the town's main intersections. All was quiet except for several bars down the street that were doing more than the usual Tuesday night trade. Behind the bank were the truck repair sheds of the Ben Thomas Logging Company, and in the yards adjacent to a prefabricated field office stood a parked pickup truck with its key in the ignition. Immediately one of the trio left the station wagon, slid into the driver's seat and started the engine. Then the two vehicles drove south again, to Horseshoe Lake Park on the outskirts of Woodland. Here the men transferred all of their burglar tools to the truck. Included was a 9-inch core drill, one of

This bank in Woodland, Washington, was the scene of Washington State's largest bank burglary. On May 14 and 15, 1974, thieves got away with $360,000.

the largest model construction tools manufactured, as well as an acetylene torch, oxygen and acetylene tanks, rope, garden hose, heavy electrical wire and a repairman's tool box. They parked the station wagon in a wooded thicket nearby and then boarded the logging truck and headed back into town.

Shortly before 1:00 a.m., Jeff Adams, the lone police officer on duty in Woodland, received a phone call from his wife, who excitedly told him of a prowler she had seen in the back of the house. She told him she had heard a loud noise in the back yard that sounded like someone tripping over a pile of lumber that was stacked next to a small shed. Frightened, but wanting to see what the commotion was, she had gone to the back door and peered out into the night. Just then she saw a man disappear around the corner of the shed. He was wearing a stocking cap and kept his head down so she couldn't identify him. Jeff immediately drove home but found no one in the area. But to be safe, he convinced his wife to accompany him in his cruiser for the remainder of his shift. Except for occasional visits, no one manned the police station the rest of the night.

The Bank of the West is a small bank in assets, but the day before a large currency shipment had been made in anticipation of the usual mid-month payroll on the 15th. Almost a half million dollars in cash, American Express travelers' checks and Series E Bonds lay neatly secure in the vault interior.

A little after 10:00 p.m., the assistant manager, who was working late to prepare for the next day's business, closed up and went home. An hour later the Ben Thomas truck was stolen.

Shortly after 1:00 a.m., the logging company truck quietly pulled up and stopped in the rear parking lot of the bank, and one heavily shrouded figure emerged in the cold drizzle. Silently he approached the furnace room door at the back of the building, knowing that the door led into a small space containing custodian supplies and cleaning equipment. A few quick pries with a piece of flexible plastic as a wedge and the wooden door swung open. Once inside the small room, he slipped the same device into an inner door latch and it, too, swung open. The safety bolt lock on the outer door had been severed earlier, perhaps by someone who had access to the premises.

When an all-clear signal was flagged, the two men waiting in the truck dismounted and immediately carried their heavy equipment inside. Each man knew exactly what to do, and no words were

This roof hatch provided access to power lines and the alarm bell.

The burglar-alarm bell was easily silenced by pouring quick-setting plastic cement in the casing louvres.

spoken. Within four minutes their task was completed. One of the bandits then felt his way through the darkened building to the bank's lobby, where he scanned the street through a line of low picture windows. His surveillance revealed nothing suspicious, so he left through the furnace room door, climbed into the cab of the truck, and slowly backed the vehicle down the short alley and again parked it in the logging company's field office parking area. The truck was to remain there temporarily until the three were ready to make their getaway.

With their equipment now piled against the wall of a first floor corridor, each of the men shed his heavy lumberman's outerwear— parkas, woolen shirts and canvas hunters' vests. Now they were ready for a long night's work.

Quickly they mounted a rear stairway that led to an employees' lounge and kitchen located above the vault and adjacent to employee bathrooms. With a ladder they had taken from the custodian's room, one member of the gang climbed up and unlatched two small eye-hooks which held a roof access cover. He carefully pushed it aside and boosted himself up through the opening onto the flat tar and gravel roof. There were still large puddles of water from the all-day rain.

Next, his two companions popped up through the roof opening carrying a piece of canvas to be used as a cover, and two 1-gallon cans of quick-drying resin, as well as six small bottles of quick-setting catalyst. Carefully, they wrapped the canvas around a large alarm bell housing that hung about 18 inches below the roof on the rear wall of the bank. Then, with a long plastic funnel, they began pouring the epoxy resin material into the bell louvers, so that the canvas which hung loosely around the bell absorbed most of the spill. As the resin hardened on the cold metal, the bell took on the look of a water-tight CARE package. As two of the gang finished the job, the third burglar crawled back into the bank and made his way downstairs to the telephone switchboard to deactivate the lines. Afraid he might cause an alarm by cutting the wires, he poured coffee and coffee grounds from the employees' kitchen into the maze of cable and terminals. Then he pulled the master power switch, cutting off all electricity to the building. This done, he returned to the roof and signalled all clear.

Next came the real test: to disconnect the alarm bell wire and determine whether the clapper had been silenced by the now hardened plastic material. Inside the bank, one burglar withdrew a large pair of wire cutters from his tool box and readied himself for the cut. In a hushed tone, he called up to his companions that he was set and to prepare themselves, in case their handiwork failed and escape became imminent.

Everyone was in position.

Snip. The steel cutting blades severed the bell cable, and instantly an auxiliary power supply inside the bell housing was activated. The two burglars standing on the roof above the bell structure heard a faint muffled ring, but almost as soon as it started, it went silent. The inner resin had not been quite hard enough, but as soon as the clapper moved, the thickened substance solidified permanently. The bank had no central station or police alarm, so the men knew they were then able to work on the vault without interruption. Feeling confident that their plan would succeed, the bandits next carried their heavy gear up to the second floor. They guessed that a clear opening down to the vault room would be just outside the lounge area in the upstairs hallway. Their principal method of attack was the formidable core drill and its heavy duty motor. Standard 110 VAC house current was not sufficient to power the rig without blowing numerous fuses, but they had known that going in. So once

This electrical line was tapped to power the core drill used in the burglary.

again two of the gang made their way onto the roof, this time toting a coil of heavy duty electrical wire. At one end of the bank building was a stand-post carrying 220 volts in from a telephone pole several yards away. Very carefully they spliced into two legs of the thick-coated wire, making sure they stayed clear of the many water pockets on the roof. A careless move would surely roast one or both of the bandits. After securely wrapping the connection with tape, they played out their new power supply back down to the second floor. Fuses or circuit breakers now posed no problems, since the men had bypassed the fuse box.

While his two friends were tapping into the power line, number three was busy with a hack saw cutting a lead-in pipe to the cold water faucet in the ladies' room. With this operation complete, he then affixed a length of green garden hose to the pipe, thus providing a remote water cooling system for the core drill. Things were going well for the three men. Time wasn't a factor, since the drill, once in place and ready to operate, would cut a clean 9-inch hole through the 13-inch reinforced concrete vault ceiling at the rate of an inch a minute. Then the drill was bolted to the floor, and the hollow cylinder pipe impregnated with diamond chips was fastened to the water-cooled electric drill head. To provide added pressure for the penetration, several long 2 by 4's were used in wedge/lever fashion. Although actual drilling would be quite smooth, considerable torque buildup was anticipated, and had they not used their new outside power supply, the men undoubtedly would have blown many fuses.

Because they had cut off the electricity—and it is not clear why— the burglars used flashlights, and this slightly hampered their operation.

Their rig was finally set and the drill was turned on. It was diamonds against concrete. As the core sank deeper into the vault ceiling, water spray and dust-turned-to-mud had to be mopped up to keep the area from flooding. Within minutes, the first heavy concrete plug fell through to the vault floor, and the hole revealed the dark interior. The gang then repositioned the device about 15 inches to the left and repeated the drilling operation. This time, however, water from the garden hose connection ran down into the vault through the first hole. It was impossible to keep the vault dry. The third and last hole created still another problem. There was little grip the core drill could bite into, since nearly half the area was now a hole itself. But somehow they managed. When the final plug plummeted downward from the core cylinder, the opening, which resembled an elongated three-leaf clover, measured about 22 inches wide and 12 inches high. Still it was large enough for a small person to squeeze through.

The men were ecstatic. Each wanted to look in the hole they had just made, and they fumbled for a Coleman lantern, tied it to a piece of rope, and lowered it into the money room. It was murky inside; dust and cold dampness from the drill and spilled water gave the room an aura which, they agreed, resembled a centuries-old tomb. To get a better look, the smallest of the trio bellied down and carefully inched his way into the opening where he could scan the interior with his flashlight. He reported the layout to his partners, who were holding his feet and belt to prevent him from slipping all the way through.

Almost directly below them was a 50-year-old screw-door money safe which was sure to contain the bulk of the cash—funds that had been delivered the preceding afternoon. It would have to be torched. But the gang had known that too, and readied their cutting torch and flint starter, together with tanks of oxygen and acetylene.

Also in the small vault room was a small portable teller's bus, the type that can be rolled out to the teller's work area to provide working cash, money orders, stamps and supplies. The thieves knew that minimum cash would be in these key-locked tin compartments, and only if time permitted would they pop the locks.

Against the walls, however, stood several metal shelves. It was here that the savings bonds and American Express travelers' checks were stored.

Still dangling upside down, the observer reported to his friends that the quantity of bonds and travelers' checks appeared to be more than they had anticipated.

Now, even more convinced they were about to score, he instructed his friends to help him back up through the hole. But getting out proved more difficult than wriggling in. Sharp edges left by the core drill cut his skin, and the little man had difficulty scrunching his shoulders enough to fit within the contour of the elongated opening.

When he was finally pulled free, his face was flushed from his being inverted so long. He sat down in the hall to regain his equilibrium while his partners prepared the torch equipment.

Now came the nearly impossible task. Again the small burglar got ready to enter the vault. With shoes off, and stripped to jeans and tee-shirt, he began the tortuous maneuver of inching his body down through the 13-inch deep concrete opening. While the core drill had apparently made a clean cut, small metal burrs and concrete chips again cut into his skin. His two companions pushed him until, inch by inch, his body disappeared, feet dangling down from the vault ceiling.

As he dropped to the floor, there was a splash. Nearly half an inch of water covered the entire room. But no matter, they were now within easy reach of the money. The vault was damp but warm, and it would get even warmer and more uncomfortable when the torch began cutting into the 1500-pound money safe. The safe was sandwiched in the rear corner of the vault, with concrete walls on two sides and a large filing cabinet on the other. It was too heavy to move, so they decided to go in from the top. Leaning over the 3-inch thick steel safe with a torch would be much harder than a side or frontal attack. And to go through the door would be nearly impossible. The robbers were certain the unit had a relocking device on it which, when subjected to the heat of the 2000° torch, would activate and deadset the locking bolts, making it almost impossible to crack.

This cloverleaf hole was cut into the vault roof with a 9 inch core drill. Burglars entered the vault through this opening.

The torch equipment was lowered to the operator piece by piece. He immediately "lit up" and started to work. Sparks, smoke and hot metal spattered in every direction, but slowly a circle 6 inches in diameter appeared, cutting deeper and deeper into the safe. Working conditions became both unbearable and hazardous. Acrid smoke and fumes filled the room, which had no ventilation except for the small hole in the ceiling. Breathing became a problem too, and more than once the torch man had to stop to rest and wipe the perspiration that covered his entire body. Finally a hot metal plug fell into the safe cavity with a convincing thud. Eagerly the two topside burglars peered down, flashlights trained on the defeated box, watching for Torch to reach inside for the loot.

"Hurry up," one of the men shouted.

"Can't," came the anxious reply. "Have to wait for the metal to cool. This crate is still a furnace. Give it another minute." So the men waited.

What seemed like an hour passed, and then a few quick finger taps confirmed that the safe had cooled enough. Reaching in carefully, Torch began to grapple for the loot. It didn't take long before stacks of banded bills began to appear in the smoke-filled room. The tens, twenties and fifties kept coming. There seemed to be no end of the beautiful green paper.

The two men on top, still beaming their lights on the safe like a center ring circus act, shouted encouragement while at the same time warning their friend not to drop any of the stuff on the wet floor. Stacks and stacks of money were placed on the open shelves, ready for exit. A quick estimate of the loot was placed at $100,000.

With the money safe empty, Torch then popped the tellers' bus lockers and took the contents of five cash drawers and over 700 pounds of rolled coins.

He was excited and confident and he wanted the easy stuff next in case they had to split in a hurry.

The time was approaching 3:30 a.m.

Meanwhile, Jeff Adams and his wife had cruised the Woodland community for over two hours with no radio reports of brawls, domestic quarrels or accidents. The bars closed at 2:00 a.m. and the streets were empty. The rain had stopped.

Rounding the corner in front of the Bank of the West, Jeff thought he'd circle the building and give it a routine once-over. Something caught his eye as he slowly passed the bank parking lot. Stopping, he got out and walked over to the side of the building. The object he had noticed turned out to be nothing more than a broken beer bottle, probably thrown there by one of the town loggers who had decided to have "one more" on the way home. He picked up the pieces of glass and threw them in a trash can next to the building. Other than that, nothing seemed to be out of order outside or inside the bank. Officer Adams had no reason to suspect that a burglary was in progress, and therefore he did not inspect the back wall of the bank with its defeated alarm.

Instead, he slid back into the cruiser next to his wife, and the pair drove off down the street.

Unaware that a policeman was within 40 feet of them, the trio of burglars continued with their work. Before deciding to hit a nest of safe deposit boxes located in a second room of the vault, Torch took another look at the open shelves. Here for the taking were piles of American Express checks and Series E savings bonds. What a break, he thought. Quickly scanning the bonds, he counted 25 $1000 certificates plus a mound of smaller denominations. A small metal box belonging to a customer was also picked off a shelf and forced open. Its contents, a bag of U.S. and foreign coins, were taken also.

The money safe inside the vault was torched open from the top. The door was opened by a bank official after the burglary was discovered.

Although the men had not yet counted the take, records the next day would show that a little over $360,000 in cash and negotiables was stolen.

More than pleased with their night's work, the men agreed it was time to depart. They passed up the safe deposit boxes in the next room but only because of the time. It was approaching 3:45 a.m.

The burglars calculated that they had no more than an hour to gather the loot, cover up any clues to their identity, reload their equipment in the logging company truck and disappear. But getting out of the vault proved to be much more difficult than getting in. The core drill hole was barely large enough to permit entry downward, and trying to pull a man's body up through that small opening was even more difficult. Besides, it would take precious time to hoist up all the currency, bonds, checks and the 700 pounds of coin. The torch man quickly decided on another course of exit. He would cut his way out through the 40-year-old vault door. He "lit up" again and then broke a protective glass window which displayed for customers the intricate bolt work and beautiful Swiss

A close up of the torched hole cut into the safe, and the red hot plug that fell into the safe interior, causing some damage to currency.

timelocks. He knew, without trying, that he couldn't deactivate the three movement clocks which revealed an opening time of 8:45 a.m. So, adjusting the oxygen flow to provide maximum heat, he aimed the blue flame directly at the master locking bolt.

Smoke and fumes again filled the tiny vault room that still hadn't had enough ventilation in the past hour to ease breathing conditions appreciably. In spite of the problem, he kept working at that single piece of metal that separated him from freedom—and fresh air. It took only 10 or 12 minutes to cut through the linkage so that the locking mechanism could be released, thus enabling him to retract the multiple throw bolts.

Then, with his shoulder to the door, Torch gave a push on the 3,000-pound slab of steel. It didn't budge. Again he tried to get the door to move. Nothing. A third effort was made with his feet braced up against the steel shelving to provide more power. Still the door didn't give an inch. Then he panicked.

"God," he mumbled, "all this frigging money and now there's no escape."

Quickly he shouted up to his companions that his retreat was cut off and they'd have to get the core drill rigged up again to cut one more hole in the ceiling.

"Wait a minute," came a muffled reply through the ceiling. "Be back in a second."

"What the hell is he going to do now?" Torch thought as he stood, perspiration soaked, in the watery smoke-filled room. Retreating down the stairs to the main floor of the bank, Torch's friend slipped out of the lobby shadows to a spot where he could be seen from the street. Then he approached the vault door. He was tense, sure that the whole town had awakened and was now watching him through the row of bank windows. Then he breathed a sigh of relief. What he saw was an old Mosler vault door with exposed pressure system and fly-wheel. It was little wonder that the big door wouldn't open, even with the mightiest of shoves.

Quickly he grabbed the five-pronged fly-wheel and gave it a spin. As the pressure system released and the two holding bars disengaged, the door finally inched open a crack. When that happened, Torch gave another push from inside and the door slowly moved outward, spilling a small stream of water onto the banking floor. "Jeez, am I ever glad to see you," Torch whispered, giving his friend a boxer's hug. "Now let's get the hell out of here."

While the second man bounded upstairs to tell his partner that all was well, Torch took a few moments to catch his breath. He maneuvered his way closer to the front window, making certain to keep within the shadows. Everything was motionless on the street, and only a thin early morning fog kept the street lamps from filling the bank with incriminating light.

Now the anxiety of success or failure began to overcome the three men. Their restless sleep the night before had started to take its toll. They had been up for nearly 24 hours and had been under intense pressure throughout the last three of those hours. The effects were increasingly obvious in the nervous movements of the trio as they wound up their night's "business" and prepared to depart.

Without a flashlight, Torch inched his way back through the darkened hallway to the place where the men had piled some of their gear. He groped for several large plastic garbage bags and then returned to the vault to bag the piles of currency, bonds and travelers' checks. As one man served as lookout at the bank window, the other two made trip after trip into the vault to retrieve every form of money. Their bounty, burglar tools, and anything that could be a clue to their identity was carefully stacked in the furnace room. When everything was accounted for, Torch returned to the vault and closed the door.

They realized that anyone looking through the front window with a flashlight would surely notice the large puddle of water caused by the core drill. But this couldn't be helped. If someone spotted the water in the next fifteen minutes, the whole caper would probably end in disaster.

All of their equipment, plus the spoils from the vault, were now piled deep in the furnace room. It was approaching 4:15 a.m., and the burglars were ready to make their exit. A quick check of the rear parking lot and the Ben Thomas Logging Co. yards across the alley revealed no signs of life, so the burglar who had originally stolen the pickup slipped out and casually walked over to the parked vehicle. He started the truck, shifted into low gear, and drove back to the bank, a mere 50 yards away. It took only a few minutes to load the bounty and move out. They took everything but three tanks of oxygen and the acetylene. Then they drove out of town and returned to Horseshoe Lake, where their station wagon had been parked in a small wooded area. Here they transferred everything again, leaving the pickup partially hidden in the brush. Within minutes they were back on Interstate 5, heading north past Woodland to Seattle. They joked, laughed and even opened a small bottle of whiskey to celebrate their successful treasure hunt.

At 4:30 a.m., an employee of Ben Thomas arrived for work as he

The door linkage had to be burned to allow the burglar to exit the vault.

always had. A few minutes later he noticed that the truck was missing, and after a thorough search of the small logging compound, he phoned the Cowlitz County Sheriff's office, 20 miles north in Kelso, Washington, to report the missing pickup.

At 8:30 a.m. the bank's operations manager pulled in and parked in his usual reserved space. He unlocked the front door and entered, but it was several minutes before he noticed water on the floor next to the vault. Nothing else seemed to be out of place. On closer inspection, however, he noticed the vault door was not completely closed and sealed. Prepared for the worst, and fearing that someone might still be in the bank, he phoned the police and reported the strange situation. Almost immediately, officers arrived to make a thorough search of the building. As one policeman swung open the vault door, a cloud of smoke billowed forth from the hot, moist interior. In utter disbelief, they all stared at the wrecked teller's bus, the broken glass, the defeated money safe and debris everywhere. Within an hour the sheriff's department was there, along with a resident F.B.I. agent stationed in Longview, Washington. Everyone agreed that it would take days and perhaps weeks to put all of the pieces together in an effort to learn who was involved and how the caper had been accomplished.

By 9:30 a.m. Wednesday, May 15, the station wagon was moving east on Interstate 90 back through Snoqualmie Pass and on to the Cle Elum exit, which was to be their resting place once more. Back over the small river bridge, the station wagon slowed to a stop next to the same open field they had visited the day before. Here, through a small section of broken barbed wire fence, the trio toted several plastic bags filled with American Express vinyl wallets (used to hold the checks), plastic coin holders, some small denomination bills and other items taken from the Bank of the West. They carried it about 325 feet across the field into a heavily wooded area thick with brush and brambles. Here they dug crude holes about 6 to 8 inches deep, and attempted to bury the evidence and some cash accidentally burned by the torch. Leaving the forest, the gang re-entered the Interstate and drove east, over the Columbia River and on through Opportunity, Washington, en route to the town where they had started.

Months passed. It was now Saturday night November 3, 1974 and a Seattle police officer happened to drive up Interstate 90 toward Cle Elum. He was despondent over personal matters. Some time late Saturday night or early Sunday morning, the officer pulled off the highway and headed up the West Nelson Siding Road, the same

This pressure system prevented "Torch" from opening the door. His accomplice had to release pressure and open the door from the lobby.

road the burglars had used months before—and also perhaps only weeks earlier. The officer parked his car on the roadside bordering the pasture less than 10 feet from the broken section of barbed wire. It is thought he sat there for an hour or more, pondering his personal problems. Unable to cope with the pressures any longer, he fired six random shots with his .45 caliber service revolver into the dash panel, apparently in a desperate effort to find the courage to turn the gun on himself. Then he pressed the muzzle of his weapon into his midsection and pulled the trigger for the last time.

The following day, John Smith, a local resident, was out pheasant hunting with his golden retriever, Sam. The dog didn't appear to be following any particular scent, Smith told reporters later, but then he began nosing in the dirt around the underbrush. Taking a closer look at what his dog was up to, Smith discovered some unearthed American Express wallets with checks ripped out, some small denomination bills that were torn and apparently burned, and some currency wrappers bearing the Bank of the West stamp. He also noticed muddy tire tracks in the grassy area leading from the scene. The tire tracks appeared to have been made a short time earlier—possibly during a return visit by members of the burglary gang.

Eventually, one $20 bill identifiable as the "bait money" that had been included in the Bank of the West loot turned up in Seattle. It had been cashed by an unknown person at a bingo game.

Several of the Series E savings bonds were cashed at an auto repair shop in Illinois. But the bulk of the money taken from the largest bank burglary in Washington State history remains unaccounted for. Nor has any of the participants been brought to trial.

Although the Woodland case has not been solved, law enforcement officials have pieced together many important facts, some of which pose interesting questions. Foremost among them is whether this expert burglary was accomplished with the aid of one or more persons familiar with the bank and the logging company. If so, whom?

When and by whom was the safety bolt severed on the furnace room door—the door through which the burglars gained such quick access to the premises?

How did the trio obtain the detailed information concerning the security system at the bank? Had they been tipped in advance, or was it merely a stroke of luck that the alarm system was connected only to an outside bell and not to the police station or another monitoring post, and that the alarm system protected the vault but not the exterior doors and windows or interior traps?

Was it negligence or secret arrangement that left the keys in the logging company truck, parked so conveniently near the bank?

Adding further to the "coincidences" surrounding this case is the fact that a police officer took his life at the very site where, one day later, part of the burglary loot was unearthed. This spot was about 80 miles from the officer's home territory. No connection was ever established between that officer and the burglary or the recovered loot.

What about the prowler who frightened Sergeant Adams' wife just prior to the burglary? Was it really a prowler, or was someone deliberately attempting to divert the attention of the town's lone on-duty police officer from the bank?

So far, there are more questions than answers surrounding this crime, and the few answers seem to lead to further, and more complicated, questions. But almost all burglaries are solved eventually. It's only a matter of time.

5
LIFETIME BURGLAR

"After 40 years as a burglar; if I had to do it over again, I'd hit private homes, not banks. The risk and the possible sentence are far less."

Harmon "Swede" Hanson
Prisoner

"Swede" Hanson is a 57-year-old professional burglar. He's been at the game for more than 40 years, and all of his adult life has been spent shuttling in and out of state penitentiaries. At present he is completing the final months of a 5- to 20-year term at one of the nation's newest maximum-security correctional institutions.

Like most repeat offenders, Swede "got off on the wrong foot" when he was growing up. He was from Cleveland's east side—a place called Hough (pronounced Huff) or "little Hollywood," as the gangs called it back in the mid-30's. A big man with greying crew-cut, ruddy face and huge muscles, you'd imagine Swede was a beer-truck driver or longshoreman. He never graduated from high school, although this self-taught technician could build or tear apart, and reconstruct almost anything. He always worked with confidence, and those who knew and worked with him respected his knowledge and ability.

Swede started his four-decade crime spree in 1937 with the help of his Uncle Bill, who was a master locksmith. When the boy was about 16, in order to teach him the trade, his uncle started to take him to neighborhood stores and offices. There the older man picked the door locks and then crudely burglarized small safes containing such things as stamp collections, dentist's gold and silver, and, occasionally, small amounts of cash.

Swede recalls that his uncle would then make a "connection" with a fence in New York, who, without question, would pay 37% of book value. It was a fairly lucrative business and was certainly more exciting than school. Swede finally quit high school in the eleventh grade to devote his full attention to burglary.

From the very beginning, Swede was never violent. He didn't use a gun until much later, when he teamed up with a gang, and then only used it as a show of strength.

Swede gained further technical experience from his father, who was a legitimate tool maker and blacksmith. It was natural for the fledgling burglar to be around drills and heavy equipment, and he learned quickly.

It was not long before the young thief made friends with other local men in the trade. Such notorious pseudonyms as "Mighty Joe Young," "Sampson," and "The Senator" (the last a pompous character who wore vests and pin-striped suits), headed the list. These burglars and con men, along with several others whom Swede met later, formed the nucleus of a gang that over a period of 35 years stole nearly 8 million dollars—a figure that Swede carefully calculated during several prison interviews.

During the war years, Swede and most of his new associates did "hard time" in various state institutions, and by 1962 Swede had crossed prison thresholds eight times. No term, however, lasted more than 18 months.

It was in prison during the late 50's and early 60's that Swede made the acquaintance of the three partners, who were ultimately to be his closest friends. There was "Stan the Man," a gutsy safe man and master locksmith who had a penchant for armed robberies, particularly of banks. "Big Joe Hampton," the only black in the group, was the alarm expert, having learned his trade as a radar technician in the armed services. "O.P." was the last to join the group, and he became Swede's most trusted friend. His companions called him "O.P." because his full Slavic name was too hard to pronounce.

On September 15, 1963, Swede and his three new friends met in a neighborhood bar on Cleveland's near east side to celebrate their recent release from prison and to form plans that would get them back into business. The story that follows illustrates the daring, the methodical planning, and the exciting "cops and robbers" chase that often made headlines during the roaring 20's. It is important to note that while the occurrences are based on fact (through Swede's recollections), names of all the places and persons have been changed to shield those who might still be effected. The purpose of recounting this incident is to illustrate the apparent excitement of a burglar's life in his quest for quick cash, the anxiety of being pursued, and the myriad experiences combining luck and fate, that befall him.

Planning a job, Swede recalled, was always the best part. "Your blood thickens and your heart pounds as you plot, in minute detail, every second of the hit! It unfolds like a half-conscious dream that you hope will come true as you lie awake in bed." Actually, the four men had talked about their next score while doing time at the Ohio Penitentiary in Columbus, months before.

Kibby's bar was perfect for the secret meeting. None of the foursome was known to regular patrons, although each looked as though he belonged in the surroundings. Stan the Man presided. Even in prison he had been the leader of the group. He had experience in bank jobs that the others had not. He was a locksmith-and-safe man, and it was he who would put it all together.

Their first job as a team was to assess their worth. There was honor among these thieves. They pooled their resources without hesitation, each member knowing that his investment would be returned—they hoped with huge dividends—after the score had been made. The total money available exceeded $5,000.

Next they planned to case the place they had selected while in prison. It was the Northside Federal Savings & Loan, located on the corner of 55th and Broad Street in Cleveland. Northside Federal was a plain yellow-brick, one-story building with standard display windows in front and several smaller casement windows facing alleys at both the side and rear. To the group, it was a perfect mark. In addition to the two main thoroughfares in front and to one side of the institution, the alley in back curved sharply around to the other side and served as egress from an adjoining parking lot for patrons. The immediate area included several bars, a pawn shop, a Polish Community Center and other establishments compatible with a lower-middle-class neighborhood.

During the following weeks, Swede and O.P. opened small savings accounts under false names and periodically made deposits and withdrawals. Each time they visited, they made note of new details of the bank's interior and surroundings. O.P., with his Slavic appearance, blended in with other patrons. Big Joe Hampton remained clear of the bank because almost no Blacks frequented the area. Instead, he cruised around the neighborhood, noting the position of telephone lines and the outside electrical conduit that led into the building.

By mid-October each gang member was completely familiar with the premises, inside and out. Floor plans were drawn so that Big Joe and Stan would know the exact location of every counter, wastebasket, table and chair. Dimensions were taken of the building by carefully but unobtrusively pacing the sidewalks outside.

The decision to go was made by Stan the Man, who selected Friday night, October 21. Swede had purchased a used panel truck on which he mounted a mechanical ladder—the type telephone linemen use. He also bought four good walkie-talkies that could be tuned to a seldom-used transmission band. Inside the van, Big Joe installed a CB radio to monitor police calls. By 9:30 p.m. on Friday, the four men assembled again at Kibby's, ordered a round of draft beer and then huddled in a corner booth for one last briefing before moving out. Swede carefully checked off supply items that were needed in the operation—drills, batteries, cutting blades, jumper cable. Everything was in order and stowed neatly in the van. Stan and O.P. had borrowed a friend's Buick; Swede and Big Joe would use the truck.

As the men finished their beer, they rechecked their pockets and wallets to make sure they carried no incriminating identification. Stan paid the waitress and started to walk toward a sidestreet exit. Approaching the door, he heard one group of Friday night bowlers joke that the foursome looked "more like commandos than neighborhood buddies out for a good time." Stan was visibly shaken by the remark and wondered if their observation might lead to later identification. No matter. He and his friends were set and that was it.

Before splitting up, Swede made a time check. It was exactly 11:32 p.m. Practice runs had confirmed that the route to 55th and Broad Street took 22 minutes. They wanted to be at the scene by 11:55 to observe a private security guard make his midnight check of area shops, knowing he wouldn't return until shortly before 4:00 a.m.

Swede and Big Joe climbed into the truck and headed out 55th Street, with the Buick following but nearly a block behind. At 11:54 p.m. they approached the bank intersection, paused and then cruised to the next block. Big Joe didn't see the security guard across the street at the Polish Community Center and radioed that information back to Stan, who was driving the Buick.

"Never mind, we got 'im," O.P. responded. "He'll be crossing over in a second."

While the conversation was going on, static from the C.B. indicated that there were no police cruisers in the area.

Both vehicles drove straight across the Broad Street intersection and turned the corner two blocks away. That would give the guard plenty of time to complete his check of Northside Federal and continue his rounds.

Swede and Big Joe were first to arrive back at the bank. Everything looked clear, so they drove into the side alley. As the truck slowed to a stop, Big Joe got out carrying a black utility bag that contained the tools of his electronic trade—black boxes, wire cutters, prepared lengths of wire, and several small batteries. It was past midnight when he began to work on the heavy conduit that brought power into the building from an adjacent telephone pole. With the precision and ability of a trained electronics expert, he bared the high voltage wire and then connected his own power cable, fastening it securely to avoid a short circuit.

He then radioed Swede, who was now parked in the patrons' parking lot, to drive up to the side of the building and raise the roof-top ladder. Stan and O.P. listened to the command from nearly a block away at their lookout position.

Swede jockeyed the van into position, climbed onto the truck roof and raised the ladder. The noise, although almost inaudible, sounded to Swede like an earthmover grading a highway.

When the operation was completed, Big Joe handed Swede the electrical cord he had spliced, a hole saw, several blades, a handbit and a drill. Then, with Swede fully equipped, he quickly climbed onto the roof of the bank. Big Joe immediately lowered the ladder and drove down the alley and onto Broad Street.

It was now Swede's turn to work. Toting his drill and other equipment, he struggled over the gravel-covered slate roof to a point close to where he calculated the vault to be. After he drilled the first hole, he used the electric saw to finish the job. Swede was careful not to let the heavy material drop through the bank's thin ceiling, an occurrence that might blow the whole caper when the security man returned with his probing flashlight.

When a man-sized section was withdrawn, Swede glanced at his watch. It was 12:55 a.m.

"Damn," he muttered, "we're running late."

After another radio transmission to Big Joe, the van reappeared, this time with the Buick close behind. Now it was Big Joe's turn again. Swede remained on the roof to act as lookout and to pass equipment to Joe and Stan, who were on their way up the ladder. O.P. drove off to his lookout point, but first he parked the van in the parking lot, leaving the keys in the ignition.

With an extension ladder, two bags of burglar tools and Joe's electronics kit, the three men on the roof were set to enter the darkened building.

It was 1:15 a.m.

Joe was the first to descend the ladder onto the rafters below. Stan followed, pointing the way with his flashlight. Then Swede played out more power cord and passed the hole saw down so that a final cut into the thin plaster ceiling board could be made. If their surveillance diagrams were correct, the drop hole would be within two feet of the vault and well protected from the front window by a line of teller work stations. The hole saw cut easily into the plaster. Zing, zing, and the blade cut a rectangular hole about 24 by 36 inches. It was their last barrier before entering the main lobby. Stan pointed the flashlight carefully into the lobby below.

"Amazing!" Their calculations had been precise. They were only 4 inches from the vault wall. Swede passed the extension ladder down from the roof and Stan and Big Joe lowered it onto the terrazzo floor. Quickly Joe made his way into the bank. Stan followed close behind.

Without touching anything, each man checked out the entire premises, looking for alarm devices. Joe's first stop was the ladies' room.

"Those bankers are all alike," Joe murmured to his friend. "They always put a holdup activator in the john, 'cause that's where the holdup men usually put their hostages."

Joe looked for the burglar alarm. "Found it," he said a moment later. "The junction box is back in the utility room."

Amid the clutter of cleaning supplies was the terminal for the bank's power supply. Big Joe returned to the vault area to retrieve his technician's carry-all, calling up to Swede on the roof to keep a sharp eye out and to radio O.P. that he was ready to defeat the burglar alarm. It was now 1:40 a.m.

The utlility room was too small for both Stan and Joe to work inside comfortably, so Stan remained in the doorway directing the flashlight beam on the box. Big Joe began to perspire. While he knew the circuits as well as any master electrician, the thought of failure was evident.

"Take your time," Stan remarked in a reassuring voice.

"Yeah," Joe responded, still nervous and now shaking visibly. "But you know, my good friend, if we get caught this time, it'll be curtains for all of us—forever and a day."

Joe was right. With their records, the judge would throw away the key.

Big Joe easily found the terminal strips and then groped for his black box. He made a few calculations on the metered box, set the potentiometer and then affixed two wires to the device.

"All set."

Before he made his connections, he traced the alarm conduit back to the alarm control which was located on a rear wall in the employees' lounge. He stood in front of the grey metal box and studied it carefully. It was a Sentinel Alarm System—one of their newest—and was connected to Sentinel's central station downtown.

"It's gonna be tough," he confided to his partner, "but I think I can do it."

"You'd better," Stan responded, thinking again of that judge and another stint in the slammer.

The pair returned to the closet. While Joe prepared to make his connection, he signaled Stan to advise the others he was ready. In a moment, Stan reappeared, nodding that Swede and O.P. were braced for the test. The operation was quick and silent. Joe held his breath as he waited for the black-box needle to move. It didn't quiver. The alarm had been defeated.

To make sure, all they could do was to wait for sirens. Stan inched over to the display window facing 55th Street. Big Joe slumped to the floor in utter exhaustion and lit a cigarette. Five minutes passed. Ten. Fifteen. Nothing. Then Stan saw a car coming up 55th at a fairly fast pace; he was sure it was the police. His first instinct was to split for the roof ladder, but the car quickly passed the bank and kept going.

"Must have been a drunk on his way home," he mumbled softly.

Satisfied that they had successfully jumped the alarm connection, they decided it was now Stan's turn. He was the hard-iron man, and it was his job to open the vault. While Stan emptied his tools in front of the vault door, Big Joe took up a position in the front window. A quick radio check to Swede and O.P. confirmed the alarm defeat and the start of their vault attack. So far so good.

Stan needed little light as he prepared to make his first hole in the plated metal door. He had carefully scribed dimensions of the door with a carpenter's chalk inward from the architrave. But like any good burglar, he first tried to manipulate the dial, hoping that any one of the various pre-set combinations had been used. After nearly fifteen minutes of fumbling, he gave up in favor of the conventional frontal attack. Northside Federal, like many savings and loan institutions, had not installed a bank-type vault door. Instead, they had used a fire-resistant, metal, concrete-filled door that measured about 7 inches thick. Even these were tough, and Stan knew it. One mistake and the relocking device would activate, deadsetting the locking bolts.

As he tested his high-speed drill, to which he had attached a ½ inch bit, Stan looked at his watch. It was now almost 2:40 a.m., which would give him a mere hour and 15 minutes to get in and ravage the teller lockers and money safe before the arrival of the security guard, who would make his rounds at 3:55 a.m.

The drill began its penetration into the semi-hard steel plate. Metal spirals fell to the floor as the bit inched deeper into the concrete-filled door. Stan pressed his arm and shoulder against the door with a thud and shuddered. He had broken through.

Now came the most difficult job—penetrating the locking mechanism without activating the relocker. With mirrors, probes and a tiny side light (called a nasopharyngeoscope), he expertly felt the intricate way through the next few steps of the operation.

"Time, time. If only I had more time," Stan cursed as he stopped to rest his weary arms. His watch read 3:23 a.m. Then, with almost no warning, he heard the familiar metal clicking sound from within the door.

"That's it," he shouted. "I've done it." In another moment, the door swung open. Inside were neat rows of lockers, a few file cabinets and a round-door money safe. Stan knew he wouldn't have time to crack the safe before guard check, but if all went well, they could drill it later. After all, they had the whole weekend.

As Stan relayed the good news of his handywork, Big Joe ducked behind the manager's desk and shouted, "Down."

Stan instantly closed the vault and dived for cover. Just then a Sentinel Alarm Company vehicle drove past the bank from the direction opposite O.P.'s lookout post. Slowly it pulled into the alleyway and around the back of the building. In another second the cruiser was gone. Evidently its driver had not spotted the van parked in the visitor's lot.

"Whadda ya' think, Stan?" Big Joe whispered.

"Dunno," came the hesitant reply. "If they'd gotten an alarm, the cops and everybody would have been down on us in minutes. I think it was only a routine pass."

At this point Swede, who had been on the roof for several hours, trundled his huge frame down the ladder to take a look.

"Did you see the Sentinel car?" Stan asked.

"Yeah," Swede said nervously. "Those guys put their light on the van but then drove off as if nothing was wrong."

"I don't like it one bit. Maybe we oughta split," Joe chimed in, having taken another check of the alarm box. "Everything's okay in there, but I don't like it."

The men decided to wait the few additional minutes until the security man had made his next inspection of the neighborhood. Swede climbed back up the ladder, Big Joe returned to the window and Stan began to hide his tools. Within a short time the bank interior was back to normal.

At 3:55 a.m. the uniformed guard appeared across the street near the Polish Community Center. A moment later he meandered over to the bank and cupped his hands around his eyes close to the window to peer in. Then he flashed his light inside, making a complete sweep of the banking floor, vault and teller stations. No-one moved. He did it again, this time aiming the beam straight at the vault door. Finally, after rattling the front door to make sure it was secure, the guard pocketed his light and strolled across Broad Street to continue his beat.

Stan was still nervous, and he called up to Swede. "I've got a funny feeling, Swede. You'd better come on down and get the truck—just in case."

Swede obeyed without comment. He too was a little shaky about the whole thing. Again he lumbered down the ladder and left quickly through the employee lunchroom window which opened onto the alley. Once in the van, he radioed O.P. to be prepared for a fast exit. Swede and O.P. revved up and moved the cars to new positions. If there were going to be trouble, they didn't want to be spotted without an escape route.

Big Joe kept watch out front while Stan began ravaging the tellers' steel lockers. Pop, pop, pop, and the key locks on each locker disappeared into the cavities. As Stan eagerly opened each compartment daily receipts, tellers' cash and travelers' checks appeared.

There was no telling how much there was, and Stan didn't take the time to count it. He and his partners would do that later.

Then there was another shout of warning, "Cool it!" reported Big Joe. "There's a broad walking her dog outside." For a second time, the pair dashed for cover.

Suddenly Stan's walkie-talkie stuttered from inside the vault, "O.P. here, do you read? Fuzz on 55th—two cars."

Stan pressed the send button and quickly answered, "Keep clear but near. Be ready for an alley pick-up."

Swede heard the transmission but didn't respond. He decided to keep his cool and cruise around within a four block radius of Northside Federal, hoping the report wasn't "for real."

It another second, one city "blue and white" pulled up in front and stopped; the other made a slow pass through the alley and out onto Broad Street. As quickly as they had come, both departed.

"That's it," shouted Stan. "I think we've been had. Let's grab what we can and get the hell out of here."

But it was too late. The two police cars reappeared and parked across the street, while another cruiser and a Sentinel alarm car blocked off the rear. As police got out with guns drawn, Big Joe could see the security guard, in a Sentinel alarm car, rounding the corner and pointing to the building. In an instant, there were spot lights trained on every window and door. The caper was over.

Stan picked up his radio, and with the coolness of an infantry commander signaled Swede and O.P. to get lost. "But bring our lawyer to the Cuyahoga County Courthouse as soon as possible," he said, almost as an afterthought.

The next morning Stan and Big Joe were brought to court and charged with breaking and entering, attempted burglary, and possession of burglars' tools. Bond was set at $50,000 each. As requested, Swede had contacted their lawyer, who showed up for the hearing and immediately posted the $100,000.

Because authorities believed others were involved, trial was postponed while a search for the others was mounted. When the case was finally heard, testimony revealed that the initial alarm defeat had been recorded as a "caution" signal at the central station. It had been heard again a short time later. The Sentinel security guard, on his 4:00 a.m. rounds, also had suspected something, and he had notified his headquarters when he got a block or so away.

In the courtroom, during the entire trial, sat Swede and O.P. They had never been picked up and charged. The brazen cohorts of Stan and Big Joe listened to the whole case and decided that their friends were doomed. During a lunch recess, all four left the courtroom and adjourned to a bar across the street. It was there that airplane tickets were distributed, and before the court assembled again for sentencing, Swede and O.P. drove with their friends to Cleveland Hopkins Airport for a get-away to Atlanta. Immediately, Ohio authorities began the search for all four—Stan and Big Joe for jumping bond and trial, and Swede and O.P., who had now been identified, for parole violation.

About 60 miles north of the Georgia city, the burglars holed up in one of several "safe houses" they and some of their northern comrades had purchased earlier. Here they remained, undercover, acting as gentlemen peanut farmers.

One day, after things settled down, Swede went out to buy groceries at a local shopping center. There he ran across an old friend who had done time with him back in Ohio. His name was J.B. Sobel. J.B.'s specialty was counterfeiting.

Swede invited J.B. to join him and his companions at the safe house, and during the next few months the fugitives bought some presses and began manufacturing high quality 10- and 20-dollar bills.

In late fall 1964, all five packed up and returned to Painesville, Ohio, where they again lived undercover, pulling a few more burglary jobs in northeastern Ohio and western Pennsylvania.

Swede eventually left the group and drifted to upper Michigan where he stayed at a hunting lodge, also a safe house, run by some friends. He and the others were then using nearly $500,000 that they had made from the sale of over 4.5 million dollars in counterfeit paper money.

All was quiet for the Ohio group until one cold morning in January, 1965. J.B. and O.P. were sitting in the kitchen of their Painesville farm house when a loudspeaker from the barn told the two men to give up and come out peacefully. Looking out the window, O.P. saw that Treasury men had the place surrounded. What happened at this point is not clear, but J.B. did give up without a fight. O.P. is believed to have made a run for it and was wounded in the back during his escape. He eluded police and Treasury agents for several hours, hiding in a nearby forest. But by early morning, exhausted and bleeding badly, he surrendered when found by officials searching the area where he was hiding. Immediately O.P. was taken to a Cleveland hospital and remained there under guard.

In the meantime, Swede heard of the incident through the underworld grapevine and headed back to Cleveland to help his friend. For many years Swede's buddies had kidded him because he looked so much like O.P.'s brother. Using this to advantage, Harman posed as O.P.'s brother and entered the hospital with a suitcase and a .38 special. Swede told the police guard he wanted to see his brother, and before a check could be made, Swede managed to get the officer inside the room, tie him up and free his partner. O.P. was still very weak and they didn't know whether he could travel, especially all the way back to Michigan. Somehow they managed. As soon as they arrived at the lodge, Swede phoned a "friendly" doctor in Detroit who agreed to nurse O.P.'s wound. The next day, while attending his patient, the doctor noticed a black suitcase on the floor under the bed. It contained about $200,000 in counterfeit bills that Swede had not yet sold. After giving O.P. a strong sedative, the physician helped himself to a bundle of the money and presented Swede with a bill for his services. Then the doctor left for his trip home to Detroit.

Swede learned a few weeks later that the doctor had been mysteriously killed, probably by an organized group that was unhappy at being paid gambling debts with bogus bills.

Later in 1965, the gang's exploits were ended. Harman "Swede" Hanson was picked up for parole violation in Newport, Kentucky, another of his favorite haunts. O.P. was apprehended about the same time and was sent back to Ohio Penitentiary in Columbus. He was sentenced to 20 years for his part in the Northside Federal job but never completed his time. He died in prison of natural causes less than a year later.

Big Joe, who had travelled south again after the counterfeiting business folded in Ohio, was spotted in Alabama. He, too, was returned to prison in Columbus.

Stan the Man was already in prison when the others arrived.

Swede was released in 1967, but he returned to the establishment twice more, in 1969 and 1970. At present he is awaiting parole for the twelfth time. He now says that he is through with crime, that he is too old. When he does get out, he says he plans to settle down "somewhere in the midwest to take up a legitimate business, maybe to work with tools." Maybe he will, after 40 years spent mostly in penitentiaries. And maybe his feeling that private homes are more available, and less risky than banks, will prove irresistible.

6

J. J.'s GOLDMINE

*"When the stakes are high, when you're shooting
for a couple million in gold, there's little you won't
do to get it. I know; I was part of the team that
tried."*

Paddy Ginzberg

Of all the means used to gain entry to bank safes and
vaults, probably the most complex, most dangerous, and
certainly the heaviest, is a weapon called the burning
bar. It is actually an oxygen lance, perfected by engineers
during World War II as an underwater demolition tool.
The lance is a long steel plumber's pipe, fitted with many
smaller alloy rods, through which oxygen is forced and
then ignited by a conventional acetylene torch. When lit,
the lance burns at temperatures exceeding 7,000°F, or
more than enough heat to burn the re-entry shields of
our space vehicles.

While the bar is truly an awesome device, it is also
cumbersome and very noisy, emitting choking gases and
acrid fumes. More than 6 hours may be required to burn
a hole in a vault wall that is large enough for a small
person to crawl through, and it may be necessary to use
more than a dozen tanks of oxygen, an untold number of
10-foot thermal rods and sundry other tools. The total
weight of the attack equipment might exceed a half ton.
Although the lance is difficult to work with in an
enclosed area, when used by professionals it is very
effective.

A highly polished nameplate with the words "James J. Calhoun"
in raised letters shimmered in the sun. Three occupants of a vintage-

model automobile squinted to make out the words. The brass plate was bolted to a stone column in front of the Calhoun estate, one of many turn-of-the-century mansions that still grace the Newport, Rhode Island, seashore.

Racing season was in full swing and as the car turned up the pink gravel driveway toward the main house, the driver and passengers could see multicolored spinnakers billowing far out in Rhode Island Sound. It was a gorgeous sight, especially to the three men who had never known such opulence or beauty.

James J. Calhoun, or "J.J." as he was known to the visitors, was obviously a man of means. Originally from Boston, he had made his millions right after World War II in the scrap metal business. He had bought old warships and military hardware and either resold them or melted down the unusable parts, selling them to companies urgently needing these scarce postwar commodities.

But Mr. Calhoun hadn't always been among the most respected men in his community. This aging captain of industry had a tainted past that included burglary and smuggling, and some old friends even suspected that he had been involved in murder. But that was long ago, and it was now 1970 and people who knew J.J. thought of him as a gentleman, sailing enthusiast and respected member of Newport's elite society.

The car slowed to a stop in front of the huge fieldstone house. The visitors were not aware that Mr. Calhoun was watching them from a bay window in the west wing as they got out of the car and momentarily stood in awe before climbing the few steps to the front door. Before the first man could touch the ornate door knocker, the door swung open and J.J. motioned them inside. Shaking hands with each man, he exchanged quiet pleasantries and then ushered them back to the west wing living room. Here he offered them brandy from a cut-crystal carafe and then passed a box of expensive cigars. The men immediately sat down and waited for their host to speak.

"Gentlemen," he said, scrutinizing the group, "I've called you here because I need a favor. It's been a long time since we've been together, and in trying to find each of you I learned that the last few years have not gone particularly well—especially for you, Paddy." J.J. was now standing at the side of Paderewski Ginzberg's chair, his hand resting on Paddy's shoulder. "You've just gotten paroled from Norfolk, and I know what seven years in the slammer is like." Paddy grinned and took another sip of the aromatic brandy.

"And Billy Howe! I guess you've made out the best. Electrician's

A burning bar will melt a hole through this safe wall in seconds. The demonstrator wears a heat-resistant suit for protection.

helper, hod carrier, and alarm installer up in Brockton before they laid you off. I hope it wasn't for your drinking problem?" Billy put his glass down on the table, obviously embarrassed, and ashamed that J.J. knew of his recent past.

"And you, Sam," Calhoun continued, walking over to Sam Tavelman. "I was sorry to hear of your family problems. Was it last year your wife died?" Sam nodded, bitter that the state hadn't taken better care of her while he was barely scraping by on welfare. He hadn't had a decent job since '62, when he had worked the docks up around Boston. Then there were his two sons, who were always in trouble. Myron was doing hard time out of state and his older boy, Sam, Jr., had run away from home more than 10 years ago. He had not even come home for Beth's funeral.

"The favor I need will involve getting the old team back together again. I know that you, Billy, and you, Sam, have been clean for the last 20 years, but because you both haven't done quite as well as me, I thought you might be interested in going back to work."

J.J. returned to a giant armchair next to the hearth and sank into the down-filled cushions.

"And, Paddy, I know you can use some help."

Paderewski Ginzberg did, indeed, need all the help he could get. His record of burglary dated back to 1942, and he had spent 21 of the past 28 years in jail.

The three men sat in silence waiting for their former boss to discuss the new mark. They knew that they would not have to think too long before agreeing to J.J.'s offer, whatever it was.

"I can't tell you too much right now, but I will whet your appetite by saying there's 300 big ones in it for each of you. And if we do it right, the risk will be minimal." The men looked at each other, dumbfounded. Three hundred thousand apiece would transform them from paupers to men of means overnight. No risk would be too great.

"Before I go any further, I want to know if you're interested. If you are, fine. If not, then please have another drink, join me for dinner and some reminiscing of the old days, and we'll forget the whole thing."

The men looked at each other, and then Paddy spoke for the group.

"J.J., we've all known you for nearly 30 years. Everything you've told us and done for us in the past has been straight. I think I can speak for the boys—we're in. Just lay it on us, and we'll produce."

"Excellent. I thought I could count on you. The score is what I jokingly call J.J.'s Goldmine. I'm a minority owner and board member of the Byron A. Thorpe Metal Findings Company over in Westerly, Rhode Island. The company deals in the manufacture of fine jewelry—school rings and company awards and incentive gifts. Their vault usually contains between two and three million in raw gold and silver."

When the four men had finished dinner, J.J. offered his guests coffee out on a huge sundeck that faced the Sound. They watched the last racing sloops lower their spinnakers and glide silently into Narragansett Bay, little more than a mile away. The bright sun was now settling over Block Island, and it became difficult to look directly at the water because of the intense reflection.

"Let's get down to business," Calhoun told his friends, who were satiated with food, drink and the picturesque nautical scene.

"Timing is going to be the key to this score. It was only last Monday that the first element of our little caper presented itself, and that's why I called you now."

The three burglars, seated in their host's expensive patio chairs, drew closer and gave their undivided attention to J.J.'s words.

"Billy, you're the alarm man. And a damn good one. Tomorrow, first thing, I want you to visit this address and ask for a Mrs. Spraytz." Calhoun handed Billy an envelope with the details and a small bundle of cash. "She's going to be your landlady for the next three months.

"I've waited over a year to rent this precise apartment, and I just learned that the current tenant moved out right after Memorial Day. You're to take a year's lease and pay her three months' advance rent. You can tell the old lady you travel a lot and might not be around much to take care of such things as the rent. Besides, the fewer times you actually see her, the better."

Then J.J. gathered his friends around a large umbrella table and unfolded a set of plans, expertly drawn, showing the entire layout of the Byron Thorpe Company in Westerly. The first prints showed the main company building that faced Water Street. J.J. explained that the old structure was the former headquarters of a shoe manufacturer who had closed up and moved south in 1958. The Thorpe concern had taken over the old brick building in '63, had made some minor renovations, and proceeded to build a very successful jewelry business. Then Calhoun, using the map, showed them that between Water Street and Mechanic Street, to the east of the Thorpe building, an alley ran north and south and split the block in two.

While their boss was talking, Billy Howe glanced at the envelope containing Mrs. Spraytz' rooming house address. It was 152 Mechanic Street.

"That's right, Billy, I think you see what significance your new rooms will have on our plan."

Then J.J. again pointed to the alley and Mrs. Spraytz' rooms that were marked with an **X**. He ran his finger over the drawing of a line of telephone poles in the alley that separated the Thorpe Company and the Mechanic Street row houses.

"Outside the bedroom window of your new home stands a telephone pole with transformer and switching box. My sources inform me that within that metal casing lie the terminals for all of the Thorpe telephones, including the vault alarm lines that are connected to the highway patrol barracks over in Charlestown."

Calhoun lay down the map and announced, "Mr. Howe, your first job will be to silence that alarm."

Billy smiled. "Right, J.J."

Calhoun then turned to Sam Tavelman and little Paddy Ginzberg. "Now for your assignments. Sam, since you're clean, I want you to rent some vacant office and warehouse space on the other side of Water Street, opposite the Thorpe headquarters. There's a vacant loft at number 158 that has loading facilities in the rear. The place hasn't been used in years, and you'll have no trouble making a deal with the real estate guy who handles the building."

J.J. handed Sam an envelope similar to Billy's containing complete details about the property, the real estate office phone number and $3,000 in cash.

"Starting tomorrow you'll be known around town as Samuel Tava, field boss of the Southern New England Construction Company, about to do some classified subcontract work for Electric Boat Company down in New London. The job you'll be doing, in case you're asked, is right over the state line in Connecticut. This way no snoopy city inspectors or state building commissioners will have any reason to check work permits or contracts."

Sam thumbed through the money, the first real green he had seen in years.

Calhoun continued, "The money will buy you a cheap lease on the construction office and also an old dump truck that one of the men at my salvage company over in Providence will be putting up for sale. Don't worry about being outbid for that piece of junk; I've made sure there won't be any competition."

Then Calhoun walked around in back of Paddy's comfortable

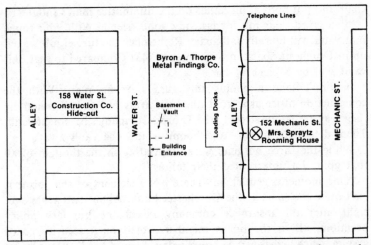

This map shows relative locations of Mrs. Spraytz's rooming house, the victim company and the construction company used as a hideout.

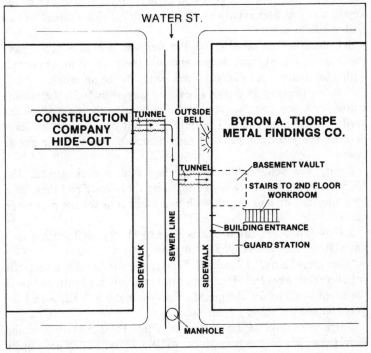

This map shows a detailed plan of J.J.'s tunnel from hide out to vault.

chair and put both of his hands on the diminutive man's shoulders.

"I've saved your job for last, my good friend. With your touch that vault will literally fall apart. Remember the tunnel job we did up in Dorchester back in the winter of '43? Compared to that, this vault will be a piece of cake."

It didn't take a genius to figure out the plan. With the construction office as a front, the little army of "moles" would dig their way across the street to the Thorpe Company's basement vault. Then, defeat the alarm—and boom!—blow the vault away.

While the three burglars were luxuriating in the thought of all that gold, J.J. interrupted their fantasy.

"One moment, gentlemen. There's one element of this job that isn't quite the same as the Dorchester bank. About two years ago, right after the insurance company raised the burglary policy premium, all of the board members voted on a security guard system which is manned 24 hours a day. I could hardly vote against it, but recently, on one of my infrequent visits to Thorpe's offices, I managed to get a copy of their operational procedures and the security devices they use. As I said earlier, timing is going to be the key to this job, and even with the new guard, I'm confident we can pull it off."

J.J. then laid out other details the men would need to know, gave them each some expense money and told them not to make contact with him again until everyone was ready to begin work.

"Oh, by the way, Paddy, it's best you stay away from the outside world for a few days, so you'll remain here on the grounds as my gardener and handyman. The only time it'll be necessary to leave here or the jobsite is for that once-a-month visit to your parole board."

Paddy was delighted to be brushing against such wealth. The Calhoun estate was certainly going to be a far better pad than the 8 by 9 foot cell he had shared with two other cons for the past seven years.

J.J. looked at his watch. It was close to 11:00 p.m. The three men knew the meeting was over, and they got up to leave.

"One more thing," J.J. added. "Today is June 12. Our target date is Labor Day weekend. That'll give us three full days with no one in the plant—except for the guards. Can we make it?" J.J. asked the question with a smile on his face.

There were three affirmative nods. Three hand shakes. Sam and Billy Howe left by the front door, while J.J. and Paddy gave quick goodbye waves and closed the big oak door.

Both men drove back to Massachusetts to pack and prepare for a three months' leave of absence, but actually they had nothing to button up. Neither of them had a job, and only Billy had a wife, and it would be a pleasure to get away from her constant bitching for a few months.

As they drove, they talked. Both were excited about the prospects of becoming wealthy; they trusted J.J. and liked the layout. But somehow they wondered about the hit. James J. Calhoun was obviously a wealthy man. He had everything any man could want— money, position and respect from Newport's elders. Why then would he risk his all for another million or so? Could it be that J.J. had ego problems? Did he just want to see if it could be done, or did he need a large sum of quiet money to pay a debt—maybe to the syndicate or some politician? Then again, maybe he was being blackmailed for some mothball problem that had happened years ago.

The two men would probably never find out, but no matter. J.J. had confidence in their talents, and there was no doubt that they and their friend Paddy were part of a team.

Billy dropped Sam off at his apartment and reminded him to be up the next day by 8:00 a.m. They were ready to go to work.

Billy parked his old Plymouth in front of 152 Mechanic Street, adjusted his tie, and walked up a small flight of wooden steps to the paint-peeled porch of Mrs. Spraytz' rooming house. The elderly landlady was watering some hanging plants when Billy presented himself. A room-for-rent sign in the front window saved him the embarrassment of explaining how he had selected this particular place, and before he could speak, Mrs. Spraytz offered a polite good-morning. Yes, she had some nice rooms upstairs, but she apologized because they were in the rear and didn't have as pleasant a view as some of the others. Billy didn't object at all.

After the details were settled, Billy went back to the car to get his suitcases and a black leather repairman's case. Once inside his Victorian apartment, which included a bathroom and a closet-size kitchen, he put away his personal effects and then opened his repair case on the bed. Drawing aside the faded damask curtains, he raised the yellowed torn window shade, and to his utter surprise stared directly into a lovely black telephone pole. Mrs. Spraytz was wrong. His *was* the perfect room, and "Ma Bell" was to be congratulated for placing her magnificent monument so beautifully close to Billy's workshop.

To get a better look at the pole and its telephone terminal box, Billy raised the window and leaned out, scanning the alley, the adjacent row houses and the Byron Thorpe Company across the way. The alley was cluttered with parked cars and two delivery trucks that butted against the jewelry company's loading dock. Billy knew that with all the daily traffic, it would be difficult to work on the alarm lines until after dark, which at that stage of summer wouldn't be until well after eight o'clock.

Then he made an almost fatal mistake. Trying to reach out for the utility pole, he lost his footing and nearly fell out the window and down two stories into a row of garbage cans.

"Damn," Billy mumbled. "This goddamn pole is too far away to work on." He pulled himself back in and plopped into the room's only chair. How the hell was he going to get to that pole without a ladder? Then he brightened at the answer to his dilemma. He'd build a ladder, but not the vertical type. What he planned was a gangplank affair that he could easily extend and retract from the window.

He searched through his tool kit and found an 8-foot retractable tape measure. Extending it out from the window sill, Billy marked the distance at 4 feet 5 inches. He estimated the terminal box to be another 3 feet above the sill—perfect working height once his platform extension was in place.

With the measurements taken, Billy drew a few rough sketches of what his work-station would look like, and then left the house to buy the lumber and other supplies to put it together.

While he was out, he also stopped at a local package store and bought a half case of good whiskey. There would be many drab days and nights spent at Mrs. Spraytz', and he thought it would do no harm to have a few drinks to help pass the time.

At 5:00 p.m. Billy again left his room and drove to a roadhouse on the outskirts of Westerly. It was here that he had told Sam to meet him. As he pulled in and parked, he noticed a rather worn and battered dump truck parked alongside the building. A faint smile came over his face. Sam had done it, he thought. He had bought the truck as planned and was already inside popping a beer.

"How'd it go today?" Sam asked his partner as the two sidled into a booth next to a blaring jukebox.

"Great, just great. Got the apartment with no sweat. J.J. sure had everything set up, right down to the most beautiful telephone pole you ever saw." Billy went on to tell Sam about the gangplank problem and his solution. All the lumber and supplies were in his car, ready for the ladder to be built as soon as the construction office was set up.

"And how about you? I see by the clunker outside that you got the truck."

"Yeah, but it was almost too easy. The guy over at Calhoun's salvage company seemed to expect me. He didn't say much, but when he set a price of twenty-two hundred bucks for the heap, I thought I'd do a little bargaining to make it look good. I finally got the thing for seventeen-fifty. I hope it'll hold up until after Labor Day."

"What about the construction office? Were you able to get that yet?" Billy took another sip of beer from the can.

"Yep, like you said, J.J. did his homework. The real estate guy nearly fell over when I told him what I wanted, and even let me go with a month-to-month lease when I told him of the uncertainty of our job with Electric Boat."

"When can we get in?" Billy asked.

Sam reached in his pocket and pulled out a set of keys, dangling them in Billy's face. "Wanna see it now?"

The men hurriedly finished their beer and then, like two school kids recessed for summer vacation, they almost ran out of the bar.

Sam followed Billy's car in his newly purchased truck. About two blocks from Water Street, Billy parked and joined his friend in the cab of the truck. It wouldn't do for anyone to see the Massachusetts car too frequently. After the heist the cops would be crawling like ants around the neighborhood, looking for clues.

Before showing Billy the inside of their new office, Sam drove slowly down Water Street and pointed to the three-story brick building that had been built prior to the turn of the century. It was almost a carbon copy of Thorpe headquarters across the street, with rows and rows of glass paned windows. There were several entrances to the property, which had been enlarged in later years as the building was divided into separate factories or warehouses. Number 158 Water Street was clearly marked, and appeared to be 60 to 70 feet up the street and across from the Thorpe main entrance.

Sam then drove the truck around the corner to the west and into another alley much like the one that separated Water Street from Mechanic Street and Mrs. Spraytz' rooming house. This repetitious layout of alley and street was typical of most old New England towns where commerce had been carried on for nearly two centuries.

Sam pulled the truck up close to the alley entrance of their newly leased facility, got out and unlocked a huge overhead door. Then he drove the truck inside and lowered the garage door. It hit the concrete floor with a resounding thud that nearly smashed three eye-level window panes.

"Easy, pal," Billy shouted, scrunching up his shoulders and expecting to hear glass shattering on the floor.

"I'll fix that tomorrow," Sam called back. "I'll put some tape on them, and it'll help keep inquisitive eyes away, too."

The two men then started on a careful search of the entire three-floor office, using Sherlock Holmes precision. Nothing of significance was in the lower truck dock area. There were a few empty 55-gallon drums probably left by the previous occupant, a small pile of used lumber stacked in a corner, and some old wooden doors that probably had been removed during a previous office renovation. Sam made a mental note that some of these items might come in handy later on.

Next they climbed up a small flight of stairs to the loading platform. This was completely empty. Entering the front office, Billy peeked into several closets, opened every drawer of an old wooden desk that had one cracked pedestal, and finally examined the six tall office windows that faced Water Street and their proposed mark across the street. Nothing was in the second or third floor rooms except for traces of decomposed rat droppings. The whole place reeked of mildew and filth.

Satisfied with the layout, Sam tugged on Billy's shirt with an expression of pride and led his friend down a darkened flight of wooden stairs to the basement. Actually it was more like a cellar. The old foundation walls facing the street were the original mortar and stone, and when Sam pointed this out, Billy laughed.

"I hope the Thorpe Company building was built by the same guy. Getting through these walls will make Paddy very happy."

The next day Billy and Sam went on a buying spree. Under false names they bought or rented construction tools and camping supplies for a long stay in their office hideout, and two very important items—special citizen-band radios to monitor police calls. Billy would keep one in his rented room and Sam and Paddy would listen to the other at the construction office.

By mid-afternoon, the two men returned to their headquarters and set up shop. While Sam prepared a makeshift campsite in the now sealed-off dock area, Billy put the finishing touches on his telephone pole platform.

The men were now prepared for a lengthy live-in. They had sleeping bags, a Coleman stove, food supplies, lanterns, and all the necessary elements to sustain them for an extended period. They were almost ready to make contact with J.J. and Paddy, but first Billy had to defeat the alarm system before actual tunnelling could begin.

It was after 10:00 p.m. when Billy left the office and walked the two short blocks back to Mrs. Spraytz' to get his car. He made sure all the lights were out inside the rooming house and then drove back to get his platform and radio. Returning once more, he silently tried to maneuver his cumbersome wooden platform inside and up the front hall stairs without waking the old lady or the other two residents. Once the platform was safely inside his room, he returned to his car for the radio and a few other pieces of equipment.

To make sure everyone would be asleep, Billy waited until after midnight before he started to mount the retractable gangplank. The only hard part of the plan would come now. Peering out the back window, Billy saw Sam's truck coming slowly up the alley. When it reached the telephone pole, Sam stopped, jumped out, and from the rear of the truck pulled out an aluminum extension ladder. He quietly placed it beside the row of garbage cans and then drove off. Billy waited another half hour before going downstairs to the alley. He was now drenched with perspiration. His adrenalin flowed and his metabolism increased to a point where he almost became unable to work. It was obvious that his 20-year absence from the business was taking its toll. He took a deep breath, exhaled, and then stooped over to pick up the ladder. So far, so good. He could see no lights, hear no one moving in the still, damp night and figured it was now or never.

As quietly as possible he extended the ladder. Click, click, click, the retaining bar sounded as it passed over each rung. Enough. Billy positioned the ladder against the pole on the side closest to his bedroom window. Then he climbed up, careful not to touch or bump anything that would make a noise. From a carpenter's utility apron tied around his middle, he extracted three heavy-duty spikes, and with a hard rubber-head mallet began driving them into the soft pine telephone pole. It was these protruding nails that would provide a firm resting place for the platform.

When that job was finished, apparently without arousing anyone, Billy retreated down the ladder, pulled the rope release that disengaged the retaining bar, and collapsed the ladder to its original 8-foot height. He carefully laid it down again and then went back inside. By the time Billy got to his room, Sam, who had been watching from the end of the alley, came around again in his truck and picked up the ladder. In another second, Sam was gone.

Billy was too unnerved to work any more that night. He uncorked a whiskey bottle and for the first time since the escapade began, drank himself to sleep.

The next morning started late for Billy Howe. He awakened at noon with a grim hangover. Glancing at the whiskey bottle on his night stand, he shuddered when he saw that more than half the stuff was gone.

By the time Billy had pulled himself together it was mid-afternoon, and Sam was more than a bit perturbed when his friend finally showed up at the office.

"Don't bother to explain," he said coldly. "I can guess what happened. I personally don't give a good rat's ass, but J.J. and Paddy wouldn't buy it at all. We've got too much at stake to have to worry about bottle problems." Billy was again ashamed that the subject had been mentioned.

"I'm sorry, Sam, it won't happen again."

"Forget it." Sam was eager for Billy to see what his handiwork had wrought that morning. Bright and early he had gone down to the cellar, and with pick and hammer he had knocked out a dozen or so stones from the old mortared wall.

"Look here!" Sam exclaimed. "We're in luck again."

Billy peered in the shallow opening and saw nothing but hard-packed dirt mixed with narrow seams of sand and gravel.

"Looks like it'll be easy diggin's," he responded, still a little shaky from the booze. "But that gravel and sand could cause problems. We may have to shore up as we move ahead or risk a cave in."

The two men spent the remainder of the day digging and clearing in order to test the holding power of the earth shaft. "J.J.'s Goldmine" had more significance as the groundhog team clawed away into the evening hours.

Finally Sam told his partner they had gone far enough. The real digging would resume after the alarm was silenced and Paddy had joined them. Billy cleaned up a bit, had a simple dinner of canned food heated on the Coleman stove, and bid his partner good night.

"If I'm lucky, I'll be back tomorrow after I put that alarm system to bed. But just in case, stay tuned to the police monitor; we may be getting some company around midnight."

The evening hours passed slowly for Billy. He wanted to finish off that bottle of whiskey, but this was not the night. He had to be sharp, and the slightest mistake could cause bells to ring and summon an abundance of police cruisers.

Billy turned his high frequency FM scanner to the several bands that monitored sheriff and local police calls. Reception on both bands was good. He chuckled when he heard a "211" go down at a local liquor store. It was probably some young kid hitting the night manager for a few lousy bucks in the cash till.

It was now early morning. Everything was quiet, and Billy's careful surveillance outside the bedroom window revealed no activity in either direction. He lifted the makeshift gangplank up to the sill and slid it carefully out the window. The far end finally hit the utility pole and dropped onto the three protruding spikes. Perfect, he thought. Now for the real test. First he applied hand pressure to the platform. It held firm. Then he crawled out the window and gave it a light shove downward. Still it held. Finally he inched out until his head touched the pole, and with both hands holding firmly to the plank, he tried bouncing on it. The heavy spike-heads sank into the plywood, creating a holding groove. Billy was pleased that his work-station was so substantial. Now he was ready for work.

Retreating toward the house, he inched into the bedroom to gather the intricate electronic gear needed to silence the alarm. When he had been fired from the alarm company, he had made sure that he took all the black boxes, meters and other testing gear he could confiscate. Everything was now neatly laid out on the bed. With his carpenter's apron again tied around his waist, Billy stuffed the fabric compartments with the tools of his trade. He also picked out a small but powerful penlight that would keep to a minimum the illumination that would be needed.

Back out on the platform, Billy sat Indian fashion in front of the terminal box. Because the metal door had no lock, he grabbed a recessed metal ring and pulled open the snapfit door. Shading the penlight with one hand, he scanned the many pairs of telephone terminals, looking for the one pair that identified the alarm. Until his eyes adjusted to the dark, it was difficult to read the color coding on the jumbled mass of wire. It's been so long, he thought, that maybe I won't be able to get the right pair. Hoping to use the process of elimination, he carefully examined each set of terminals.

"Here," he mumbled, stopping about midway down the terminal strip. Quickly he extracted his test equipment, and with the precision of a watchmaker placed alligator clips, first on one terminal, and then ever so carefully on the other. Then he trained his light on the needle of the meter. "Oh, my God," he thought. It had already jumped into the red position which, Billy knew, meant the alarm had sounded at highway patrol headquarters.

"Damn," he said out loud. Quickly he pulled his connections free, closed the metal door and slid back into his room. It took another minute to retract his platform and hide it behind some clothes in the closet.

Billy looked at his watch. It was 1:32 a.m. Subtracting two minutes from the time the signal was transmitted, Billy waited to see how long it would take for the police to show up.

Although he couldn't hear it, Billy knew that the alarm bell, high up on Thorpe's Water Street front wall, was clanging away loudly. Sam was the only recipient of the racket, and he too was timing police response.

At 1:36 a.m., two Westerly police cruisers screamed around the corner down Water Street. One stopped in front and the other kept going, circling the block in an attempt to capture any would-be burglars. Then a highway patrol car raced up the alley, screeched to a halt by the Thorpe loading dock, and two troopers piled out, guns drawn.

Sam stayed in the shadows of the second floor office windows and peered down as the security guard, who was stationed inside, motioned one of the policemen up to the front door. For more than 15 minutes police and highway patrol officers investigated the possible intrusion. Finally the bell was silenced, which greatly reduced Sam's tension.

At 2:05 a.m. an unmarked car pulled up in front of Thorpe's, and a man dressed in pajamas and bathrobe emerged. It was probably the plant manager or a company vice president who had been routinely summoned by the guard inside. Police and the company official remained on the site until after 2:30 a.m. and then, apparently satisfied that it was a false alarm, they drove away.

Billy was mad that he had bungled the job, but he was glad the police didn't suspect anything was awry at the telephone junction box. That, he thought, would come the next day when there was sure to be a visit by the alarm company repairman. Both Sam and Billy flipped off their scanners and went to bed shortly before 3:00 a.m.

Very early the next morning, Billy was back at the construction office trying to explain to Sam what had gone wrong the night before. The two men chatted about the problem while they stood at an upstairs window, watching to see if and when the alarm repairman would make an appearance. They didn't wait long. At 8:10 a.m. a panel van drove up in front of Thorpe's, and a uniformed serviceman went inside. Billy took this opportunity to slip out the back door and return to his apartment. He wanted to be right there when the alarm guy made a check of the terminals. He waited for more than an hour, but no one came. It figured, he thought. The alarm company man had found nothing wrong with the system inside the jewelry company and must have left.

The day again passed slowly, and all Billy could do was wait till night and try again. He and Sam prepared for the same routine, with one variation. Billy altered the time of attack in case he failed again. He didn't want the guard or the fuzz to begin putting together any patterns.

At 11:30 p.m. Billy set up his platform again and went to work, changing his meter readings and terminal connections slightly. Then it happened again. The bell sounded and within minutes the same police cruisers were on the scene. Could it be that J.J.'s information was incorrect and the Thorpe Company had some new kind of system Billy was unfamiliar with? Sam thought of contacting J.J. to tell him of the problem, but Billy talked him out of it, reminding his friend that Calhoun had specifically told them not to call until they were ready to go.

"We'll try it again tonight," Billy said, outlining a new technique he would use. But the third try was no more successful than the first two. Billy was becoming despondent. He was sure he had lost his touch. A fourth, fifth and sixth attempt also failed, and it was on this last try that the alarm repairman finally went to the alley to check out the terminal connections in the junction box.

Billy was waiting inside his room. When he saw the van park next to the pole, he pulled aside his window shade and looked through a rip in the faded blind. The repairman was within easy reach as he stood on his ladder and fumbled with the connections. Fortunately he never even glanced at the rooming house window, and Billy felt confident the man didn't suspect any foul play. Although Billy couldn't be sure, he also thought the alarm man didn't notice the three protruding spikes. Billy continued to watch as he descended the ladder, racked it on top of his van and disappeared down the alley.

Billy returned to the construction office and told Sam of the incident. The two men reviewed the situation, trying to pinpoint the cause for six failures. But Sam was of little help. He didn't know the difference between a diode and a resistor.

They decided that Billy would try one more time, employing the most complex equipment he had. If that failed, he'd have to give up.

He chose 5:00 a.m. for his last attempt. Again he extended the platform and set the dials of his expensive black box. Again he took the alligator clips and placed them on the terminal strips. He waited two, three, four, five minutes. No sirens. He checked the metered dials. They stayed in the green position, and he knew that this time he had been successful.

To make sure, he left the clips in place, withdrew the meters, closed the metal box door and climbed back in his room to check the scanner. He heard nothing unusual while he waited for more than 20 minutes. Then Billy retrieved his gear from the pole, retracted the platform and left the rooming house to tell Sam. It was getting light when he unlocked the loading dock door and jubilantly ran in, shouting his triumph.

"We did it, Sam. We did it!"

It was a little before noon when Billy's old car drove up the pink gravel driveway of the Calhoun estate. Paddy, who was leisurely clipping some hedges in front of the stone mansion, saw them coming and was the first to greet his friends as they got out of the car.

Lunching on the patio was delightful. The sight of sailboats silhouetted against the horizon, the comfortable setting, the brisk ocean breeze, all seemed to transform Billy and Sam from dedicated burglars to part-time gentlemen. The two men gave J.J. and Paddy a blow-by-blow account of the previous nine days. Then they discussed what appeared to be their last roadblock before they could resume tunnelling operations full tilt.

"That godawful bell has to be silenced," Sam told his friends, remembering the piercing clatter six nights in a row. "That thing is on a circuit that is independent of the police signal, and we gotta shut it off. It has to be done in such a way that no one will know it's been beaten. If we take it down, the cops and the guard will notice it's missing. Besides, as soon as we pull it off the wall, the son-of-a-bitch will start ringing."

Paddy thought for a moment. It sounded like a job he could handle. Anxious to get in the action, he turned to J.J. and offered a simple solution.

"Diversionary tactics should do the trick," he suggested, and he drew his chair closer to the others and started some invisible finger painting on the luncheon table.

"The Fourth of July is coming in a couple of weeks, right?" he continued. The three men nodded. "During the evening we create a diversion by popping some homemade stuff around the Thorpe complex—just enough to be noticeable for the occasion but not enough to do any damage. Then, at the right time...bang. We'll plant a load big enough to raise a sewer cap or two. It'll surely draw the guard away from his post long enough for Billy to do a number on the bell."

"What kind of number?" Billy queried, not sure what Paddy had in mind.

"Again, simple, my friend. You pull a B&E on the factory beforehand, locate the bell cable and prepare to splice into it. On the night of the Fourth, and at our signal, you cut the real wire, insert a by-pass and, in effect, shunt out the bell. From that time on, we can do it whenever we want.

"As soon as that sewer lid flies and the guard comes to the door to check it out, Sam will give you a signal on the walkie-talkie. When you cut the real cable, the bell will sound momentarily and will light up at the guard's monitor panel downstairs. But he won't be there to see it. Even if he hears the damn thing ringing for a few seconds, he'll probably think the concussion caused it."

"Sounds pretty risky, Paddy," Calhoun interrupted, not too sure of the scheme.

"Leave it to me, J.J., I know human nature, and I know the guard will bite. Those guys sit at the board night after night with nothing to do. They gotta be bored as hell. A little fireworks will draw him away like a fly looking for cow dung."

Sam looked at Billy for a long moment and then relaxed in his chair. "Don't worry, Billy. If you can silence that telephone line, you can certainly do a number on the bell."

Everyone took a sip of brandy in an expression of joint approval, and then prepared to adjourn.

"One moment, my good friends," J.J. cautioned. "There is still one more problem that needs a solution.

"Mr. Thorpe and his security director have always been deeply concerned about the gold vault. They figure they're pretty safe when it comes to a burglar's attack—that's been pretty well verified by the problems Billy and Sam have faced so far. What Thorpe is really worried about is employee theft during working hours. A number of goldsmiths have access to the vault every day, and with a couple million in gold bars inside, it wouldn't be too hard to make off with one of those beauties."

J.J. went on to explain that each bar weighed 27½ pounds and measured, in inches, 7 by 3⅝ by 1¼. "Those little beauties are worth just over $16,000 apiece. And as of yesterday, there were exactly 137 bricks neatly stacked on the floor."

Paddy did more fingerwork on J.J.'s glass top table and pretended to wipe his brow. "Men, you won't believe this, but if my scratchings are close to correct, that adds up to over $2,200,000."

J.J. added that the amount didn't include the 53 silver bars also stored inside. "Only if time permits will we take the silver. Those damn things weigh 97 pounds each, and it'll take an earthmover to get them all out of there.

"Because of the theft problem," J.J. continued, getting back to the point, "the security guy had some photo-electric beams installed and wired into a permanent daytime alarm circuit. If anyone passes through the light beam which separates the vault storage from a small pickup point in the front of the protected room, an alarm sounds at the guard station. This device is not wired into the police or the bell."

"No sweat, J.J.," Billy joined the conversation. "Those lights are easy to douse."

"Hold it a minute," Paddy interrupted. "Now we've got another problem. Those photocells are sensitive, and if we blast the vault, even with a small charge undetectable to the guard, the light source may go out of kilter and blow the whole thing." Paddy was right. Those light beams might force them to take another course of action.

After another half hour of discussion, Sam finally settled the matter. "We'll use a lance." He was referring to a thermal lance or a burning bar. It was the only possible way to get through 12 inches of vault wall plus another 10 inches of basement concrete or stone.

The switch from explosives to a lance created a whole new strategy. They'd now have to buy or steal burning bar rods, a supply of oxygen tanks, and a fire-resistant entry suit to protect the operator from asphyxiation and noxious gases that were sure to blanket the poorly ventilated tunnel. Time would certainly be a factor.

All of their plans were now set, they hoped. J.J. lifted his glass in a toast to the complete success of the operation, and the three men rose to leave. Paddy was glad to be joining Sam and Billy. It was like the old days again.

While Billy brought his car around to the courtyard, the others stood on the portico exchanging friendly goodbyes. J.J. squeezed

Paddy's arm gently, letting him know that the little man was his favorite. His final words to Paderewski were, "Good luck. See you when it's over." Paddy winked, got into the car with the others, and the three men drove away.

The next few days went quickly as Billy and Sam bartered for the new construction equipment needed for the job. On the third night after the meeting with J.J., Paddy and Billy drove down to Mystic, Connecticut, and rifled through a construction yard for such essentials as burning bar rods and the much-needed asbestos protective suit.

While they were gone, Sam took a walk out on Water Street. His seemingly nonchalant stroll had a purpose. Carefully he stepped off the distance between the construction office and the middle of Water Street, where he knew there was a sewer. Other measurements were similarly made, including the distance from Thorpe's main entrance north to where Sam thought the basement vault was located. Even though he had J.J.'s blueprints, he couldn't be sure, within a foot or so, exactly where the vault's midsection was. They would have to wait until the tunnel progressed further to take final measurements.

Next day Paddy and Sam were up early, ready to start excavating operations. Billy arrived from Mrs. Spraytz' in time for a last cup of coffee. Then the three men went to the basement, each carrying tools, lumber, and heavy canvas bags in which they planned to transport the tons of dirt back upstairs to their dump truck. It would take days, perhaps weeks, of loading and unloading to clear a tunnel under the street. Paddy thought that, depending on the size of the sewer and its drainage conditions, they might be able to utilize this man-made passageway and go south about 10 yards before heading east again to the Thorpe basement and the vault.

"Let's get started," Sam insisted, dropping a pile of 2 by 4's on the basement floor. As agreed, they would take turns, two men using picks and shovels while the other two filled bags with dirt and carried them upstairs. It was back-breaking work, and they had to rest often.

Paddy had the tunnel plans all worked out. From the Dorchester job 30 years earlier, he remembered the team's problems and mistakes, and as a result he redesigned the passageway, making it slightly smaller and more boxlike. This would make shoring easier and stronger. The size of the tunnel at the entrance point measured 5 feet high by 36 inches wide. It was snug but large enough to work in comfortably. As the men dug deeper under the sidewalk and street, their corridor decreased slightly to 32 inches wide and 4 feet high. Digging operations went smoothly for the first few days, and minimal braces and supports were necessary.

The chief problem for the men continued to be dirt removal. They estimated the number of cubic yards to be removed and decided that one out of every four loads could be piled in the basement, reducing the number of arduous trips upstairs to the truck. At night Billy or Sam would take the truck out to a local landfill and dispose of the load.

On the fifth day, during Paddy's trick in the hole, his pick struck something solid. Using a short-handled shovel, he chipped and scraped away enough dirt to discover that he had at last hit the sewer pipe that ran down Water Street. He scurried back through the 25-foot shaft to announce the good news to his companions.

"It looks like a 5-foot-diameter job," he said "But a thought just occurred to me. If we bust through now, we're liable to blow the whole deal."

Sam knew what he meant. "Yeah, over the Fourth, when we blow the sewer lids, those city maintenance guys may start checking the pipe to see if there's any damage."

"Right. We better stop right here until Billy takes care of the bell."

It was now June 29th. They had five days to wait. On the 30th, after they had cleared away all the residue and added a few additional support beams, Billy suggested that they enter Thorpe's during the night and locate the bell wires.

"Good idea," Sam agreed. "Let's all go. We can get a good first-hand look at the entire layout, including the downstairs vault."

Getting into the building presented no problem. Paddy was an expert B&E man, and within seconds he had picked the simple tumbler lock on a personnel door adjacent to Thorpe's loading dock near the back alley. Using the map supplied earlier by J.J., they had no trouble finding their way upstairs to a third floor production room. It was here, on the front of the building, that the menacing bell was mounted equidistant between two windows. Billy located the bell simply by counting the number of windows from the end of the building. He had earlier taken a sight reading from across the street.

The production room was a large open work area with rows of benches, well illuminated by fluorescent lights hanging from a high ceiling. The original heavy beam rafters and support columns would make it easy to conceal extra wiring that Billy would install as by-pass connections. The alarm bell cable was fully exposed, appearing through the exterior brick wall, snaking its way up toward a set of cross beams and then finally across the room into an interior wall.

"Great," Billy whispered to his friends. "This will be easier than I thought. Why don't you two guys snoop around downstairs, locate the guard station, and try to get to the basement and the vault. While you're doing that, I'll get busy setting up what I have to do for our Fourth of July celebration."

Sam and Paddy agreed, saying they'd be back in 20 minutes to report their findings.

Silently the two intruders made their way down the front stairway to the Thorpe Company's main entrance. As they neared the first floor reception area, they could see a faint light coming from a glass enclosure off to one side. Anxious to get a better look at the guard's cubicle, they inched along the darkened corridor and, staying in the shadows, peered through the window. A uniformed armed security guard was sitting, feet propped up on the alarm control counter, reading a girlie magazine.

"Just as I thought," Paddy whispered. "That guy is in never-never land. I'm surprised he's not asleep."

In another second the corridor was empty. Sam and Paddy slipped away downstairs to a secured room where the vault was located. A grilled metal gate and fence temporarily blocked their way into the gold work area, but Paddy again slipped his spring-steel picks into the lock and swung open the gate. An old black heavy steel vault door halted any further approach. Sam stood in front of it, admiring the fancy artwork painted on the door. It was typical of late 19th-century craftsmanship. There was intricate gold striping around the border and a Rocky Mountain scene painted in the center. The words "Victor Safe and Lock Company, Cincinnati, Ohio," arched over the painting, and hand-lettered patent numbers dated 1899 graced the lower section, below the door handle and the intricate pressure system.

"A thing of beauty," Sam commented. "A tough nut to crack."

The 20 minutes were nearly up when Sam and Paddy interrupted Billy, who was putting the final touches on the shunt switch mechanism.

"All set?" Paddy asked.

"All set," Billy replied. In another three minutes, the men exited by the door they had entered and headed back to Water Street.

For the next few days, there was little for the men to do. They played cards, drank beer and read. Billy finally went back to his rooming house and gathered up what was left of his half case of whiskey. Surely there would be no harm in popping a few corks. Besides, it would help pass the time.

As the holiday weekend approached, Sam walked down to a neighborhood drug store to stretch his legs and to buy a paper. All three men were sports enthusiasts, and they liked to keep up with the ball scores and pennant races.

When Sam returned, he offered Paddy the front page while he curled up on his cot with the sports page. It was some time before Paddy got around to picking it up, but as soon as he did, he shouted, "My God, J.J.'s missing. It's right here on the front page." Sam and Billy bolted upright, startled, not quite believing what they had heard.

"It says right here, 'James J. Calhoun of Newport, Rhode Island, yesterday was reported missing overboard from his racing sloop J.J. II. Three sailing companions, all from out of town, told police and coast guard officials that Mr. Calhoun must have fallen overboard during the annual Race Week Regatta. Sailing with Calhoun were three house guests, Nino Bengelluti, John Shuttleworth and Masme Scarpanzo. A search of the area, some 12 miles east of Block Island, revealed no trace of the well-known Newport resident.'"

Paddy continued reading the story to his friends, then dropped the paper on his cot and started crying uncontrollably.

"Those dirty bastards threw him overboard," he sobbed.

Radio reports and the evening newspaper were filled with stories of J.J.'s disappearance, but after nearly 48 hours, all search efforts were disbanded.

Next morning the little gang of thieves plotted their next move. Their good friend and financier was gone; there was nothing they could do about that, and they agreed to go it alone. But they were puzzled by J.J.'s death, which they were convinced had been no accident. They had never heard of Nino Bengelluti or his friends, but they figured that J.J. was probably in hock to them. If their suspicions were correct, it was obvious why J.J. had engineered this gold strike.

Paddy was worried.

"What if those guys know our plan? It's curtains for all of us if they do."

"I doubt it, Paddy," Sam blurted. "If J.J. did spill the beans, those guys would already be here."

Billy agreed. "What we've got to do now is finish the job and get the hell out of here. We're way ahead of schedule, and unless J.J. had some special reason for going in over Labor Day, I say let's do it as fast as we can."

Paddy had planted explosive charges under two manhole covers the night before. He had other lesser concoctions set to go off in the alley behind Thorpe's and on Water Street two blocks away.

During the day and evening, firecrackers could be heard exploding in the vicinity, creating an auspicious atmosphere for the blasts later that night.

At 10:30 p.m., Paddy again slipped the lock of the Thorpe personnel door and let Billy inside to do his number on the bell. Then he returned to the office. Everything was set. Each man had his own job to do and everyone was ready. Sam had worked out a contingency plan in case the diversionary operation failed. He pulled the truck out of the garage and parked it some distance away in the event they needed getaway wheels.

Billy sat motionless at one of the production room benches and waited, hoping that his telephone line defeat would hold when put to the real test.

At 11:35 p.m. it happened. Boom! The charge on Water Street blew. A few seconds later, two sewer lids blew off in quick succession. The one closest to Thorpe's. main entrance hit the pavement and came to a stop like a 25-cent piece rolling on top of a cigar counter.

Almost immediately Sam, who was watching from his second floor lookout point, radioed to Billy across the street and told him that the guard had taken the bait and was unlocking the front door for a look-see. Smoke was rising from the manhole as the security man leaned out to get a better look.

Billy went to work. He was in position with wire snips, tape and connector wire. He had already bared the bell cable down to copper wire and all he had to do was cut.

Snip. Instantly the bell clanged, and the guard spun around and looked up. Then the noise stopped. By that time, the guard had disappeared back into the building to monitor his alarm panel. Everyone held his breath. It would only take minutes for the police to respond—if they were summoned at all. Sam waited, Paddy waited, and then Billy broke the silence and transmitted over the crackling walkie-talkie.

"Did we make it?"

"Dunno," came a quick response from Sam, who was watching

the seconds go by on his watch. "Give it another three minutes, and I think we're home free."

At that moment the guard emerged from Thorpe's. Both Paddy and Sam saw him.

"Either he's waiting for the cops, or he's trying to sight the kids who blew that lid off," Sam muttered.

Five minutes passed. Then ten. No cops. Sam radioed Billy to finish concealing the shunted-out wires and come home.

As Billy slipped back in the construction office, Sam, who was still at the upstairs window, noticed a yellow flashing light coming up Water Street. But before he could call out a warning, he breathed a sigh of relief. It was a city utility truck to replace the manhole covers and check out the damage.

The next morning the men went to work again. Paddy got a chisel and hammer and disappeared into the shaft. His first job was to break through the concrete sewer main and survey what he hoped would be a clear passage down about 30 feet to the section where the men could start tunnelling straight for the vault. It took more than an hour to hammer out an opening big enough to stick his head in. His puncture was made at eye level, in case the water level inside was high. It was hard work, and perspiration drenched his body. Finally he broke through. Shining a powerful lantern up and down the culvert, he was overjoyed to see that only 2 or 3 inches of water were trickling by.

Paddy emerged from the shaft and reported the good news. "Unless it rains hard during the next few weeks, we've saved about ten days. Billy, you finish cutting out the rest of the water main, but make sure you don't remove any concrete below 8 or 9 inches from the bottom. That way we've got a bulkhead to keep a reasonable amount of water flow inside the pipe. If we have a downpour of rain, we could be in real trouble. The whole shaft and basement would flood."

By late afternoon the trio had finished the first opening, waded through the muddy sewer, and started breaking through the opposite side. They were now only 28 feet from the gold.

Digging from that point went extremely slowly. The further they penetrated, the longer it took to remove the dirt and stone. There was no way for them to pile their diggings in the sewer; too much dirt would cause a water backup and flood the shaft. It had to be lugged back out through the basement to the truck.

Light became a problem, too. It was hard enough to struggle with the canvas bags, but when they couldn't see, their operations slowed even more. Sam went out to buy some miners' lights but could find none. Then Billy decided to string up some regular bulbs, and he tapped into the construction office power from the basement. It took nearly two days to run wire and connect the makeshift lighting system, but when it was finished, digging resumed at full speed.

The intense heat and humidity began to take their toll. Sam was first to catch a cold, and then Paddy became ill. The men reduced their work shifts to two hours on and four hours off.

On July 15, it started to rain. It rained all day, and the men took turns working, as they watched the water level slowly rise in the sewer. The water stabilized at 6 inches, but that was enough to halt operations. Even if they wore waterproof boots, plodding through the murky water would only increase their chances of catching pneumonia. The rain continued on and off for the next few days, and Sam and Paddy took the respite to nurse their ills. It was during this time that Billy drove Paddy back to Massachusetts for his monthly parole board visit.

By dawn on the 19th, the storm clouds abated and bright sunshine filled the sky. Paddy was feeling much better, but Sam was still a little under the weather. It was agreed that Billy and Paddy would resume work and Sam, when he felt up to it, would transport dirt from the basement to the truck. He stayed out of the tunnel altogether.

On the 23rd, Billy, who was working with the pick and shovel, jabbed his sharp instrument onto solid stone, and he knew immediately that he had reached the Thorpe Company's basement wall. Excited, as with all of their previous victories, Billy turned around in his cramped work space and started back to tell the others. Then he saw a mound of loosely packed earth in the tunnel ceiling crumble and fall about 10 feet in front of him. Panic struck. While the cave-in didn't completely fill the crude passage, enough of the black stuff lay there to prevent him from using the exit. Billy scrambled up to the barricade, tried to scratch away a larger opening, and then he yelled for help. Paddy didn't hear him; he was trucking another load of dirt back to Sam.

Billy continued clawing at the loose material, but no matter how fast he scratched, the overhead kept collapsing, and eventually the lights shorted out. His heart pounded as he envisioned being permanently trapped. He crawled back toward Thorpe's to retrieve his shovel. Maybe that would help, he thought. And maybe Paddy would notice the tunnel lights were out and realize there was trouble. Billy used his shovel as a scraper and frantically pushed aside the heavy dirt in order to keep an air supply intact. Then he saw a faint light up ahead.

"You okay?" came the welcome sound of his friend.

"Yeah, but I hope the rest of this frigging hole doesn't come down."

Both men dug at fever pitch until they made an opening large enough to permit Billy to wriggle out.

That was enough for the day, both men agreed. The next day they'd shore up the tunnel, fix the lights and resume the last, most difficult part of their task.

Now all that separated the burglars from two million dollars in gold was 22 inches of stone and concrete. Setting up the burning bar rig was no easy job, especially in their cramped quarters. It was decided to expand the shaft at the base of the basement wall in order to provide more working room. More digging and chipping and clearing away took another day and a half, and then Sam suggested that they use the old wooden doors, still piled up on the loading dock, to fashion a ceiling for the earthen room. Good idea, they agreed, and the stack of lumber would come in handy for braces and pillars.

Next they brought in several large fans, the kind used to ventilate bedrooms and attics. This required more wiring, and the tunnel began to look like an electric power station.

It took two men to carry each large bottle of oxygen through the shaft, and soon the sewer was filled with gas masks, oxygen tanks, fans and torches. These filled every inch of usable space, and the congestion hampered the operation even more.

Because Paddy was the smallest of the group, it was decided he would become chief lance operator. He suited up in the stolen fire-entry costume, ready for a dry run in their basement hideout. In the strange apparel he resembled a creature from outer space. The suit was heavy with fire-resistant asbestos and proved cumbersome to work in. Sam attached an air hose to the garment's headgear so Paddy could breathe. Then Billy hooked up the air tanks to a 10-foot burning bar rod and lit the wand with his acetylene torch. Sparks flew as the torch ignited the lance, and Paddy thrust it into a section of basement wall to see if it would work. Almost immediately the stone and mortar melted, dripping molten slag onto the floor. The devastating tool worked like a charm. They were now ready for the real thing.

The work day began early for the three. Everything was set—tools, supplies, fans and especially their enthusiasm. They had plenty of time to execute this last penetration to the booty, as they determined by checking the calendar that they had four days to cut through the outer basement wall—10 inches or so—and then they would confine their work on the vault wall to night-time operations when no employees were present. It was now Tuesday, and they hoped to be ready to make final entry after work ended Friday evening. That would give them until early Monday morning, August 3, to finish the job and split.

Paddy again got ready, and in the small tomb-like room he prepared for several days of tedious and extremely uncomfortable work. Standing behind Paddy were Sam and Billy, gas masks in place, who would control the flow of oxygen and assist their friend with the long cumbersome lance. It burned like a child's sparkler, but with far more intensity. Within minutes, smoke and noxious gas filled the tunnel, forcing Paddy to stop because he could no longer see the wall in front of him. They'd have to change the fans around. The largest unit was brought up front and positioned to blow the smoke out toward the water main. Two other blowers faced downstream to help the convectional current. No one knew where the smoke would be emitted, but they were sure that it would eventually filter out and be noticed.

Burning continued well into the night. When Paddy quit, the fans were left on in an effort to clear the air enough to resume work the following day.

By Thursday noon, Paddy had burned and chopped his way through the Thorpe basement wall, and then he suspended his frontal attack to clear the rubble for a final thrust. Now they were only 12 inches away from their mark.

On Thursday night Paddy suggested they burn another 6 inches into the actual vault wall. Apparently they were right on target. Their only concern now was whether the first gusher of sparks penetrating the vault would interrupt the light beam emitted by the photoelectric cells inside the vault room. Too much smoke filtering between the balanced light source could signal the guard upstairs. If that happened, two months' work would go down the drain.

Friday arrived, and the men used most of the day to pack up the things they wanted to take with them on Sunday or early Monday morning. Billy cleaned out his room at Mrs. Spraytz'. But before leaving that night, he set up his platform and crawled out to the telephone pole one last time to defeat the police alarm. Later Paddy let him in Thorpe's back door to shunt-out the bell connection. By midnight Friday, all they had left to do was burn those last few inches to the gold room. Paddy directed the burning bar up as high as he could and to the left of the center of the vault. When he did break through, he wanted the smoke to filter in as far away from the photocell as possible.

At 3:50 a.m., he calculated he was only an inch or two from the inner wall of the vault. He motioned to Billy to cut off the oxygen which fueled the lance, and all three men splashed back through the sewer to their basement hideout across the street.

"Sam, I think we better make sure that guard doesn't blow the whistle," Paddy remarked, still worried about the light beam. "You let yourself in the back door again and pay a visit to the security shack on the first floor. You can get a good look at the security guy through the window, and if his monitor panel lights up, don't give him a chance to use the phone. His first reaction will be to press the alarm button, not knowing the bell and police connection have been silenced. Then, as a backup, he'll dial Westerly police headquarters. You know what to do if he reaches for that phone."

Sam looked at his watch. It was 4:15 a.m. "Give me twenty minutes to get into position and then start burning again. It's too dangerous to use the walkie-talkie, so I'll give you an hour. At 5:35, you stop wherever you are, and I'll come back and report."

Sam disappeared up the basement stairs, while Billy and Paddy retreated into the smoky tunnel.

At 4:35 a.m., Paddy aimed the huge sparkler at the concrete wall once more and poked the rod the last 2 inches into the imposing cavity.

Almost without warning the lance broke through into the vault, and Paddy quickly pulled back, nearly falling to the debris-filled floor. Instantly, Billy knew that his partner had made it, and he turned off the oxygen. With hammer and chisel, Billy chipped away at the tiny aperture, and then motioned for a flashlight. Intense smoke filled both sides of the vault wall, but Billy could see the interior well enough to notice the photo beam about 9 or 10 feet to his right. There was no telling whether the acrid stuff had tripped the alarm—they would have to wait for Sam to return.

Once again Billy and Paddy withdrew from their attack site and meandered back to the basement, where it was much easier to breathe.

It was close to 6:00 a.m. Saturday when Sam finally returned. They knew without asking that the photo-electric beams had held fast. Otherwise Sam would have come back much sooner.

"Did you see the gold?" Sam asked, out of breath.

"Nope," Billy replied. "Too many shelves and boxes in the way. But I could see those photo-electric cells through the smoke."

All three men were exhausted from their night's work, but anxiety and the thought of all that gold would keep them working until they got inside.

For the next few hours, they kept the fans going full blast, and used conventional means of hammer and chisel to enlarge the opening enough so that they could crawl through. It wasn't until late Saturday night that their man-made door measured 26 by 24 inches—just large enough to squeeze little Paddy inside.

With his flashlight as a guide, Paderewski Ginzberg inched into the gold room. Once inside, he got his bearings and carefully scanned every corner of the room. Fortunately the smoke had settled sufficiently, and Paddy could see much better than before and was able to breathe without his gas mask.

"Stay away from those photocells," Sam hollered into the opening.

"Gotcha," came a muffled reply.

"Do you see the gold yet?" another voice asked. Paddy said nothing for moment, and then he stuck his hand out through the vault wall.

"Amen!" Sam carefully took a little yellow brick in his hands and kissed it. He turned to Billy and let him hold it.

"We're rich, my friend, we're rich."

Paddy counted the precious gold bars that lay neatly on the floor. Then he counted again. There were only 65—less than half of what J.J.'s tally had been almost six weeks earlier. Paddy searched the rest of the vault, making sure he stayed clear of the incriminating photo-electric ray, but he could find no more bricks. All he saw was a criss-cross stack of silver bars, and they numbered only 21.

What the hell, he thought, could Thorpe have used that much gold? He reported the disappointing inventory count to Sam and then said he was coming out.

"Pass out a few more bricks before you leave. We might as well make every trip count," Sam suggested.

With the gold bars each weighing 27½ pounds, it was all the men could do to carry one bar apiece back to their hideout.

Billy voted to take a rest, eat something, and then try to sleep a few hours. No one argued, for they knew it would take most of Sunday to empty the vault. While they heated the last of their canned rations, Paddy calculated the weight and worth of their spoils. If they got it all, they'd have just over $1,100,000 in gold, totalling slightly less than 3,000 pounds. Would the old truck carry all that weight? They decided a million bucks was enough—they would leave the silver where it was.

Sleep didn't come easily, but at least their minds and numb bodies would have a chance to relax for a few hours before the final installment of their score.

Billy was first to wake from a half sleep. It was past 11:00 a.m. on Sunday, and time had now become their biggest enemy. Quickly they pushed Paddy back inside the vault, and while Sam took one brick at a time from him through the crude opening, Billy began hauling them back to the basement. Hours passed. The work was backbreaking, and soon Billy fell behind. It was more than 90 feet from vault to basement, and each round trip took longer and longer, dragging out to more than 10 minutes. Sewer water, lingering smoke, and the strain of plodding along in a crouched position brought such aching pain to the men that it forced them to take more breaks than they had planned for. By late afternoon, Paddy heisted the last gold brick out of the vault and handed it to Sam. Then he crawled out of the vault and sank to his knees. His fingers were raw and bleeding. He had just "liberated" 3,000 pounds of precious metal.

It was 3:00 a.m. Monday. Paddy, Sam and Billy Howe sat huddled around the small pyramid of gold bars they had piled on the loading dock platform next to the old dump truck. The anti-climax of having finished their work had left them physically and mentally spent.

"Well, whatta we do next?" Paddy asked, running his finger tenderly over the precious metal. "In another five hours the Feds and fuzz will be down on this place, and it won't take them long to find out who they're looking for."

Paddy was right. It would have been impossible to wipe clean every fingerprint made during the past two months. Beer cans, tools, equipment, toilets, windows and the vault itself bore incriminating marks of the trio.

"We gotta split," Sam said matter-of-factly, reminding his accomplices of the fact that escape had become their most imminent concern.

"But where do we go?" Billy wondered aloud. "We can't go back to Boston. I don't give a damn about the old lady, but we'll get nailed before dark if we head east."

Then Sam came up with a solution that made sense. "New York," he said. "That's the only place we can fence the stuff. There are close to a thousand dealers in gold bullion down there, and you know that at least one of them will be interested."

With no further conversation, the three men clasped hands in agreement, and then began a hurried clean-up campaign that they hoped would delay detection. While Paddy and Sam retrieved essential and incriminating evidence, Billy jumped off the loading platform and headed directly for the two 55-gallon drums that stood in the corner of the garage. He pried the lid off one metal can and peered inside. There were about 2 inches of dirty machine oil on the bottom.

"This is where we'll hide the gold," he yelled back to the others, as he rolled the heavy container over to the truck's tailgate. Sam helped lift the drum topside, and then they went back for the other can.

By 5:30 a.m. the burglars had carefully loaded all 65 gold bars into the barrels and filled in the cracks with dirt. Hurriedly they gathered their belongings, threw them onto the truck and shoveled in more dirt to make it look like a construction load. Then all three men took one last look around. They checked out the office, basement, tunnel and second-floor lookout post. If they had missed anything, it was too late to worry about it. They had run out of time and were forced to leave.

Daylight had arrived when the truck pulled out into the alley, and Billy closed and locked the garage door. Sam and Paddy stayed with the truck, while Billy followed close behind in his old Plymouth.

The little caravan left Westerly, Rhode Island, heading west on Interstate 95 toward Groton and New London, Connecticut. It was a journey of 18 miles, and they expected to get there by 6:30 a.m.

After crossing the Thames River, Sam pulled off the superhighway at the New London exit and followed signs pointing the way to the ferry for Orient Point, Long Island. They were in plenty of time to catch the first boat, which was scheduled to leave at 7:00 a.m. Taking the ferry would save at least an hour to New York City and would, they figured, reduce their chances of being stopped at one of the roadblocks which were sure to be set up within the next two hours.

It seemed like an eternity before the boat crew lifted the control gate and motioned Sam onto the steel ramp. Billy Howe was second in line, and then the other early morning motorists inched aboard. The ride would take at least an hour and a half, so the three men decided to sit in Billy's car and monitor police calls on their C.B. Half an hour passed. Eight o'clock, 8:10. And then they heard it. Police were dispatched to 153 Water Street to investigate a burglary.

At 8:40 a.m. the huge ferry reversed its engines and inched into the Orient Point dock on Long Island, New York. In another 10 minutes the Southern New England Construction Company truck eased off the boat onto solid ground, followed by a Massachusetts-registered Plymouth. They were free at last.

About a mile down the road, Sam spotted a diner and nudged Paddy. "Let's stop for breakfast. I'm starved." Paddy agreed, and rolled down his window to motion Billy to follow them into the gravel parking lot. As he completed his circular hand signals, a New York State police cruiser started to pull out of the diner's driveway. With panic instinct, Sam slammed on the brakes in an effort to avoid the turn-off, and as a result nearly hit the police car.

"Play it cool, real cool," Sam nervously told his friend, sure that the cop would want to question the abrupt action. "I'll do the talking."

Sam was dripping with perspiration. His hands shook as he turned off the ignition and opened the cab door. Paddy didn't move. At first glance Sam thought the cruiser would continue out onto the highway. Then his heart sank. He could see first the brake lights and then the white back-up lights go on. Slowly the cruiser backed up and stopped alongside the truck.

Sam didn't know what to do, so he sat there, staring at the blue and white car with its shiny gold star painted on the side.

Then he caught sight of Billy cruising by and continuing down the country road.

"Sorry about that," Sam said, half smiling to the trooper as the uniformed man got out of his car. "Blue doesn't go with the lousy paint job on my clunker. Good thing I saw you in time." The officer didn't return Sam's comment right away. Sam felt sick and dizzy, and for a moment he thought he would throw up.

The trooper gave the truck a good once-over and then, spotting the two metal drums marked "flammable" in faded stencil letters, asked, "What are you carrying in those things?"

A Concluding Note

Although all the incidents in this chapter really occurred, the event itself is a composite of three burglaries executed or attempted between 1967 and 1972, and is the case referred to in the introduction as the exception to the statement that "all the cases actually happened." This episode does depict the way in which certain burglaries are planned, the methods used, and the possibilities for failure at every stage.

The main characters—Paddy, Sam and Billy—are true to life. Paddy was returned to prison, where he remains in custody. Sam was killed in an aborted liquor store robbery in a state not too distant from Rhode Island. Only Billy Howe is on the streets today.

PART II
The Robbers
—"A Most Dangerous Game"

7

FROM MASKED BANDITS TO TV CAMERAS

"...because that's where the money is."
Willie Sutton, on being asked why
he had spent nearly his whole life
robbing banks

It was February 13, 1866, and shortly after noon several of Liberty, Missouri's, shop owners saw twelve men ride quietly into their nearly deserted town. Each was bundled against the cold in traditional greatcoat, floppy range hat and leather knee boots. Each had a six shooter strapped to his hip, and displayed the butt of a soldier's carbine protruding from his mount's saddle sheath.

When the dozen horsemen reached the center of town, they stopped. Several of the unshaven gang dismounted and took up positions along the street on both sides of their proposed mark— The Clay County Savings Association. Others remained mounted, holding the reins of their friends' horses.

With the aplomb of prosperous cattle ranchers, two of the desperados strode up a small flight of wooden steps and entered the bank. What was about to take place was an event that would mark the start of one of our nation's most serious and dangerous crimes. It was the beginning of armed holdups in financial institutions. Incredible as it may sound, it wasn't until this day, February 13, 1866—84 years after the first American bank was chartered[1]—that a gang actually planned to stickup a bank in broad daylight.[2]

[1] The first federally chartered bank in the United States was established in 1782 with the opening of the Bank of North America.

[2] Only two other recorded holdups occurred prior to the Clay County Savings Association incident. The first robbery took place on December 15, 1863 at the Malden Bank, Malden, Massachusetts, and was perpetrated almost as an afterthought by Edward Green. Seeing only the 17-year-old son of the banker on the premises, Green went home, retrieved a pistol and then returned and shot the boy dead, taking $5,000 in cash before he fled. The other incident occurred the following year at a Vermont bank where a Confederate guerilla gang plundered the institution during the Civil War.

Although it is still not proved, one of the intruders was believed to be a James—either Frank or his younger brother, Jesse.

While one robber engaged the bookkeeper in conversation, the other asked the cashier to change a $10 bill. Then, in a steady and direct manner, the gunman leveled a long barreled revolver at his victim and demanded all the money. This action not only signaled the first bank holdup, but also marked the beginning of the James gang's 15-year crime spree, which included 12 bank holdups and 12 train and stage-coach robberies in 11 states. Little known is the fact that the boys had earlier earned their illegal spurs while serving Quantrill and Bloody Bill Anderson during the War between the States.

Within moments, while the cashier and bookkeeper stood in silent, utter disbelief, the two bandits filled their sacks with an estimated $60,000 and then fled as quickly as they had come.

Outside the bank, the now spirited gang remounted and galloped

Jim Paragin

away shouting and shooting wildly in the air. It was unfortunate that one young boy who saw the wild bunch make their escape was shot as he tried to take cover. Although a posse was immediately formed to track down the bandits, no trace of their whereabouts was found. It wasn't until years later that officials confirmed the identity of some of those who actually took part in the Liberty raid.

For the next 50 years the number of holdups continued to mount, with the problem of positive identification still unsolved. Individual stickup men and notorious gangs spread their reign of terror through the roaring 20's, with local police, sheriffs and G-men doing their best to stem the plague that was costing millions of dollars and taking scores of lives.

It was a little past 7:00 p.m. on March 12, 1934 when Harry Fisher, assistant cashier, at the First National Bank of Mason City, Iowa, strolled into the living room to finish reading the evening paper.

There was a knock at the door. Mr. Fisher laid aside his paper and went to the front hall. Through the glass-paneled door he could see a man unfamiliar to him standing outside on the porch. The stranger was Eddie Green, a good friend of John Dillinger. He was there as the gang's "gay cat" or advance man, and he wanted a good look at the cashier for the robbery planned for the following day.

Green asked the small aging banker for an address.

"It's up the street a few doors."

"Thanks," came the polite reply. Green turned and left. He had had to see for himself the man who held the combination to the bank's vault.

The next afternoon Green and Homer "Wayne" Van Meter waited outside the town, in a Buick sedan, for the rest of the gang that included John Dillinger, Tommy Carroll, John "Red" Hamilton and George "Baby Face" Nelson. It was 2:00 p.m. when another sedan pulled up and parked. Dillinger and his friends transferred to the Buick, and the six men, laden with pistols and machine guns, headed for the bank downtown.

At 2:20 p.m. the big car pulled up in front of the bank and Green, Hamilton and Van Meter went inside. A typical bank of the early 30's, the First National's lobby looked like an impenetrable fortress. High wooden teller cages with metal grills and etched glass windows separated customers from employees. Upstairs, on a mezzanine that overlooked the banking floor, was a bullet-resistant glass-enclosed guard station. Tom Walters, the uniformed guard, sat at the gunport holding a shot gun loaded with a teargas pellet.

No one expected a holdup—that sort of thing always happened to the other guy. But Walters was ready. Bank officers had instructed the guard to fire a few rounds onto the banking floor if trouble should ever start. Within seconds the choking, acrid gas would fill the room, forcing any bandits out onto the street and away from the customers and the cash.

Harry Fisher was waiting on a depositor when the yelling started. Customers and employees looked up and saw the three gangsters waving pistols and machine guns in the air, motioning patrons against the nearest wall.

Bank President Willis Bagley quickly swiveled out of his chair and darted for his private office. Van Meter was in hot pursuit, and as Bagley tried to slam and lock the door the gunman wedged his pistol in the door frame to prevent it from closing. Bagley worked the gun loose and then slammed the door and locked it, but not before Van Meter had fired a shot, wounding the banker superficially.

Tom Walters, momentarily dazed by the confusion, pointed his shotgun through the gunport and pulled the trigger. The 8-inch-long gas cartridge slammed into Eddie Green's back, and the impact caused the cartridge to burst and spew teargas through the lobby.

Green cried out in pain and then swung around to fire a volley at the protected guard enclosure. Several bullet splinters ricocheted through the gunport, wounding the guard. While Tom Walters tried to reload, Hamilton and Green rounded up several tellers for hostages. Then the pair ravaged as many cash drawers as time would permit. They took $32,000, but it wasn't enough. They wanted the vault cash, and Harry Fisher was the man to get it for them.

Pointing his gun, Red Hamilton ushered approximately a dozen hostages out onto the street. Here Dillinger, Carroll and Baby Face Nelson stood watch. With all the hostages lined up on the sidewalk to form a human shield, Dillinger then relinquished command of the outside operations to Hamilton and darted inside, his machine gun ready for action.

About that time, a bank official hiding behind a desk on the balcony fumbled for a teargas canister. He pulled the fuse and lobbed it down to the lobby floor. Almost immediately it exploded, emitting billows of smoke and gas, and choking everyone nearby.

Dillinger then used his automatic weapon to herd more people out to the street. A crowd had gathered by now, and cars stopped in their tracks, the drivers too frightened or confused to proceed. One of the bandits fired a shot into a car radiator, and another gang member triggered a burst from his machine gun into the air.

From a business building across the street an elderly local judge who had been watching the incident pulled a revolver from his desk, took careful aim at John Dillinger and squeezed off a single round. The bullet found its mark, striking Dillinger in the shoulder. Grimacing from his wound, Dillinger whirled around and sprayed the building with a burst from his Tommy gun. The judge had already ducked to safety.

It was now apparent to Dillinger that the stickup plan was rapidly turning into all-out war. Clutching his bleeding shoulder, Dillinger shouted to Van Meter to get his men out of the bank with whatever money they had. "Let's get the hell out of here," he yelled.

One gang member called back, "Give us three more minutes." Red Hamilton found Harry Fisher and forced him into the vault. The assistant cashier obeyed instructions, but tried desperately to find a way to save the $200,000 stored inside. Slowly he handed Hamilton bundles of money that contained only $1 bills.

"Hurry it up," Hamilton urged, "or I'll shoot you."

Finally Van Meter ran inside and shouted, "We're leaving." Hamilton then bagged the last of the cash given him in a huge sack, grabbed another hostage and fled from the bank.

The Buick was ready to go. Six bandits and at least two hostages crammed inside, while other hostages were told to climb on the running boards and rear bumper. The gang had removed the rear window beforehand to provide a holding grip for the frightened hostages, and also to give themselves unobstructed freedom to shoot at police who were sure to follow in pursuit.

As the car inched away from the curb there were at least twenty-one people, either inside, or hanging on for dear life on the outside. Because of the load and the hampered vision of the driver, the get-away car crawled out of town at 20 miles an hour. It was like a scene from a Mack Sennett movie, but to the participants it was not funny.

The Mason City, Iowa, job ended later that afternoon. All the hostages were eventually released, and the Dillinger gang escaped with slightly over $50,000, ready to strike again.

The number of bank robberies remained relatively constant during the 1930's. There were 114 attempts and successful attacks in 1935, 147 in 1936, and 133 in 1939, as the decade ended.

Because of the notorious gangs who perpetrated these crimes and the violence that surrounded them, the federal government enacted a highly important anticrime bill, the Federal Bank Robbery Statute, which gave the F.B.I. jurisdiction to investigate holdups involving federally insured financial institutions in all states. President Roosevelt signed the bill enacted by Congress on May 18, 1934—just 66 days after Dillinger and his men robbed the First National Bank in Mason City.

The G-men didn't have long to wait before logging their first case file. On June 4, 1934, 17 days after the bill became law, F.B.I. agents at Washington headquarters created File 91-1 (Code 91 designates bank robbery; 1 was shown as their first case) and the chase began. It was a case that remained open for six long years. The principle character in this episode was named Eddie Bentz.

The criminal career of Edward Wilheim Bentz spanned roughly half a century and included distinctions that would arouse envy in professional hoodlum circles even today.

Known in later years as "King of the Bank Robbers," Eddie began his career like most other robbers—as a small-time thief. He began stealing cars in 1915, a time when stables outnumbered gasoline stations.

Born in Pipestone, Minnesota, on June 2, 1894, he was one of nine children and lived a very modest life until he was 16. He was then arrested for petty larceny and sentenced to serve 18 months in the State Training School at Chohalis, Washington.

During the next 14 years young Bentz was incarcerated five more times, each time for a crime more serious than the one before. When he wasn't in jail, Eddie planned increasingly intricate and cunning crimes. He gained a reputation for being intelligent and methodical, and eventually such well-known underworld figures as Machine Gun Kelly and John Dillinger sought his advice.

But before Eddie Bentz started robbing banks, he dabbled in less violent action. He first became a "weeder"—a type of burgler who used skelton keys to enter stores in small communities. He would then "weed" through merchandise, stealing only small quantities of a variety of items. Upon leaving, he'd lock the door again, and since he hadn't cleaned out the store, the shop owner seldom would know he'd been victimized.

As his underworld skills increased, so did the sophistication of the jobs he pulled. During the late 20's Bentz learned how to boil nitroglycerine from dynamite sticks. He also became highly skilled in the use of the acetylene torch—a tool he used to cut open safes and vaults.

In 1925 and '28 he was arrested in Michigan and Wisconsin and served time under the alias of "Ned Dewey." When he finally emerged from prison in late 1928, Eddie Bentz was convinced that the only way to make real money was to join the growing list of well-publicized daylight bank robbers. He accumulated a small arsenal of hand guns, rifles and submachine guns and then set out to earn for himself the title of "King of the Bank Robbers."

From the very beginning, Bentz' armed assaults on banks were trademarked by his uncanny knack for selecting the right mark. Meticulous planning and thorough casing of each financial institution often took a week or more. He became acquainted with the roads in and out of town, selecting primary and alternate escape routes. He studied financial statements, watched armored cars deliver and unload cash, and even watched the daily routine of key bank officials.

So highly regarded did he become within the underworld that other stick-up men would often approach him for a piece of the action. Eddie also found it profitable to sell complete jobs to other bandits—jobs that he was not sure of. And for this service he was paid either a specific sum or a percentage of the loot.

In less than two years, Eddie's reputation spread throughout the greater midwest, and each time a bank robbery occurred police were sure that Bentz was involved. Such was the case when, on September 30, 1930, the Lincoln National Bank and Trust Company of Lincoln, Nebraska, was hit for a reported $1,000,000—the largest single bank robbery in U.S. history.

Automatically, F.B.I. officials figured it was a Bentz job. Underworld reports that filtered to law enforcement agencies gave additional weight to the speculation that Bentz had led the assault, but Eddie later denied having been near Lincoln when the robbery occurred, and Nebraska authorities were never able to link him to the crime.

From 1930 through early 1934, Eddie and his underworld confederates pulled jobs from Colfax, Washington, to Grand Haven, Michigan, to Upper Marlboro, Maryland.

Then in February 1934, while Eddie was vacationing in Florida with his young wife—a girl who was the sister-in-law of a recently killed accomplice—he was joined by his younger brother, also a bank robber and fugitive from justice.

The younger Bentz said he wanted to go straight. He had had enough of the criminal life. He convinced Eddie to join him in a legitimate business in a section of the country where neither of the men had a record or was known. Eddie finally agreed, and the two men moved to Portland, Maine, with their wives—Eddie and his wife as Mr. & Mrs. Frederick Wendell, and his brother and his wife as Mr. & Mrs. Theodore Craig.

They quickly settled down, finding suitable business offices on St. Johns Street under the name of "Ultra Products Company."

Eddie had always prided himself on his complete knowledge of the law; he had used this information when planning his jobs. "If you violate state or local law," he reasoned, "you can always move to another part of the country and disappear. But the federal law—that's a different thing. State boundary lines don't mean a damn thing to the F.B.I. There are G-men across the entire country. And if you commit a violation within their jurisdiction, they'll keep on your trail no matter where you try to hide."

During the humdrum weeks of spring, Eddie tried to become involved in the daily operation of legitimate business. But he soon got bored and his mind wandered to other interests—the many banks of New England. So acutely was his attention focused on another robbery that he failed to notice newspaper headlines that announced the signing, by President Roosevelt, of the federal Bank Robbery Statute, on May 18.

One particular bank, the Caledonia National Bank in Danville, Vermont, caught his attention. He liked the whole setup, particularly because the town was small and quiet, and the sole source of protection was the county sheriff about 10 miles away.

Near the end of May, Eddie had completed his thorough casing of the small bank and had mapped out his escape route to Albany, New York. He then phoned a close friend in Chicago and said he had a "soft job" all lined up. "Meet me in Portland this Saturday," he told the confederate, "and pick out another reliable man. The three of us will be able to handle it."

On Saturday, May 26, Avery Simons and Clyde Hamilton Nimerick were waiting at Portland's train depot for Bentz to outline details of the hit.

The next week the men wrapped up a few loose ends of their proposed caper and drove down to Massachusetts in Eddie's Terraplane to steal a getaway car and a set of license plates. The car they chose was a black Ford sedan with yellow wire wheels.

Unknown to the bandits, as they explored the countryside the proprietor of a small cafe became suspicious and recorded the license number of Eddie's car. It was a Maine plate AW 628. This clue later helped F.B.I. agents to trace Bentz back to Portland and the Ultra Products Company's owner, "Frederick Wendell."

On Monday, June 4, a black Ford drove into Danville, Vermont. Clyde Nimerick was at the wheel. At 1:50 p.m. Avery Simons, dressed in a blue suit and felt hat, casually walked into the Caledonia National Bank, followed closely by Eddie Bentz, wearing farmers' overalls and a straw hat. Only four employees were present.

Once inside, the pair drew pistols and commanded the unsuspecting tellers to lie on the floor. After searching the bank for other employees, Bentz told the manager to open the vault. As soon as the big door swung open, Eddie hurried inside and pulled two cloth sacks from his overall bib and began filling them with $7,221 in cash, $8,025 in bonds, $160 in money orders and $3,440 in travelers' checks. It all happened within five minutes with no violence and few words spoken.

As the pair was about to leave, Simons ordered all the employees into the bank's washroom with instructions not to leave. Then the two men dashed from the bank and into Nimerick's waiting car. The three men fled without leaving a trace.

On June 6, 1934, police found the getaway car parked in Schenectady, New York. From photographs shown to Caledonia National Bank employees, one woman teller exonerated John Dillinger and Homer Van Meter. "They're not the ones," she said. "But that one," pointing to Eddie Bentz, "is the man who wore the overalls and straw hat."

The cafe operator came forward after reading about the robbery, and told F.B.I. agents about the Maine license he had jotted down. That led agents to Portland and the arrest of Ted Bentz, Eddie's younger brother. He was wanted for parole violation and also for his connection with a Grand Haven, Michigan, robbery. Ted was eventually convicted of that crime and sentenced to life imprisonment at Michigan State Penitentiary.

Eddie and Avery Simons eluded police for nearly two years, during which time Bentz robbed more banks in Vermont, North Carolina, New Jersey and Pennsylvania, netting more than $100,000.

Then on March 13, 1936, F.B.I. agents closed in on the "King of Bank Robbers." On a tip, they traced Eddie to a Bushwick Avenue, Brooklyn, apartment. Guns drawn, they burst in and captured their elusive fugitive, who was dressed only in his underwear. He gave up without a struggle.

Two months later, on May 14, Simons was picked up in Los Angeles. At the time of his arrest, it was found that he had mutilated the ends of his fingers and removed a tatoo from his left arm in an effort to conceal his identity.

Now two of the three robbers on case 91-1 were behind bars. But Clyde Hamilton Nimerick was still at large. It wasn't until July 3, 1940, in a Burlington, Vermont, court that Nimerick was found guilty of the Caledonia National Bank robbery and sentenced to serve 20 years at a federal penitentiary.

Since 1935 (the first full fiscal year that federal bank robbery statistics were recorded), holdups in this country have risen from 114 in 1935 to 6,148 such incidents in 1979—a record that, according to the United States Justice Department, will almost surely be broken in the years to come.

Ever since case 91-1 was closed in 1940, bank robberies have increased—slowly after the war years, but doubling every five years since 1955. Law enforcement officials credited this epidemic surge of crime to one basic element—lack of positive identification. "If we only knew who these characters were, our apprehension and conviction rate would escalate," was their defense.

A partial answer to their complaint was given during the spring of 1957.

On April 12, 91 years after Jessie and Frank James robbed Liberty, Missouri's Clay County Savings Association, another savings institution was to become a different holdup "first."

This time it was the St. Clair Savings & Loan Company of Cleveland, Ohio. The event was the first holdup in which a surveillance camera was used to film an actual robbery. For law enforcement officials and the entire security world, the event could not have been arranged better. St. Clair Savings was selected as a pilot location by Cleveland police because of its previous high incidence of robbery. On the afternoon of April 11, less than 24 hours before the holdup, two technicians entered the bank carrying cartons of electronic gear, including a 16mm motion picture camera. Quickly, the men began to install the electronically operated, remote-controlled device behind the teller line. As closing time approached, the installers packed up and prepared to leave, explaining to the manager that they would return the following morning to finish the job. Meanwhile, across the street stood two people, a man and a woman, both of whom went unnoticed by St. Clair employees. The bystanders were there for only one reason—to case the bank for the next day's planned robbery.

They had done their homework well. They knew when the branch office opened and closed. They knew how many tellers and employees would be on hand, when they arrived for work, and who would enter first. They had also planned their escape route with a second woman (not present) and they calculated that opening time would be the best time to strike.

Shortly after 8:00 a.m. the following day, the camera installers returned to complete the job. They wired the new camera, control mechanism and holdup activators. Then they loaded the camera with film. Unfortunately they did not have time to run off test pictures, make final adustments for lens settings or light exposure. They planned to do that later.

It was approximately 9:15 a.m. when the workmen left. Fifteen minutes later, as the manager unlocked the door to open for the day's business, a man and a woman entered the lobby. They were the same two who had watched from across the street the day before.

Almost immediately they made their intentions known, demanding all the money in the cash drawers. Understandably startled, but

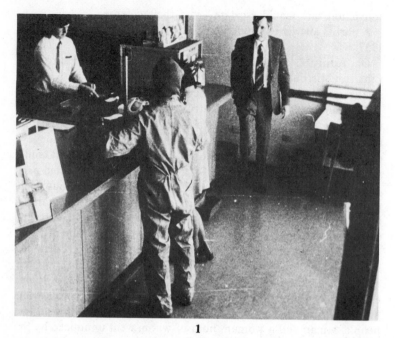

1

The following 13 photographs are actual frames of film shot with a bank camera much like the ones seen in bank lobbies across the country.

in command of the situation, one of the tellers triggered the brand-new holdup activator without being noticed. Instantly the concealed camera behind a wall partition began to roll at twenty-four frames per second. At the same time a conventional silent police alarm recorded "holdup in progress" at the Cleveland police communications center downtown. Within two minutes the first cruiser arrived at the scene, but the bandits had left the bank.

Officers, in obtaining descriptions of the escaped couple, encountered the usual generalities and contradictions that seem to be the rule in situations where emotion dominates reason. Soon afterward, composite descriptions were made and broadcast over police radios, but, as so many times before, officials knew they would fit any two of 10,000 people.

Almost as an afterthought, the St. Clair manager alerted the lawmen to the fact that they had something else going for them that would supplement the confused and frightened verbal descriptions given by witnesses. It was the camera. For the first time, this device

2

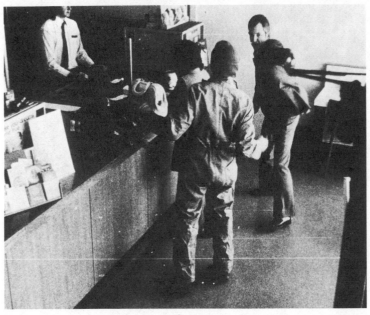

3

4

5

6

7

8

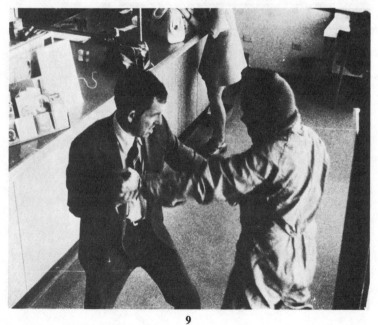

9

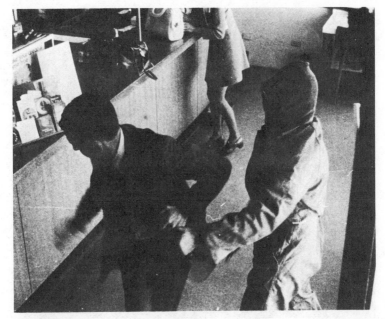

10

11

12

would prove to be an infallible silent witness to the crime. For the
first time, motion picture films of an entire robbery were waiting to
give expert unemotional testimony.

In accordance with previous arrangements, the film was rushed to
a film lab and then to detectives assembled at Cleveland police
headquarters. At first, authorities were apprehensive about picture
quality and definition, because they knew that focus and exposure
tests had not been made. But the film was more than adequate—and
incriminating. In fascinated silence, the officers intently viewed the
holdup from start to finish.

They saw a masked bandit brandish his pistol. They could
actually see one teller press the holdup alarm, undetected, and then
raise her hands obediently. They could see the male bandit, using his
gun as a threat, move one employee against the counter. They saw
his female companion walk behind the teller stations with an
unusual mincing gait. They noticed the practiced motion with which
she snapped open the paper bag into which she placed the money. It
was almost as though she had done it a thousand times before,
perhaps as a supermarket check-out clerk. Noticeable too were the

13

peculiar prancing and erratic steps taken by the masked robber.

Veteran detectives then watched in amazement as the bandit whirled from the frightened clerks to confront a bewildered customer who had wandered in unknowingly. Finally, the officers watched the hasty exit of the masked man and his accomplice as they backed out of the lobby, covering the victims with the pistol as they retreated into the street.

Silence followed the end of the film. Police had just participated in the unprecedented viewing of a smoothly executed robbery. In one minute, fifteen seconds they had observed more of an actual bank holdup than any of them had seen in their entire careers.

The film showing was repeated many times, and each showing produced new clues to the identity of the criminals, largely through the mannerisms of the subjects.

Within minutes after the unsuspecting actors were put through a final command performance, detectives were fanning out over the city putting the pieces of their puzzle together.

Later that day, motion picture films of the holdup were shown to millions of viewers on network television. Still photos by the

1

This bank robber is shooting out the lens of the bank camera that took these photos. The camera was destroyed but the film was undamaged.

The robber shot the camera just under the lens, putting it out of service but not damaging the exposed film.

2

3

Unusually laced shoes (above) and a tell tale scar over his right eye (right) provided crucial clues to this robber's identification, and led to his arrest.

thousands appeared across the land in evening newspapers. Wherever the bandits might go, they couldn't escape their mug shots being on public display. Their criminal act was being discussed everywhere—in bars, at dinner tables and in theater lobbies. It was the most publicized robbery in the 91-year history of bank holdups.

Steven Thomas, the masked gunman, after successfully eluding a police dragnet in northern Ohio, made his way to Indianapolis by nightfall. He checked in at a local hotel to "cool off" and almost immediately saw himself on television. He quickly decided he had had enough of being a star on TV and in the newspapers, so he returned to Cleveland and calmly walked into police headquarters where he surrendered, saying, "I knew I couldn't get far."

Excellent investigative work by detectives established the identity of the woman, whose mannerisms were helpful clues. But for an entire day a police dragnet combing the city for her was fruitless. She could not be found in any of her usual haunts.

Later that evening an anonymous person called police and said in

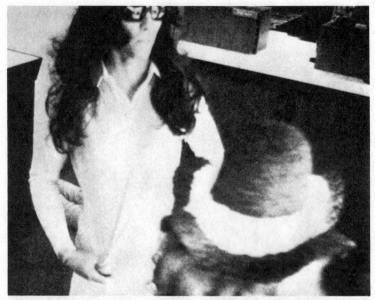

For obvious reasons, robbers disguise themselves. In this photo two men are disguised as women.

This is the more traditional disguise, a nylon stocking over the head.

This now-famous photograph of Patricia Hearst, while a member of the Symbionese Liberation Army, participating in a bank robbery.

Another increasingly popular disguise of bank robbers is the ski mask.

a hushed tone, "I saw the girl you are looking for on television. She can be found at...."

The wanted girl was picked up for questioning a short time later at the given address.

The woman driver and lookout, realizing the futility of hiding, also walked into police headquarters and surrendered. Still another accomplice, who had supplied the gun and automobile, was named by those in custody, and she too was brought in.

The total time from holdup to arrest of those involved? Just 36 hours.

The new surveillance camera technique instantly earned it's place in modern criminal investigation and law enforcement identification. The effectiveness of recording the motions and mannerisms of those who were masked or disguised had been clearly established. The man in this case was identified by his erratic movements; the girl, by her unusual gait.

The results of this documentary were amazing. While the incidence of holdups continued to climb elsewhere in the United States, Cleveland did not experience a single financial institution robbery attempt for the next 15 months. Law enforcement leaders estimate that this was the longest "holdup free" period in the history of any major U.S. city. It is a record that may never be broken.

Who knows what the consequences would have been if the infamous James brothers, Frank and Jesse, had existed at the same time as TV surveillance cameras? The entire history of bank robberies would undoubtedly have to be rewritten.

8
NO BETTER PLAN

*"Even the electronic wizardry of a sophisticated
security system is worthless when, against it, you
have to weigh the lives of your family."*
Harold Wilcox
Bank President

From his Mt. Adams apartment window, Jamie Kemper could look
down on most of central Cincinnati, a good stretch of the Ohio
River, sections of Columbia Parkway that were not obscured by
meandering hills that followed the river, and almost all of Newport
and Covington, Kentucky, on the far bank. It was a good sight—far
better than the confining walls of prison he sporadically had known
as home for nearly 30 years.

The time was 4:30 p.m. that late March afternoon in 1971, and the
rush hour traffic was beginning its eastward blitz for the suburbs.
Kemper had managed to get himself together after a disastrous
night in Newport, drinking heavily and trying to play "Big Stud" at
every bar he frequented. At age 57, it wasn't so easy to find the type
of companionship he craved unless he was willing to shell out good
bucks. But at 5:00 a.m., he had decided to give up because of a
hangover that was beginning to settle in.

As he sipped a beer from his window lookout, trying to escape the
thumping in his head, Kemper wondered how he'd now survive in a
world that wouldn't give him a job or befriend him because of his
record. The whole thing was bullshit. This was a standard question
he had asked himself after every parole, but one that had meaning
for only a few days before vanishing in favor of yet another scheme
that would probably cause him to give more of his life to the state.
Most of his cellmates were gone now, and those he had known in
earlier days hadn't kept in touch. Only Wanda, his cousin, had taken

any pity on him, and she had offered her apartment—temporarily—until he got straightened out.

Kemper needed a stake. If only he had a couple of bucks he'd head down to Keeneland or try his luck with the trotters up at Lebanon Raceway. When another beer didn't settle his mind or his body, he collapsed on Wanda's new sofa and drifted off in a late afternoon nap dreaming of horses, booze and the broad that he was sure he's score with that night.

When he woke up, it was past 10:00 p.m., and the lights from across the river reflected unevenly on the water, interrupted occasionally by ice floes that would melt somewhere downstream.

Feeling a little better, he popped another beer, shaved, and then headed out for another night on the town. Back to Newport and Covington, he thought, as he waited impatiently for the bus.

"Damn! Wish I had some wheels," he mumbled, shuffling back and forth in the cold night. "This ain't my style. It's low class riding with all these bums who haven't got a pot to piss in."

It started to rain as the Metro crossed the bridge onto the Kentucky side. Kemper got off in Covington and began to wander aimlessly through streets that were lined with neon signs offering: Girls—Whiskey—Entertainment. The Padded Bra Lounge looked good for starters. Kemper knew the place from years back, when he and some of his old friends from up north would stop off on their way to Florida to unload loot from house burglaries. He wondered if "Thorney" still ran the place. Howard Thorne was the fence they used to contact back in the 50's and early 60's. He didn't pay the percentage his Youngstown friends did, but it was a convenient stop-off when they went south. Kemper pushed his way through a group of young patrons and squeezed up to a bar stool between two middle-aged men who were hoping to keep the seat open for some action that probably would never come. He chuckled silently as he sank into the cushion.

"Yep, the place hasn't changed a bit." The seat cushion, like all the room decorations, resembled voluptuous bosoms. The music was loud and the crowd was lively. It was the first time in months that he, too, felt energetic, ready to dive into something. Anything.

Kemper inquired whether Thorney was still around.

"Nope," came the curt reply from the bartender.

"Know where he is?"

"Nope!"

But Kemper knew the man was lying and watched him for nearly 20 minutes as he mixed more cheap drinks for the noisy, raucous crowd. Then a well-padded bunny sidled up to Kemper and asked if he was Jamie Kemper from up Cleveland way.

"Er, yea," he stammered, almost in shock.

"Good," the bunny replied, handing him a scotch and water. "You do still drink scotch, don't you?"

"Sure, baby, I sure as hell do. Who do I owe the compliment?"

Before he could get an answer, the cottontail had disappeared in the crowd of horny animal flesh. Kemper waited longer, drinking the scotch and ordering another. He had good vibes now and knew that he was going to make a contact—but who? God, if he could only think who was out of stir and who would be down here in Kentucky. The only reason he was here was because of Wanda.

Just then the bunny came back, tugged on his arm, and said to follow her. Kemper gulped the rest of his drink and nearly fell off the stool trying not to get lost behind his beautiful leader. As the two wended their way to the rear of the club, Jamie felt as though it was old times. He knew that behind that locked door, if nothing in recent years had changed, were private booths—each a separate room where fencing operations took place and where deals were made. The barmaid unlocked the door and led him down a dark corridor to another room. She stopped and knocked, and then retreated the way she had come, leaving Kemper to fend for himself.

"Come in," came a muffled command.

"Come in, Jamie," demanded the unfamiliar voice again. The door swung open, and Kemper entered the booth, trying to adjust his eyes to the new light level. Seated on a semi-circular lounge, with the same padded bosom cushions, were two men dressed in priests' habits. And then in an instant he recognized the shorter of the two.

"Mac Bates, you old son-of-a-bitch. I haven't seen you in nearly 20 years. Where the hell have you been hiding?"

As the two shook hands and exchanged a few more friendly greetings, Kemper turned to Bates' partner and gave him a hug.

"Duncan, you old bum, it's great to see you."

Don Duncan slapped Kemper on the back, and then the three men sank into the comfort of their padded seats. Before the trio became involved talking about the old days, Cottontail reappeared, this time with a whole bottle of Scotch, a bucket of ice and new glasses.

Kemper gave her the once-over and said to his two friends as she departed, "Who the hell is she?"

"Thorney's girl," Bates quickly interrupted, giving him a hands-off look.

"No wonder. I made an inquiry about an hour ago and the bartender clammed up tight."

"Is Thorney in trouble?"

"Dunno for sure," Duncan chimed in, "but when you asked the question, word got out in here that you might be fuzz, so we took a peek. When we saw it was you, I told Phyllis to bring you a drink and ask your name. You're just the man we've been looking for, and after we talk a bit more, we might have something for you."

They poured another drink and got down to business.

Bates and Duncan were both "hot." Each was wanted on federal stuff, so they had to keep moving. The priest idea was Bates'. He had been attracted to religion in the slammer and had assisted at Mass on Sundays.

Leighton "Mac" Bates, born in 1922 in central Ohio, was an unusually bright and witty man, teller of a thousand jokes yet serious when it came to business. He could look the part of a vicar, a statesman or a corporate president. He was affable, glib and popular with women.

Duncan was his opposite. Born in Europe, he had been in trouble with the law since the early 30's and had done hard time in several of America's leading institutions—Atlanta, Lewisburg, Alcatraz and Leavenworth. Taller than Bates, muscular and with hard-as-nails features, Duncan was the heavyweight. He wouldn't hesitate to shoot it out with anyone. He had proved that on earlier jobs.

"But why me?" Kemper asked after his friends had given him a rundown on the past 15 years. "I've never been a big hitter like you guys—you know that from our stint over at Chillicothe. I'm a second-story man, peanuts compared to what you've done."

"Right," snapped Bates, the obvious leader. "That's just it. You're clean around here. No one knows you. You can drive, can't you?"

"Yeah, but..." and Bates cut him off again.

Whatever they were planning, they weren't about to expose it to Kemper yet. But after more conversation, they reminded their potential partner that he was pretty good at the track. He had bragged a lot in prison that he knew every track in the midwest, and had good inside info on the jocks, horses and betting.

It was nearly 3:00 a.m. when the group finally wound up their discussions and decided to call it quits. Bates and Duncan promised to meet Kemper the next day at the Holiday Inn in Fort Mitchell to give him the plan.

"Are you interested?" they asked.

"Count me in."

The three men got up to leave, the priests exiting through a rear door to the alley, and Kemper by the way he had entered.

Jamie Kemper slept till early afternoon, and when he got up he felt like a new man. He now had a purpose to his life and he told Wanda he'd probably be moving out soon. She never questioned her cousin but, knowing all of his "priors," she had a feeling that Jamie was probably headed back to jail—or maybe worse this time.

The Holiday Inn meeting was brief. Bates and Duncan had agreed before Jamie arrived that they'd cut him in, but that they wouldn't give him any specifics yet. The job they had in mind would take some time to set up, and they would do that while Jamie stayed loose. They gave Kemper some cash to keep him going and out of trouble.

"Don't blow it on the horses," they warned.

"And make damn sure you keep in touch with your parole board. We don't want to lose you to no quota buster," Duncan added, deadly serious. The men agreed that they wouldn't meet again for several weeks, but that when the signal came, Jamie should be ready.

The days passed slowly. He sat around Wanda's place drinking beer, seldom going out except for cigarettes and more beer. He stayed off the hard stuff, knowing he could put away nearly a fifth a day, and he wanted to be sharp when his friends called.

On April 1, the phone finally rang and Kemper leaped to answer it.

"We're all set to move," came the voice on the other end. "Take a cab over to this address and we'll meet you. And, Jamie—a bag."

In less than half an hour Kemper, suitcase in hand, knocked on the motel room door. This time, however, the hideout was the posh Carrousel Inn on Reading Road north of Cincinnati. The men had a drink and went over a few details.

"Jamie, we want you to drive up around Hamilton and rent an apartment for the three of us."

Duncan threw Kemper the keys to a not-quite-new Thunderbird and $500 in cash. "Try to find a furnished place you can get on a month-to-month deal, and tell the landlord you're a lumber salesman relocating and will probably have visitors occasionally—home office types or whatever. Try to keep it cheap, but most important, make sure it's up by LeSourdsville, near the Route 63 cut-off that leads over to Interstate 75."

Jamie did as he was told, never asking any questions. Just being around Duncan made him a little nervous, and he wasn't about to do anything to betray his trust. He was no canary and they knew it. His reputation in stir was that of a regular guy who would never violate the confidence of a buddy.

Finding an apartment wasn't all that easy. North of Hamilton on Route 4 there were scores of trailer parks, but few, if any, places to rent. In desperation, Jamie saw an apartment building on a side road—not made to order, but, he hoped, acceptable to his associates. The landlord had a place that looked okay, but it would take a while to get it furnished. Jamie paid the price and said he'd be back. When he returned to the Carrousel, Bates and Duncan were ready to move out. They were both dressed in civvies and anxious to go.

When Duncan heard of the delay he blew his top, and only after Mac Bates heard the whole story did he cool his partner down and get him to accept the fact that there would be a delay.

"What the hell," Duncan conceded, "let's go have a ball. We've already got our bags packed, so let's take off and try our luck at the track."

The Keeneland track was open down in Lexington, so they'd spend a day or two at the horses.

Jamie would drive. He knew that without asking.

Bates sat in the front seat, while Duncan stretched out in back and fell asleep as the Thunderbird crossed over the river into Kentucky.

With Lexington less than two hours away, Jamie felt better, knowing he'd now have a chance to do some real betting again. He felt good too that Duncan was in the back, out of the way.

Bates didn't say much on the trip, and it was unlike him to be so quiet. No jokes, no wisecracks. Jamie thought something was wrong, or that maybe Keeneland or some bank in Lexington was going to be the mark and Bates wasn't quite ready for it. Still, he dared not ask any questions.

"Feel real lucky today, Mac," Jamie said, keeping the car at a respectable speed and trying to break the ice. "Been reading the forms and..."

At that moment he felt a cold tickle at the back of his neck, and he could hear Duncan hunching up closer to the back of the front seat.

"Jeez," Jamie cried, nearly driving onto the median. "Get that goddamn gun off my back. What the hell you think you're doing?"

Mac spun around and ordered his partner to cool it.

Duncan only wanted Jamie to know that he was boss of this caper and that *he* had authority and could use it. Kemper continued to drive in absolute silence, thinking now that this dumb bastard must really be wacko and would probably shoot his mother to make a point. All of a sudden the track seemed meaningless. His day was ruined.

The next day was Saturday, so they decided to spend the weekend at the horses and to drive back to Hamilton on Monday to check on the apartment. Fortunately the landlord had hustled for his new tenant, and said some furniture had already been set up when Jamie phoned ahead to make arrangements to pick up the key. Bates and Duncan agreed privately that upon their return to Ohio they would then let Jamie Kemper in on their plan.

The Boar and Partridge was filled that evening as it was almost every night of the week. The centuries-old inn was one of the most popular watering holes in southern Ohio, and families travelled from miles around to dine and visit the shops and restored bedrooms that served notable travellers as early as 1804, when the original coach stop was opened.

"Let's wait in the bar until we can get a window seat over there," remarked Bates as they inched their way close to a waitress taking drink orders.

Kemper was impressed by the respectability of the place and the fact that the two priests fitted right in with the family surroundings.

It wasn't long before the hostess announced a table for three for "Father Bornman and his party." Perfect, Bates thought, as they took their seats at the window. From their vantage point, the men could look up and down Main Street, but more important, they had an unobstructed view of the Niles Center National Bank across the street.

Turning to Kemper, Bates said in a low voice, "That, my friend, is our score. And within 30 days each of us will come away with more than a hundred big ones."

Duncan smiled as he sipped the last of his martini, and Kemper dumfounded, sat in silence, afraid to ask the thousand questions that suddenly filled his head.

After dinner Jamie paid the check, and the three men thanked their waitress for a very enjoyable evening. Jamie was anxious to get back to the privacy of the Thunderbird so he could begin to ask the ever-growing host of questions.

Rather than head back to their Hamilton apartment, Bates said Kemper should drive up the highway to Lebanon Raceway.

"The horses, Jamie. That's where our money is coming from."

"Of course." And immediately Jamie Kemper was aware of the scheme. The Lebanon racetrack receipts had to be kept somewhere for safekeeping, and Niles Center National Bank must be the place!

Feeling like part of the team now, Jamie asked his two partners the next logical question—how? None of them were burglars—at least not professional bank burglars. How did they plan to pull it off?

"There are certain things you'll need to know about this caper, Jamie, and other things it's best you don't know. Let's just say that I got a tip. A very expensive tip," Bates continued. "We know where the money is kept in the bank at night and how we can get it— without cracking a vault."

It was warm for so early in April and the track was dry and fast. Seated in the clubhouse area, Kemper made all the bets. He didn't want the public to think his clerical associates were spending their congregation's plate money on the horses and thus possibly remember later that they were involved in a stick-up.

Duncan sucked on a beer and occasionally wiped his lips with the black cloth of his sleeve. Bates became visibly annoyed by these gestures and snapped at him to maintain a better image, considering his position. All three men were getting anxious as the last race on the card ended. Now it was time for them to get to work. From up in the stands, the trio watched as the people on the field headed toward the parking lot. Because of the weather, the crowd was unusually large, and it took more than 20 minutes for the cars to file out to the highway. In order not to arouse suspicion, the three men exited slowly to their car and took their time leaving. Already in place near the office area, below the stands, were two Niles Center police cruisers, each with night-duty patrolmen standing by.

It was 11:20 p.m.

A minute later a station wagon pulled up and sandwiched itself between the blue-and-whites, and an armed civilian got out and opened the tailgate. Then two armed racetrack employees carried out canvas bags of receipts and carefully put them in the wagon. The officers were out of their cars now, and they could be seen scanning the nearly deserted parking lot for possible trouble. But because it was a routine assignment, one that occurred each night during the racing season, their surveillance didn't catch the late departure of two priests and their driver. At 11:23 p.m., with the money bags locked in the station wagon, the small caravan headed out of the parking lot and south to Niles Center a few miles away.

It would have been too risky to follow the money to the bank that night, so Jamie was instructed to wait another moment and then head back to their apartment. It was obvious as the men drove down the lonely state road to Hamilton that they were excited, each counting in his own mind how much loot was in those canvas bags. Two, three, maybe five hundred thousand.

During the next few weeks, Kemper, Bates and Duncan took turns going to the track. At the conclusion of each night's racing, they would write down the exact time the station wagon and its escorts left the parking lot for the bank. The time never varied by more than five to ten minutes. The latest pickup was recorded at 11:35 p.m. On alternate nights, two of the men, generally Duncan and Jamie, would leave the apartment about 11:00 p.m. and drive to downtown Niles Center and cruise around the area, waiting for the station wagon to pull up in front of the bank. Coming in from the north, the two cruisers and the wagon had to go around the block so they would avoid a U-turn on Main Street. Once in front of the bank, an assistant cashier would unlock the front door while a racetrack man opened the tailgate where the money was stored.

Police security was good. They used this front door method of transferring the bags to the basement vault because of their complete visibility up and down the street. It was a smart defensive tactic. If there were ever to be an ambush, the officers didn't want to be penned in, as they would be if they used the rear alley entrance. Besides, at 11:30 p.m. there was generally a fair amount of automobile traffic still moving, and street lights kept the downtown area as bright as high noon. On most nights there were three or four bags of money, made up of gate receipts, horsemen's money and bank money—about $100,000 in cash to cover bets at the cashier windows.

While police remained on guard outside, the two cashiers carried the canvas bags into the main lobby. Here one of the men would turn off the alarm system, permitting them to proceed down a back stairway into the basement where the two old storage vaults were located. One of the vaults was used expressly for the Lebanon Raceway money. The total time to make a deposit, lock up the vault, and reactivate the alarm was never more than five minutes. They were always gone by 11:50 p.m.

Satisfied that the pickup and deposit routine would not change, the bandits switched their attention to the most critical element of the crime. Sitting around the kitchen table at their apartment, Bates pored over notes he had taken during the past weeks and began reading aloud some of the specifics to his partners.

"Howard Wilcox, President, Niles Center National Bank, 45 years old. Wife's name, Audrey; daughter Kristin is 17 years old and is a junior at the local high school. The family lives at 47 Applewood Drive, just south of the bank, four minutes drive away. Wilcox is a good-looking man, a smart dresser and always arrives at work in one of his two cars before 8:45 a.m. A son, Mathew, 20, is a student at Miami University up in Oxford, Ohio, and is not home during the week."

The next step in their plan was to familiarize themselves with the bank, inside and out, get a fix on the Applewood Drive house and surrounding neighborhood, and then check out possible drops where the money could be left after Wilcox picked it up for them at the bank. It all looked so easy—except for that hour or so when they would wait at the Wilcox home, holding his family hostage during the critical cash withdrawal.

During the next week, it was back on the street again for the trio. Jamie went into the bank to inquire about an automobile loan. He checked out the lobby and the main floor vault, and tried to look at the alarm system but couldn't find it without causing suspicion. They cruised around the Applewood Drive area during the day and late afternoon, and logged the times when Kristin, Audrey and Mr. Wilcox returned home. At night they watched the house from a number of vantage points, including the rear, where a patio door led into the basement family room.

On one of their many trips back and forth from Niles Center to their Hamilton hideout, Kemper spotted a natural place for the money to be dropped off. It was on the now-familiar state route about four-and-a-half miles west of the bank. Beyond a large tree nursery on the right side of the highway, the road began descending a long hill to a remote curve by a railroad crossing—Golf Port Road intersection—and a meandering irrigation canal. Cover and concealment were excellent at this point. A large overgrown mound of dirt, about 50 feet in on Golf Port Road, would provide an excellent lookout for the entire scene, especially at night. Most important, however, was the fact that there were three routes of escape, should that become a problem.

All was set. They had thought of everything.

By this time the men, especially Duncan, were getting nervous. They had to pull it off soon or something might go wrong. Bates was worried that the Thunderbird might be a giveaway to some smart cop or junior detective who noticed the flashy car around town. And why wouldn't somebody get suspicious? Wasn't it strange to see two or three men riding round all the time? Didn't they have jobs? It was now Monday, May 3. They would pull the job on Wednesday. Duncan volunteered to check out the bank deposits by himself on Monday and Tuesday to make sure the pattern held. When he got back to his waiting companions shortly after midnight Wednesday morning, he reported business as usual. The Monday escort had dropped the bags off at 11:36 p.m., and tonight it had been 11:38. If all went according to plan, the next day at this time Duncan, Bates and Jamie would be speeding south on Interstate 75, richer by many thousands of dollars.

None of the men even thought of sleeping. The adrenalin flowed in their veins, and to keep off each others' backs, they tried to keep busy. Duncan packed his bags and smoked cigarettes. Bates destroyed his voluminous notes by shredding them into minute pieces and flushing them down the toilet. This process took nearly an hour. Jamie decided to clean the apartment, wiping fingerprints from everything in sight—a job he would only have to do again the next afternoon. As each was busy doing his own nervous thing over and over, none of the men realized how late—or early—it really was. Booze had numbed their minds, but perhaps that was good. It prevented them from coming apart during the tense, pre-robbery hours.

Bates was up first, but already it was early afternoon. After a meal of canned food, they finished packing and set their bags near the front door. They decided not to take their gear out to the car until after dark, to minimize the possibility of curious neighbors identifying them to the search party that was bound to arrive in the morning. Every shred of evidence in the apartment had to go. For hours the men cleaned, wiped and scoured every hard object that would produce fingerprints. They wore gloves during the cleanup, but on one trip to the apartment complex incinerator, Jamie forgot to take them off.

"You damn fool," Bates screamed on his return inside. "You want those idiots to finger you tomorrow when the cops climb on this place looking for clues?"

It was a dumb move and Jamie was visibly shaken by the reprimand.

Dusk turned to night, and the trotters started to run over at the raceway.

The apartment was now space-station clean. Even footprints left in the shag carpet were raked over by Jamie Kemper as he retreated out the apartment door on hands and knees, brushing carefully with wide, sure strokes. With their bags now secure in the truck, Bates took one last look inside before closing and locking the door. Before he got in the car, he pitched the apartment key into the incinerator.

"Let 'em try to find it," he laughed as they drove off on their way back to Niles Center for the last time.

For that night's job Duncan wore black pants and a black uniform jacket that didn't quite match. On the seat next to him lay a policeman's hat to which was affixed a "Special Police" badge—the type a Pinkerton or Burns guard would wear. On the floor in the back seat and covered by a blanket was a loaded army-type carbine. Bates and Kemper wore work pants and windbreaker jackets. All three had black stocking masks stuffed in their pockets and automatics in their belts. They all wore gloves.

As they headed east on the state highway, the three sat silently anticipating each step of their well-planned hit. Traffic picked up as the Thunderbird passed over the Interstate bridge, and gas stations bordering the exit ramps were doing a good Wednesday night business. The trio decided to make one unscheduled stop before heading into town. They pulled off the main highway at Golf Port Road, beyond the yellow flasher lights of the Penn Central railroad tracks. Bates wanted to be sure the drop area was free of lover's-lane teenagers, and that their selected lookout point behind a huge earth embankment was hidden from traffic both ways. Satisfied that they could do no more than actually pull the job, Kemper put the car in gear for the four miles into town.

The time was 9:55 p.m. when the white Thunderbird turned the corner onto Applewood Drive and began its slow cruise down the now-darkened road. Harold Wilcox's home was easy to spot. Out near the street was a mailbox on a pedestal. Over the box was a sign that read *Wilcox—47*. The porch light was on, as were several lights inside the fashionable split-level home. No one was on the street, and most of the residents were preparing to retire for the night. Kemper turned the car around at the end of the street and headed back, making one more pass in front of the Wilcox home. Then he stopped the car. Duncan uncovered the carbine and drew the stocking mask over his face.

"See ya," he whispered to his companions while opening the door of the large coupe. He squeezed out from the back seat and walked up the Wilcox's driveway. The white car moved silently up the street and parked.

Harold Wilcox was relaxing in the lower-level family room watching television, while his daughter Kristin was up in her bedroom trying to concentrate on homework, her TV tuned to a different station. Audrey Wilcox was still out, attending music classes at a local night school. It was 10:15 p.m. when Wilcox heard the unlocked front door open.

"Audrey, is that you?"

There was no response. Harold started to get up, calling to his wife again.

"That you, honey?"

Still nothing.

Maybe she hadn't heard him, he thought, so he started up the family room stairs. Standing in the middle of the living room, dressed in his makeshift policeman's outfit, was Duncan, leveling his steel-blue army carbine at the startled bank president.

"Wilcox?" demanded the bandit.

But before Harold could respond, Duncan thrust the weapon forward and cautioned, "If you don't want anyone to get hurt, you'll do exactly as I tell you."

There was a nervous pause as both men stared at each other, not knowing what the other would do next. In another instant, Duncan took charge and motioned Wilcox back down to the family room. As they both emerged from the stairway into the comfortable setting of the family's second living room, Duncan quickly scanned the four corners for Kristin or Harold's wife.

"Anybody else at home?" he commanded in a voice much too loud to be secretive.

"Only my daughter," Harold answered, trying to do exactly as he was told. "She's upstairs in her room doing homework."

"What about your wife, Audrey?" came the next question, as Duncan cautiously scoured the basement level for other people that their research might have overlooked.

"She's at school and won't be back for a while yet—er, what is it that you want?" Wilcox asked, collapsing in his favorite lounge chair, visibly shaking.

Duncan didn't answer. He kept his carbine partially trained on his hostage as he nervously pranced back and forth, drawing the patio door drapes closed.

Suddenly Wilcox heard footsteps outside, and Duncan slid open the glass door and let Kemper and Bates in. Their shoes were covered with mud. Harold made a mental note that the two accomplices must have run through the field that joined his back yard. Both men were out of breath.

"Everything okay?" Bates asked, careful not to name his partner.

"Yeah," Duncan sighed, glad to know his friends were at his side. Like Duncan, Bates and Kemper had masks that concealed their identity. Bates carried a small handgun, but Mr. Wilcox could not immediately make out the caliber or brand. Jamie also had a handgun, but his was still in his belt.

Now Bates, with an air of authority, took command of the situation while the other two stood guard at the patio door and the stairway.

"Wilcox, I'm going to make this brief. Do exactly what we tell you and nobody gets hurt. Where's the kid?"

"Upstairs. I told your friend she's upstairs in her room." Wilcox was now afraid for his family. It was the first moment he had had to think of anything, and he was suddenly afraid that physical harm might come to him and his family.

"Okay. I want you to go up there and get her. But don't try to be a hero. We've spent a lot of time and money on this caper, and I wouldn't hesitate to shoot you or your daughter if you try something foolish."

"I understand," said Wilcox, getting up from his chair and heading for the stairs again. But before he fully got to his feet, Duncan thrust the barrel of his carbine under the bank president's chin.

"Just keep it cool, baby, and nothing will happen."

Wilcox fell back into the chair, almost too frightened to get up again. But he somehow managed and went upstairs to the living room with Duncan and Bates right behind him.

Kristin emerged at the top of the bedroom level stairs. "Anything wrong, Dad?"

But it was too late. She saw the two masked men and immediately darted for the hall bathroom, where she slammed the door and locked herself in. Bates jabbed Wilcox in the back with his automatic and yelled, "Get her down here quick. And tell her not to scream."

Harold ran upstairs and tried calmly to get Kristin to come out of the bathroom. In a moment the door slowly swung open, and Wilcox took his daughter by the arm and led her downstairs.

"What do these men want?" she repeated over and over as they descended to the living room.

"I don't know, honey, but try to keep calm and do exactly what they say."

"Atta boy, Mr. President, very good. You do as your daddy says, Miss, and we'll all get along fine."

By this time, Kemper had come upstairs and taken up a position next to the picture window in the living room. He did not speak as the others retreated to the lower level.

Kristin and her father were instructed to sit on the couch.

"Now, while we wait for the Mrs. to come home, let me explain our mission." Bates' tone showed that he was gaining confidence. He knew the tough part was almost over.

"When Mrs. Wilcox gets home we want you to go down to your bank and get tonight's raceway receipts that are kept in your basement vault. We know all about the alarm system, and we know there's no timelock on the vault. All you gotta do is open it up, take the money to your car and drive to a drop-off place we'll tell you about later. And when that's done we'll tell you where you can find your family."

Wilcox looked at his daughter and squeezed her hand. They said nothing.

It was now 10:30 p.m. Harold Wilcox later recalled this clearly, because the television announcer signaled a station break and the usual three minutes of commercials filled the screen. Nobody saw the commercials or, later, could even remember what program was playing. They sat in silence, Harold and Kristin on the sofa and Duncan and Bates trying to act casual.

A little before 11:00 p.m., Harold told his captors he had better go upstairs to wait for his wife. He said she might get nervous and scream when she saw Jamie in the living room with his gun and mask. Bates motioned with his weapon that it was okay, so Wilcox climbed the stairs again and disappeared into the living room.

He had no sooner gotten there than Audrey opened the front door and walked in. Immediately Harold took her by the hand and told her to sit down. Kemper was now looking right at her, gun drawn.

"Easy, hon," Harold tried to reassure her. "There are three men in here to rob the bank, and as long as we do as we're told they promised to leave us alone."

Audrey didn't shatter as her husband had supposed. It all happened too fast for her to comprehend. Without his being told, he helped his wife downstairs where Kristin and the others waited. All three sat on the couch and waited for the bandits' next move.

"Well, now," Duncan began sarcastically, "we've got the whole family together. You good people relax and watch the news for a while and we'll tell you when Mr. President can go for the money."

Bates didn't care for his partner's bravado and cut him off

abruptly. "Cool it, friend," he cautioned, almost forgetting to keep Duncan's identity secret.

Then Bates began to outline the plan in detail. "At 11:50, we're all going upstairs to the garage. I want you, Wilcox, to get in your car and drive to the bank—around in back, through the drive-in lanes, and park by the back door. You're to unlock the door, cut the alarm system with your key and then go downstairs and open the special vault where the receipts are kept. We know they'll be deposited no later than 11:45 by the raceway guy and your assistant cashier."

Harold interrupted his captor, telling him he didn't know for sure whether he remembered the vault combination.

"Bullshit," Duncan exploded, waving his carbine in the air. "You better remember it, pal. Don't forget, we'll be following you every step of the way, and we've got momma and the kid. Anything goes wrong on your end and we blow 'em away."

This was the first time that any strong language had been used by the intruders, and again it had its effect on Bates.

"Okay, okay," Bates said soothingly. "While you're at the bank we move the family out of the house. And when you've gotten the money, you drive over to Golf Port Road, past the tree nursery. You know where it is?"

Wilcox nodded.

"When you get there, you check to see if there're any cars coming either way. Got it?"

Wilcox nodded again.

"When all's clear," Bates continued, "you back into Golf Port Road next to the railroad tracks—two car lengths—and push the money out the passenger side. Make sure it goes out in the grass."

Harold's head began to spin. The bank, combination, alarm system, Golf Port Road, money bags. How would he ever remember everything?

"Err.., what next?" he stammered, afraid he might have missed something while all the instructions were being thrown at him.

"Simple," came Bates' answer. "You come on home. We'll have instructions here where you can find your wife and daughter."

Again there was silence. Mrs. Wilcox and Kristin sat close together, holding hands. Harold was next to them in deep thought, trying to remember all he had been told and staring blankly at the TV tube.

At 11:50 p.m., Jamie Kemper, who was still at his window lookout, called to his partners downstairs that the money should have been deposited and it was time to go. Bates looked at his watch, nodded to Duncan, and then told the Wilcoxes to move on upstairs. As they got up, Duncan prodded Harold with the business end of his rifle while Mrs. Wilcox, through habit, turned the TV off and followed the group upstairs.

"Remember, Mr. President, no phone calls, no heroics—drive to the bank, get the money and take it to Golf Port Road. We'll be watching you the whole time."

Bates' instructions were very clear. Harold got his keys from the kitchen counter where he always left them.

"Where are your keys, Ma'am?" asked Bates as an afterthought.

Without speaking she took them out of the purse that she had not given up from the time she had come home from music school.

"Good, let me have them," Kemper demanded, in one of his rare statements since he had come in through the patio door nearly two hours earlier.

Everyone went out to the garage together. Wilcox got in his car, and Mrs. Wilcox was told to get in the back seat of her 1968 Cougar with Kristin. At that moment, Duncan raised the garage door and told Wilcox to get going. Without hesitation, Wilcox started the engine, and through the car window gave Audrey and Kristin a loving farewell look before backing out onto the street. As his car started moving down Applewood Drive, he looked back at his house to see if the others were following, but the split-level house disappeared from his view before he could see the Cougar back out onto the driveway.

Harold reduced his speed to let the others catch up. "If they're going to follow me I'd better slow down," he thought, now driving less than 20 miles an hour. Keeping his eye on the rear view mirror, he kept waiting for a car that he finally suspected would never come. "Better speed up a bit," he reasoned, "or I might catch the attention of the few motorists still on the road. God, what'll I do if a patrol car comes along and pulls me over?" He increased his speed even more.

By then he had driven into the middle of town, The Boar and Partridge Restaurant on his left and Niles Center National on his right. Now his thoughts turned from the extortionists and his family to the bank vault. Fear mounted inside him as he tried to recall the numbers of the combination. It had been months since he had worked the combination on that downstairs vault. What if he couldn't get it open? He remembered that the last time he tried, he had needed help from his cashier. Maybe that was good. It would help him correct the mistakes he'd made earlier.

Over and over, he tried to recall the numbers. Left 4 times to

83... or was it 84; right 3 times to 12 and back again 2 times to 16. His hands were wet and trembling on the steering wheel as he pulled into the drive-in lanes that led to the back of the bank. He parked right next to the building, trying to hide his station wagon in the shadows. He was sure his abductors had a fourth man, yet unseen, hiding somewhere near the bank to make sure Harold did what he was told. Maybe the man had a walkie-talkie and could call his friends if something went wrong. But that didn't make sense. None of the men at his house had a receiver—at least he hadn't seen one. "Don't get smart," he reasoned, trying to calm himself. "Don't play detective at this critical time. Simply do what you're told, Harold, and nothing will happen." He caught himself talking to himself and all it did was confuse his already throbbing head.

Wilcox got out of the car and fumbled for the key to the bank. He nearly dropped the whole key wallet in the dark, and had trouble inserting the right one in the lock. Click. The back door to the bank opened and, not knowing why, he entered quietly, almost as if he himself were a burglar. Thinking about it for an instant, he chuckled. But he *was* a burglar, and now he was here to rob his own bank. Disgusting, he thought, as he inched his way in the dark to the alarm control panel. With a special round key that was easy to distinguish among the many on his ring, he deactivated the burglar alarm that could transmit a signal to police headquarters located around the corner. So far, so good. It was five past midnight.

Now for the hard part. Open up the vault. Wilcox held the handrail as he carefully descended to the basement. Feeling his way through the downstairs corridor, he groped for the light switch he knew was somewhere nearby. His fingers touched it and he flicked it on. He knew that no one could see the light from outside because of the many twists and turns of halls and stairs. He was now ready to open the vault.

Back at 47 Applewood Drive, Bates, Duncan and Kemper had other plans for the Wilcox family. The instructions they had given Harold were, in part, a feint. These men had no intention of rustling the mother and daughter off to some remote hideout and releasing them later. It would complicate the scheme and add to their risk of apprehension. No, they would keep it simple. As the bandits and the two ladies watched Wilcox back out of the drive, Bates motioned to the women to get out of their car and go back into the house.

"I'll handle this," Bates told his friends, not wanting Duncan near Mrs. Wilcox or Kristin.

"Give me the wire," he said, motioning to Kemper, who had remained silent through most of the ordeal.

Kemper handed him two small lengths of insulated wire he kept in his jacket. As Kemper and Duncan stood guard upstairs, Bates led the two hostages down to the family room and arranged two small chairs, back to back, against one of the basement support posts. "I'll try not to hurt you," he said, telling them to sit down. He tied Kristin first, arms behind her back, and laced the wire tightly around the post. Then he tied Mrs. Wilcox the same way. "You both have been very cooperative all night and if you promise not to start yelling, I won't gag you."

Audrey spoke for them both and offered her word to keep quiet.

"Oh, to keep you honest, we'll be in the living room until your husband comes home," Bates added as he went upstairs.

The two women heard the basement door close and in another minute detected something being wedged against it. Several more minutes passed before Audrey whispered to her daughter. "At least we're alone, Kristy, and those terrible men don't plan to harm us."

It was five past midnight when the gang went out through the garage, climbed into the Cougar and drove away down Applewood Drive.

Jamie spoke to his friends, much relieved that they were finally out of the house. "Even if we blow it now, at least we won't get caught."

"Bullshit," came one of Duncan's standard remarks. "We're not goin' to get caught and we *are* going to make the score. In twenty minutes it'll all be over."

Kemper pulled up behind the parked Thunderbird and, as he let Duncan out, reminded him, "Meet you at the Lexington Square apartments up the street."

The two cars pulled away from the curb again and headed toward town.

Bates decided to leave the Wilcox's car at the apartment complex for two reasons. First, it was on the way downtown and on their now familiar highway escape route. Second, the apartment parking lot would conceal the unobtrusive vehicle in a sea of other three-year-old cars. It took only a second to find a vacant space and Duncan pulled in, turned off the car lights and rejoined his companions in the Thunderbird.

Time was now slipping away, and Mr. Wilcox should have been about ready to leave the bank and make his drop at Golf Port Road. The Thunderbird headed west in an effort to get there first.

Harold Wilcox now had the combination numbers clearly
engraved in his mind, but his hands were shaking badly as he tried
the tumblers for the first time. 83...12... 16 he said over and over,
trying to make the slippery dial do its thing. Take your time,
Harold. It'll open. Take your time. He was talking to himself again.
Three, four, five more times he tried to open the old vault.
"Damn," he muttered. "I know I'm doing it right."
Racing through his mind was the thought of calling the police, the
F.B.I. or his cashier. Don't do it, Harold, they'll only blow the
whole trick and Audrey and Kristin will get hurt. His mind was now
racing ahead of his fingers.
"Why did I ever let this happen?" he worried. "But even the
electronic wizardry of a sophisticated security system is worthless
when, against it, you have to weigh the lives of your family."
Harold Wilcox tried it one more time. Slowly and easily he
moved the dial to the precise numbers he could now visualize. Then
came a click as the last tumbler fell into place. He stood back for an
instant, took a deep breath and tried the big brass handle. It opened.
As he walked through the vestibule, he noticed how hot and stuffy
it was inside. Maybe it was just nervous excitement, but his shirt
sleeves were soaked from the ordeal.
On a table in the middle of the vault lay three canvas bags with
letters stamped on the side: Niles Center National Bank. Harold
quickly grabbed two of them but couldn't manage the third bag, so
he left it behind. Then he headed back the way he had come. Down
the hall, up the stairs into the dark, and out the rear door. As the
outer door started to close, he caught it with his foot in an effort to
keep it from locking behind him.
"Oh, no," he said out loud, wedging his shoe in the doorway and
dropping the bags to get a better grip. If that stupid door had locked
shut, he'd be dead. He remembered his keys still dangling from the
alarm control. Carefully he let the steel door close but not latch. He
then opened the passenger door of his car and dropped the bags on
the floor. Leaving the car door ajar, he went back again to retrieve
the last bag of cash. As he did, he wondered why he needed to give it
all to this bunch of thieves. But on second thought, maybe they
knew how many there were and he rationalized it was better to be
safe than sorry. On the last trip out of the basement he turned out
the light, switched the alarm system back on and left the building,
locking the door on the way out.
Wilcox threw the last bag on the front seat and closed the door.
His only thought now was to make the drop and get home. He

started the car, backed up and then headed out to the street the way he had come. It was 12:18 a.m. as he caught sight of his watch dial under the downtown street lights.

At 12:19 the familiar blue and white of a Niles Center police cruiser appeared in the back alley of the bank. The night shift officer made a note in his log that the bank and drive-in facilities were normal, and drove off to make his rounds.

Wilcox was relatively calm as he pointed his car down the state road toward Golf Port Road. He had the window open to cool his overheated body and to dry out his shirt. The car passed the tree nursery and headed down the long hill; no one was behind him, and he could see no headlights approaching from the Interstate a half-mile away. Slowing down at the Golf Port Road cut-off, he did what he had been told. He stopped, put the car in reverse and slowly backed onto the side road about two car lengths. Wilcox glanced in the rear view mirror to try to see the approach of one of the bandits, or perhaps the unknown accomplice he still supposed existed. It was too dark to see anything, so he reached over and opened the passenger door. With all his strength he pitched the first bag out onto the gravel berm that bordered the road. Then he heaved the other two bags out, and they too tumbled to the ground. None of the bags made it to the grass, but they were close enough. He shut the door and drove off.

It was 12:35 a.m. when he pulled into his driveway. The headlights slowly circled the garage and showed that nobody was inside. Harold pulled the car up to some bicycles and a lawn mower, and ran into the house to look for a note telling where to go or call for his family. Then he saw a dining room chair wedged against the basement door. At first he felt a chill in his back, a feeling that something terrible waited for him downstairs. He released the chair and started down the steps.

"Harold, is that you?" his wife called.

At 12:40 a.m., Thursday, May 6, 1971, the phone rang at police headquarters.

"This is Harold Wilcox, President of the Niles Center National Bank. I've just been robbed. Can you send someone over right away?"

Jamie Kemper rested comfortably in Wanda's Mount Adams apartment, sipping his second beer and watching a coal barge on the Ohio River negotiate the suspension bridge that separated Cincinnati from Newport. It was late afternoon, and he hadn't yet been to bed. The anxiety of the previous night was still with him, and he was hoping to sleep for a few hours after his cousin came home from work. Then he'd take her out to a fancy restaurant in town to celebrate his most profitable heist and explain his return to the Queen City.

Under his bed in the other room was a black suitcase that contained more than $45,600 in cash—his split of a cool $137,000 in raceway receipts.

Somewhere in northern Ohio, Don Duncan and Mac Bates were relaxing or drinking or betting the horses with their share of the loot. The three men would not meet again until early September—a time that would mark the beginning of the end of their life-long bout with crime.

Duncan and Bates had asked Jamie to meet them again at the Padded Bra Lounge. Their purpose, he knew, was to invite him to join them in retirement down in Florida. Kemper wasn't too enthusiastic about the offer, knowing full well that his friends were still hot and couldn't afford to settle down in one place too long. Besides, he knew they couldn't sit still for more than a few weeks before another job would begin churning in their minds. It wasn't for him, but he thought he'd better meet them anyway for a drink. A request, particularly from Duncan, was one you didn't refuse.

It was September 6, and except for some new bunnies on duty, the Padded Bra looked pretty much the same. Jamie Kemper was the first to arrive, and he decided to sit in the lounge rather than at the bar. He ordered his usual Scotch and water and watched the floor show with mediocre interest. Waiting for his friends, Jamie noticed a well-dressed man in a business suit sitting at the next table, the ice melting in his nearly full drink. He wondered what this "out-of-place" individual was doing here—not drinking, not smoking, not really watching the action. The bunnies didn't even bother to ask him if he wanted a refill.

Duncan and Bates showed up in the the middle of Jamie's second Scotch, and they greeted one another affably and sat down to watch the finish of the show. Because their conversation didn't require the privacy of a back room booth, the men remained in the lounge exchanging small talk.

After a while Jamie poked Duncan and told him of his increasingly nervous feeling about the "business-type" sitting close by. Both Duncan and Bates gave the man a quick glance and immediately could smell trouble. They agreed to leave. Bates stood up and walked over to the bar to pay the bill, dropping $20 on the cash register, and then wended his way through the crowd to the front door. The businessman followed him. As Bates disappeared from view, Duncan and Kemper dashed out the back, past the private rooms and out into the alley. Somehow they managed to escape a web of detectives who had surrounded the building. Mac Bates wasn't so fortunate. He was apprehended outside, charged with a number of offenses including parole violation, and was sent back to the federal penitentiary. He was never tried for the raceway job.

Knocking around the south, particularly Florida, Kemper and Duncan also did hard time for various offenses including fencing stolen property. Then, in late 1976, Duncan met his fate in a shootout in southern Florida. He was killed trying to rob a businessman and his family.

Jamie Kemper, the quiet, unassuming bandit from Ohio who had done his biggest job with the two hardened criminals, vanished, probably to take up with Wanda again—to drink beer, to watch river barges, and to wonder at the sparkling lights of Newport reflected in the river.

No one was ever brought to trial for the 1971 Niles Center National Bank robbery.

9

INCIDENT ON AVENUE P

"Perhaps the longest holdup in New York City history, this 14-hour robbery involved nine hostages, hundreds of law enforcement officers, the death of one bandit and ultimate apprehension and conviction of the remaining two perpetrators."

Gerald VanDorn
Vice President
Chase Manhattan Bank

It was slightly past 11:30 a.m. Tuesday, August 22, 1972, when John Wojtowicz stepped from his lower Manhattan apartment, affectionately known as "Boystown" by its residents, and headed straight for his favorite bar in the middle of Greenwich Village's gay section. The 27-year-old Vietnam veteran, thin, dark and morosely handsome, made up his mind then that he was going to get even with society for a bagful of grievances which he felt more than justified in settling.

Out of work, divorced and almost pitiful in his attempt to "get even" with the world, he would this day take what he wanted in order to start a new life, a life he was convinced would not last much longer. He had been under psychiatric care for much of the time since his honorable discharge from the army, and he was sure he was dying of cancer or some intestinal malady that gnawed unmercifully at his insides.

John had no police record, but in recent months he had associated with those who did. He was down on his luck. He couldn't get a decent job, and the few he got he couldn't keep. Those he kept company with were drifters, on drugs or openly anti-establishment. He had left his wife and children and most of his newer friends were homosexuals.

During the late morning hour there were few patrons in the dirty little watering hole, and the cleanup man hadn't yet shown up to put the disco back in order after a busy Monday night.

John was glad to be inside, out of the sweltering heat that had seen the mercury top 90° before noon. He was glad to be out of sight of friends and inside the relative security of a quiet bar. Maybe a drink would settle his nerves as he waited for his two companions, so that they could put the final touches on a score he had planned for later that afternoon.

John slid onto the plain wooden bench of an inconspicuous booth at the far end of the lounge and waited for his friends.

"Gin and tonic," he ordered, clearing his throat and trying to speak casually to the vaguely familiar day-shift bartender. "Has Sal been in yet?"

"Sal who?" the bartender retorted.

"Never mind."

John sat there in silence, sipping his drink and squeezing the lime between his fingers to extract the last bit of tartness. A wall-mounted air conditioner blew gusts of cold damp air on the young man, drying his perspiration-soaked shirt. Even if it hadn't been so hot, the nervous sweat would still have oozed from his lean body. He had never thought of pulling off such a job until a few weeks earlier when his boyfriend, Ernest Aron, demanded more personal attention. Ernest had told John that if he really loved him he would do something to prove it. He would provide him with the money for his much-yearned-for sex change operation. Ernest desperately wanted to become the woman he felt he ought to have been.

For whatever reason—sex change operation, stomach cramps, no job, mixed-up sex life, divorced real wife or make-believe wife— John had to prove something to make peace with himself and put his life in order. The bank robbery would achieve that end.

After that none of his friends would dare laugh at him for being the clown of the party, for being the pathetic little jokester known in gay circles as "Little-john Basso." He would show them all.

When it was over he'd flash a bankroll as big as your fist, and he'd buy drinks for the house, take care of Ernest Aron, buy a dozen expensive suits and do all the things he had ever dreamed of—before his meeting with the death which he believed was not far off.

Just before noon Salvatore Naturile sauntered into the dimly-lit bar and peered through the darkness for his friend.

"Over here," a voice filtered through the sound of the air conditioner. Sal, a bony, scraggly kid barely 18 years old, made his way over to the booth and slid in beside John. He blinked a few times, adjusting his eyes to the light, and then brushed back his long wiry hair. He waited for John to unfold the last details of the hit which he still thought was scheduled for the next week.

Sal had been a loser from the beginning. As a kid, growing up in New Jersey, he had been picked up and arrested on countless charges of truancy, burglary and drugs. He spent most of his teen years in and out of state reform schools, and within the past three months he had been charged with possession of burglar tools and possession of narcotics. As a youngster trying to survive in a prison world, he had succumbed to numerous acts of sodomy. He had told John and others that he'd never return to prison; he'd die before going back.

As John signaled for another gin and tonic and a beer for Sal, the third member of the little gang entered, made his way to the back of the room and sat across from his partners. Twenty-one-year-old Robert Westenberg, like John Wojtowicz, had no prior record. All that is known about him is that he frequented the same haunts as his new-found companions. Still unsure of this proposed adventure, he sat, fidgeting and silent, as John recounted the holdup plan from start to finish.

"Today's the day. We're going this afternoon, not next week like we talked about. I got a tip that Brinks is making a delivery around closing time, and we'll be right there to accept it."

The excitement of John's new plan was quickly caught by the two young men, and they sat frozen, stunned with the news that soon, probably within hours, they would be rich.

"You guys cool it awhile. I'm going over to Brooklyn, to the old neighborhood, and rent us a getaway car. I got the guns and ammo, and when I get back, about 2 o'clock, I'll meet you at the house and we'll split. It should all be over by 4 o'clock and we'll come back here to celebrate."

John got up to leave, and as he did he reminded his two friends to dress for the occasion. "Business suits, guys. No jeans or tee shirts." He paid the bar bill and left, walking out into the muggy dog day afternoon.

Steam rose from the hot pavement in Manhattan's Wall Street section, producing a thermal mirage that distorted skyscrapers to look like fluttering monuments. A Pepsi Cola thermometer hanging under the faded awning of a downtown deli read 96°. Even the American flag perched atop the Battery's Port Authority building stood at parade rest. There was absolutely nothing to disturb the heavy August air.

It was just past 1:30 when Gerald Van Dorn and his associates,

James Cummings and Philip Cooper, emerged from their favorite lunch spot—Armato's, a posh financial district restaurant. Jerry directed his companions back to their office at New York Plaza by way of shadowed streets in order to avoid a glaring sun. As they ascended the granite steps leading into their building, Cummings joked that even the stainless steel letters reading "Chase Manhattan Bank," affixed to the promenade deck didn't glisten because of the dense haze.

As they passed through a bank of revolving doors, an icy blast of air gushed out to greet them, instantly chilling their skin, clearing their minds for what they hoped would be a quiet afternoon. Entering the elevator, Cooper pushed the button marked 22, and the express silently whisked the security men up to the comfort of their offices.

VanDorn was handed a few telephone messages and then disappeared into the confines of his corner suite. A small triangular sign on the oak desk identified the occupant as vice president, Security and Protection Division. Gracing the otherwise plain walls were plaques and certificates of merit from the F.B.I. and New York City Police Department. It was easy, even at a quick glance, to learn that Mr. VanDorn was a long-time Bureau agent and professional security director with an international reputation.

Unaware that this would be the longest day of his career, VanDorn stood momentarily in front of his lofty picture windows, from which he could scan most of Chase Manhattan's banking domain. North and east he could see Manhattan and Queens, and to the southeast most of Brooklyn showed through the hot mist. Although they were barely visible, he could make out the giant piers of the Verrazano Narrows Bridge, which emptied cars into the very heat of Brooklyn's Bath Beach, Bay Ridge, Bensonhurst and Flatbush districts. The last soon would become the scene of tragedy and terror.

Uptown in a building on the corner of 69th Street and 3rd Avenue was another man who would play a key role in the events that were about to unfold. The old brick building housed the headquarters of the New York field office of the Federal Bureau of Investigation. Richard Baker, Special Agent in Charge (SAC) of the Administrative Division, had returned from lunch and was, in fact, the number one executive on duty, filling that role during the temporary absence of John Malone, assistant director in charge of the F.B.I.'s New York field office.

Dick Baker was an imposing man, over six feet tall, gracefully handsome, with a gray receding hairline. He actually looked more like a bank president, attired in his crisp, blue pinstripe suit. The only telltale clue to his true identity was his service revolver in the holster on his belt, which made a slight bulge in his jacket. A veteran of nearly 25 years of service, Baker had recently been appointed to his current post after organizing and heading a division of nearly 250 special agents dedicated to investigating organized crime.

Fred Fehl, his good friend and special agent in charge of the criminal division, was also out of the office. If something broke, Dick Baker would be in command. But he wasn't anticipating anything big, and he hoped the day would end as it had started— quietly—because he had a dinner date with his wife, and they were looking forward to an evening alone.

Down on the seventh floor, Joe Corliss, bank robbery desk supervisor, had finished talking on the phone with one of his rover teams—mobile agents who patrolled Greater New York on the lookout for bank robbery suspects or other felons.

So far, the only criminal activity within the city that day had been a foiled bank robbery in midtown that had occurred earlier in the afternoon. Corliss had received a call from the manager of a branch bank who reported that a suspect had passed a note to one of his tellers. "The woman simply told the bandit she didn't have authorization to give him any money," the manager stated. The culprit, hearing this unorthodox response, had spun around and fled the bank without uttering another word. Corliss asked the bank official to have the surveillance camera unloaded. Possibly the exposed film would provide a clue to the criminal's identity.

In another part of the city, down on Centre Street and hidden in the cavernous headquarters building of the New York City Police Department, was the other law enforcement officer who would play a key role in the soon-to-be-historic bank robbery. Newly-appointed Chief of Detectives Louis Cottel sat in his high-ceilinged office poring over lists of promotion recommendations, reviewing the more important cases, and putting the final touches on a graduation speech he was to make at the Police Academy. Lou Cottell was an unassuming man in both personality and stature, but he had a solid frame that befitted his new three-star rank. He was not a voluble officer, nor did he appear overbearing, but he was a professional, long-time, up-through-the-ranks street cop who had won the respect of those who served with him.

The time was now 2:55 p.m., and the Pepsi thermometer downtown seemed to have stuck at the 96° mark. Across the East

River and over in the Flatbush section of Brooklyn, Robert Barrett, manager of Chase Manhattan's branch number 252, located at Avenue P and East 3rd Street, was sitting in cool comfort at his desk, signing auto loan applications and preparing to close out the day's business. Mrs. Dolores Goettesheim, the assistant manager, was behind the tellers' counters helping one of her girls, Shirley Ball, balance the accounts.

Back in Manhattan, F.B.I. agent Joe Corliss was about to free his mind from thoughts of another robbery, since 3:00 p.m. was bank closing time, and he knew things would be less hectic, at least until the next day.

As uniformed bank guard Calvin Jones was letting the last customers out the door, three young men dressed in business suits walked in while Jones held the door for them. Bobby Westenberg casually walked over to a customer check desk and placed against it what looked like a large florist's box about four feet high. Visibly nervous, he then turned, apparently unaware of his companions, and quickly walked out. Jones again held the door and politely smiled as Westenberg left, but the young man didn't return the smile.

Mr. Barrett hardly noticed the second man approach his desk until the stranger sat down. Sal was wearing a dark blue suit and carried a small attaché case. Barrett looked up from his stack of papers and asked, "Can I help you?" Sal mumbled something, then pulled a revolver from inside his jacket.

As he shakily displayed the weapon, he jumped to his feet and demanded, in a low tone barely loud enough for Barrett to hear, "Freeze. This is a stick-up."

Barrett looked startled, as though he had not heard correctly.

"Get that guard over here and have him stand there next to the wall." Sal made some quick motions with his gun, pointing to the wall next to Barrett's desk.

"Don't try anything dumb," he continued, now waving the gun with authority. "I've got a partner over there and he means business."

Barrett quickly glanced at John, who at the moment was standing at a teller's cage removing his sunglasses. Barrett motioned to the guard to come over to the desk.

Calvin Jones, an elderly man and unarmed, didn't need an explanation as he approached Naturile and Barrett. He could see the threatening pistol.

"Cal," Barrett instructed before Sal could get the words out, "stand over there against the wall and don't start anything." Silently the guard obeyed.

Mrs. Goettesheim was now approaching Barrett's desk, and he spoke to her very calmly. "Dorothy, we're being held up. Try not to get excited. Keep quiet and stand over against the wall with Cal."

As she took her place, Sal backed to the front windows and pulled the drapes. When he had sealed off the bank to outside eyes, John retreated to the check desk, popped open the loosely-tied flower box and withdrew a shotgun and a 30.06 army-type rifle.

"This is a stick-up. Nobody moves," he repeated loudly for the benefit of six more employees who until then had been oblivious to what was going on. Everyone froze. Shirley Ball looked up from her adding machine and stared at the bandits in utter disbelief.

There was a moment of silence as John, not quite sure what to do next, stood transfixed, shotgun leveled at Barrett. Then he quickly took command and declared to his hostages, "I don't want anybody hurt. Do what we say and everybody will be okay." Sal was still standing next to the manager with his snub-nose pointed at Barrett's head.

John lowered the barrel of his weapon a little and walked over to Barrett.

"Now listen, listen carefully. I want all the money. Tens, twenties, fifties and hundred dollar bills. No fives, no ones. I want the list of serial numbers in the girl's book, and I want all the traveller's checks and the book you list them in. I know all about the book, and I want it."

John felt easier after he had made his demands. Everything was going smothly, as they had planned. His shotgun touched the floor, and his manner and the reaction of the tellers became less tense.

"You have a Brink's pick-up in a couple of minutes, and I want that money from the vault too," he continued almost as an afterthought.

"Oh, Mr. Barrett," cried Kathleen Amore, one of the tellers, "they picked up that shipment at 11:30 this morning."

John spun around and faced the girl who was half hidden by counters. "I thought Brinks didn't come until 3:30. Open the vault. I want to see it."

Barrett started to get up from his desk but hesitated as Sal again leveled his pistol close to the manager's head. "It's okay," John said, nodding his head in approval.

Still cautious, Barrett rose and started for the vault, motioning to Kathy to follow. The vault had a dual combination, and it required

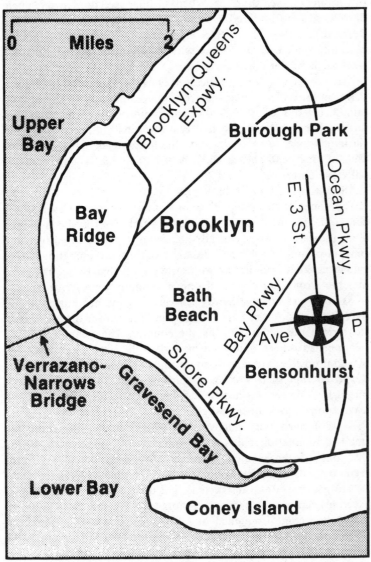

The branch of the Chase Manhattan Bank where the robbery took place is located on Avenue P, in the Bensonhurst section of Brooklyn, New York.

two people to open the door. When the huge steel door swung open, Barrett went in and retrieved $4,000 in a bag marked "Federal Reserve."

John prodded Kathy Amore with the tip of his gun and the two went back to the tellers' area.

"The traveller's checks. Get the traveller's checks and log book."

Kathy looked at Robert Barrett as if to get approval and then said, "They're locked up down here," pointing to an undercounter locker. The steel safe also had two combinations, so Barrett and Kathy stooped down and twirled the locks open. Kathy extracted piles of traveller's checks and stacked them neatly on top of the tellers' counter.

"Now the log book," John pressed.

The young teller hesitated a moment and then withdrew a ledger containing recorded serial numbers of purchased traveller's checks. John took it from her, casually glanced at the written entries, and smiled, proud that he had thought of this incriminating bit of evidence. What he didn't know, however, was that Kathy had given him the wrong book, an old one containing useless entries.

As John was busy gathering cash, checks and other negotiables, Sal left his position at Barrett's desk and headed for the check desk to retrieve the 30.06 lying on the counter. The ominous-looking weapon had a telescopic sight affixed to the barrel, and when Sal picked it up an expression of power and confidence crossed his face. Surprised that their work was going so well, the bandits almost forgot the time. It was nearly 3:15, and the two men would have to leave soon or risk being caught.

As John piled more money on the tellers' counter, discarding the small denomination bills on the floor, Barrett interrupted, saying that one of the women, Maureen Andrews, the safe deposit secretary, was in the restroom, unaware of what was taking place.

"Go get her," John instructed, "but don't try anything." Barrett asked his captor if he'd lower his shotgun and step back so Maureen wouldn't become frightened or hysterical. John didn't argue, but obeyed the request and stepped aside to let Barrett through to the ladies' room. The manager informed Mrs. Andrews of the situation and led her back to her desk to answer phone calls.

At almost that same time, the phone rang and Barrett, now close to his desk again, picked up the receiver. The caller was Joe Anterio at the personnel office downtown. Barrett looked up at John, shrugged his shoulders as if to say, "What'll I do now?" and John whispered, "Nothing funny or everyone gets hurt."

Joe asked Barrett to send one of his tellers, Joan Saunders, to the 75th Street branch the following day to fill in.

"Instead of sending Joan," Barrett answered, "I'll send Steve Marzano."

Anterio, puzzled because Marzano had been fired a few months before, hesitated. "You're talking funny, Bob. Are you in trouble?"

"Yes," was the monosyllabic reply.

"Do you need help?" Anterio asked quickly.

"Yes." Barrett hung up.

Wojtowicz seemed satisfied with Barrett's brief conversation and returned to the tellers' area and the money.

As soon as Joe Anterio finished speaking with Mr. Barrett, he phoned the Security and Protection Division. He asked to speak to Phil Cooper, then gave him the few facts he had. Cooper looked at his watch. It was 3:20. He called one of his bank investigators into his office. Nicholas Albanese stood in the doorway and listened as Cooper told him about the call he had received from Joseph Anterio, assistant treasurer, Manpower and Administration Division.

"Bob Barrett is in trouble. I want you to call the branch and see if you can find out what's going on. Be careful. Don't let on who you are in case someone is in there and listening."

Nick went back to his desk and dialed Branch 252. It was now 3:25.

When Barrett answered, Nick repeated Anterio's questions and got the same double-talk reply. Then the phone was silent. At 3:30, Nick called again and this time Dolores Goettesheim answered. In this conversation, Albanese detected there was real trouble at the branch, but feeling now that there *was* someone listening, he pretended it was a routine call and hung up.

Nick then reported back to Cooper, who was now giving the information to Jerry VanDorn. VanDorn told Nick to call the police, and said that he himself would phone the F.B.I.

At 3:40, Nick called Lt. Maurice Beers, 10th District Detectives, Robbery Squad, and explained what he knew. Lt. Beers informed Nick he would call the police emergency dispatcher and have them send a radio car to the scene. Nick expressed his fear that if uniformed officers were sent, the bank and its personnel might be endangered. He then asked the lieutenant to respond as quickly as possible with plain clothes detectives and to conduct a discreet investigation. Before hanging up, Nick gave Lt. Beers the protection division telephone number, and the officer said he would get back to the Chase Manhattan headquarters when he had more information.

Meanwhile, at the bank, John ordered Sal to herd the tellers into a rear conference room where he could keep an eye on them more easily. Mr. Barrett, still at his desk, suddenly noticed smoke spiraling from behind the tellers' counters. He rushed over to see what John was doing. The log book, in a wasketbasket, was smoldering amid old calculator tape, discarded bank forms and sundry wastepaper.

John nonchalantly looked up from the little fire and asked Barrett, "You got another exit from this place?"

"Yes, there's a back door."

"Does it have an alarm on it?"

Barrett said it did and asked Dolores Goettesheim to get the keys from her desk. John continued to watch the flames to make sure the fire didn't get out of hand. Then for some reason, he looked up and glanced at the front of the bank. With the drapes still drawn across the windows, John could see only through the opening at the two glass entrance doors. But that was enough to spot a police cruiser parked across the street.

Keeping clear of the door, he dashed over to the drapes, lifted a corner, and scanned the quiet street. One police car was visible, but it was sufficient to convince the robber that escape now would not be a certainty.

Rushing back to the conference room, he yelled to his partner, "Sal, we got company."

The telephone on Robert Barrett's desk rang again. The manager looked at Wojtowicz before answering it. John nodded and Mr. Barrett picked up the receiver.

"This is Lt. Maurice Beers, 10th District Police. I've got a report of a suspected robbery in progress. Is this true?"

Barrett knew the doubletalk games were over and confirmed the situation.

"Can you put one of the subjects on the phone?"

Barrett turned to John and said, "It's for you," and handed him the phone.

Lt. Beers repeated the message and apprised John of the situation.

"We've got the bank surrounded. Put down your guns and come out through the front door with your hands up. If you surrender now, no one will get hurt and things will go much easier for you." John remained silent, not knowing what to do or say. After a long pause, Lt. Beers asked, "Are you still there?"

"Er, yeah," John responded, almost defiant. Again there was silence, and then John slammed the receiver back on the hook.

By this time Sal had left the women alone in the conference room and was standing next to John and Barrett.

"Was that the cops?"

"Yeah," John informed his partner, slumping in Barrett's chair. "I gotta think . . . " Then he bolted from the chair and ordered Sal, "Go to the back door and see if you can spot any more fuzz out there."

For the first time since they had entered the branch, both bandits experienced adrenalin highs. They were caught in a box and they knew it.

In a moment Sal returned to the manager's desk and reported that he could see a patrol car out back, and that two officers were visible outside their car, partially hidden by the crusier's hood.

"Great. This is just great," John yelled at Barrett. "We got all the money and now we can't get out."

Downtown, Jerry VanDorn called the F.B.I. Joe Corliss was handed the details of the robbery and immediately ordered his dispatcher to radio the rover team closest to Avenue P and East 3rd Street. Within minutes an unmarked Bureau car pulled up close to the bank, and the agents were immediately filled in by police already at the scene.

By 3:50 newsmen from around the city were racing to Brooklyn with camera crews and photographers. Their radios, tuned to police bands, caught enough of the official reports to know that a holdup was in progress and that a possible hostage situation existed. By 4:15 there were more than a dozen patrol cars surrounding the small Chase Manhattan branch, and more than 50 policemen were in position, guns ready for possible action.

In the meantime, VanDorn dispatched Nick Albanese with Jim Cummings and James Bannon, other Chase Protection Division investigators, to Brooklyn to coordinate with the F.B.I. and police and to set up a communications command post. With them they took blueprints of Branch 252 which showed all exits, electrical work and the floor plan of the building. VanDorn instructed Jim to phone in every half hour to give him an update on the situation.

Up on 69th Street, Fred Fehl, special agent in charge of the Bureau's Criminal Division, had recently returned to the office, and he and Joe Corliss left for the scene in an official F.B.I. car.

By 5:00 there were more than 200 law enforcement officers, three dozen cruisers, police vans, ambulances and even a Red Cross wagon to serve coffee.

Across the street from the bank was a small barber shop Fred Fehl wanted to use as a command post. Anthony Finizio, owner of the Palestinian Barber Shop, agreed to cooperate and allowed police to set up additional phones in the rear of his store. By 5:30 the telephone company had a half dozen additional lines in and operating, and Jim made his first call to VanDorn, advising him of the situation and speculating that it looked as though it might be a long night.

During the next hour and a half several events took place which would later provide the F.B.I. and police with clues to the mental makeup and bargaining potential of the assailants. Shortly before 7:00 John released bank guard Calvin Jones, apparently as a good faith gesture to further escape negotiations which, up to that point, had been conducted by police. A little earlier John had exposed himself to possible gunfire by coming out on the street to talk to two police lieutenants. He had asked for pizzas to be delivered for himself, Sal and their captives. He also had demanded that Ernest Aron be brought from Kings County Hospital where Aron was confined as a mental patient, having tried to commit suicide because of worry over his sex change problem. Aron was later brought to the bank but refused to talk with John, saying he was afraid that John might kill him.

While all this was going on, John and Sal permitted all the bank employees freedom to use the bathroom facilities and to make telephone calls to their families. Relatives informed police that the captors were treating the hostages as well as could be expected, and that they often joked with one another about their predicament.

One of the tensest moments came when Sal, completely uptight, surveyed the street and alley area that was now filled with flak-vested officers. Each officer was poised and ready for all-out warfare. Sal fired a single shot through the back exit door, thinking police were trying to break in. From inside the bank, the shot sounded like an explosion, but from outside all police heard was the staccato of a racing bullet as it pierced the barricaded door. In an instant the early evening air was filled with clicks of rifle and handgun safeties in preparation for return fire. But nothing happened.

As Dick Baker was about to leave his New York Headquarters to meet his wife for dinner, he was told of the incident on Avenue P and suddenly changed his mind. Normally he wouldn't get involved, but this robbery appeared to be developing into a major case.

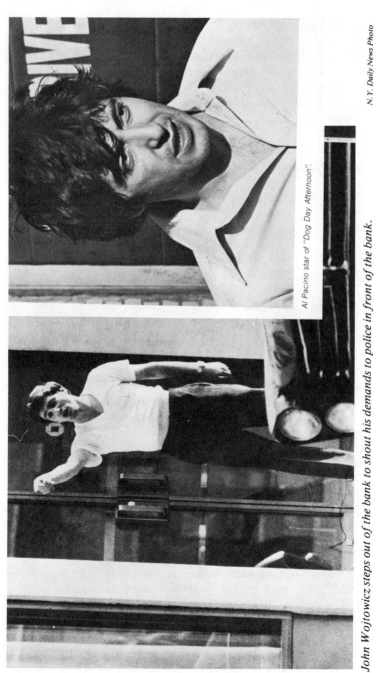

N.Y. Daily News Photo

Al Pacino star of "Dog Day Afternoon".

John Wojtowicz steps out of the bank to shout his demands to police in front of the bank.

During an average day in the city of New York there might be two, three or as many as six holdups, and rarely would a top-ranking official like Baker or Fehl get involved personally. But the lives of an unknown number of hostages hung in the balance, and Baker felt that his presence was required. He left the office with other agents and arrived in Flatbush about 6:00 p.m.

Chief of Detectives Louis Cottell pulled into the driveway of his modest Hollis, Long Island, home shortly after 6:30 p.m. He was tired after a full day that had begun at 7:30 that morning. As he sat down for dinner the kitchen phone rang. The chief reached for the wall-mounted receiver; it was his office calling. He, like Baker and others in command positions, were regularly notified of situations like the Chase robbery, but unless it was something really big, he left the investigation in the capable hands of his district commanders.

"Send a car over for me right away," the chief ordered after hearing the report. "We should be able to make the scene in an hour." Lou snapped on his police special, kissed his wife goodbye, and walked out the front door to wait for his driver.

By early evening the crowds, TV crews, off-duty police and neighborhood residents had found viewing places around the two-block-wide barricaded streets. One woman with a baby stroller defied police blockades and meandered through the maze of uniformed officers and parked vehicles. Hotdog carts and soft drink wagons parked behind the official perimeter were selling their wares to hungry, thirsty and perspiration-soaked onlookers.

Outside the bank there appeared to be mass confusion, but it was mainly because of the sheer number of people. When the chief arrived, he was furious. He told his unit commanders that the scene looked more like a carnival than an investigation.

"Get these pedestrians moved back," he ordered. "And reduce your manpower to a manageable size," he told those in charge.

Fred Fehl, Joe Corliss and Jim Cummings were in constant communication with police and their respective headquarters. A good working relationship prevailed among those in authority at the scene.

Inside the bank it was another story. While John seemed to have settled down slightly, Sal remained jittery and trigger-happy—ready, if need be, to shoot it out. As recounted later by Barrett and his tellers, Sal often spoke of the tremendous power of his 30.06 and his ability and willingness to use it. It was he the hostages feared most.

During the late afternoon and early evening the phone rang

N.Y. Daily News Photo

Bank guard, Calvin Jones (center), describes the situation inside the bank to police officials.

constantly inside the bank. Newsmen phoned, wanting to talk to the bandits. Others called to encourage the pair. One man called every fifteen minutes or so and in a whispered weird voice told John, "Kill them all."

By 7:30 all of the principal law enforcement officials had arrived and were formulating their strategy and evaluating possible courses of action. The little Palestinian Barber Shop was hot and sticky, and the lawmen were uncomfortable as they mapped out their plans. It was agreed that Chief Cottell would command all of the activities outside the bank including placement of officers, crowd control and possible sniper action. The F.B.I. would take over any negotiations with the suspects, since robbery of a federally-insured financial institution was a federal offense. Although Fred Fehl headed the criminal division, Dick Baker was actually senior to his close friend, and therefore, by F.B.I. chain of command regulations, Baker would make all final decisions.

Baker asked Chief Cottell whether snipers were in position at critical locations around the building. The answer was affirmative. Through spaces between the drawn drapes, and through the exposed glass entrance doors, police marksmen equipped with high power scopes could see the hostages and robbers clearly. The safety of the hostages was the uppermost concern of the lawmen, and only if the criminals intensified their threat to snuff out these innocent lives, would F.B.I. agents try to lure them to the front of the lobby where snipers might have an opportunity to end the seige.

Joe Corliss told the small conclave, "It's too dangerous. The rooftop marksmen will be shooting at the suspects down on an angle, and there's a possibility their bullets might be deflected as they pass through the glass. If they do and miss, one of the hostages might be hit." Baker, Fehl and Cottell agreed that this plan would be used only as a last resort.

Dick Baker wanted to talk to John. He wanted to get inside the bank to determine the exact firepower the robbers had and to confirm that the captives were all right. A police bull horn had been used to communicate with the bank several times earlier but with no results.

Baker got on one of the phones the telephone company had set up earlier and called across the street. He knew John's full name by this time because of the many conversations the media and police had had with him during the past several hours. He also knew that John had no prior arrests. And from other investigative intelligence he was aware that John had a real wife (divorced) and two children and

Wojtowicz's lover, Ernest Aron, was brought to the scene in hopes that he might be able to talk him into surrendering to authorities.

N.Y. Daily News Photo

also a homosexual friend, Ernest Aron, who had been brought to the command post hours earlier. He was puzzled, however, by the name Wojtowicz had given police in identifying his partner Sal. John had told them his accomplice was named Donald Matterson. For two hours local TV stations, live from the scene, had been telling their audiences that it was Wojtowicz and Matterson who were holed up inside the Chase Manhattan branch. Police computer files showed no such name. It wasn't until later that Salvatore Naturile, alias Donald Matterson, was identified as a young man who had been picked up in Manhattan three months before on the charge of possessing burglar tools.

The phone rang on Barrett's desk and John immediately picked it up, expecting another crank call or a TV reporter wanting to know the latest developments to update his viewers.

"Mr. Wojtowicz?" Baker asked to make sure it was one of the bandits.

"Whadda ya want this time," John replied, matter-of-factly.

"This is the F.B.I. My name is Richard Baker and I'd like to come over and talk to you."

217

John thought for a moment and then asked, "Yeah, what about?"

"John, I'm sure you're aware that your situation, and your friend's, is hopeless as it exists. I'd like to talk with you to explain how we can end this terrible thing with no one getting hurt. Right now the basic charge against you is armed bank robbery." Baker made every word count. He talked intelligently to John and described the situation exactly. He was careful not to threaten John or talk down to him. His articulate manner and honest appraisal kept John on the line, an accomplishment that others had failed to acheive.

"Why can't we just talk over the phone?" John asked.

"John, I'd really like to talk to you on your ground. I'd like to see for myself that those people you're holding are all right, and it would be a show of good faith if you'll agree to see me. I'm across the street in the barber shop and I'll come over, unarmed. You can watch me through the window."

"Are you the head guy in the Bureau, the guy that can make the decisions?" John interrupted.

"Yes, I am. Chief Louis Cottell of the New York Police Department will also accompany me. We'll both be unarmed." John didn't accept or reject the plan, but hung up without further conversation. A minute passed and the two commanders started across the street. John left Barrett's desk and headed for the front doors, hesitated for a moment and then opened one section a crack. When the two officers got to the middle of the street, they saw that John appeared to be buying the plan. Baker took off his suit jacket, removed his pistol, and handed them to another F.B.I. agent. Chief Cottell did the same.

"John, we're coming in," Baker stated as he started to move forward, not waiting for a negative response.

John dropped the barrel of his gun and retreated into the semi-darkness of the lobby, permitting Baker and Cottell to enter.

John did all the talking for the robbers. Sal, still nervously toying with his rifle, stood far back, out of the way of any possible action the cops might start. At first John spoke in foul four-letter words, trying to justify his being there. Then he quieted down and seemed interested in what Baker had to offer.

"I don't want to talk to the cop, only to you." Baker looked at the chief and, sensing it would be futile to argue the point, told John that this was acceptable.

"You have eight hostages—Mr. Robert Barrett and seven female tellers. I'd like to know if they're all okay."

Negotiations with the robbers continued into the night. FBI Special Agent, Richard Baker, left, talks with Wojtowicz.
N.Y. Daily News Photo

John didn't confirm or deny the headcount, but a quick glance at Barrett got an affirmative nod that this was true. While Baker continued to talk, Chief Cottell noted that the bandits had a high-powered rifle, a shotgun, a pistol and an automatic.

Suddenly John interrupted. "We want out of this place. I want you to arrange for a helicopter to take me and my friend and some hostages to Kennedy, and I want a plane ready to take us to another country."

Baker was quick to respond. "That'll be impossible, John. The street isn't wide enough to land such a machine, and the roof is too small. I can't promise you anything, but if you'll let these people go, let them out the front door one at a time, and then you and Matterson come out, I can tell you you'll not be harmed, and we can end this thing right now."

John didn't buy it. He started using foul language again and repeated his demands, this time changing his request for transportation to the airport to two cars. "I'll go in one car with four hostages, and Sal will go in the other with the rest."

"Who is Sal?" Baker asked.

"Sal! Salvatore Naturile. That's my friend over there. I told those press guys his name was Donald Matterson because that's the name he uses once in a while."

Baker didn't like the idea, but saw it as an opportunity to bargain. First, it would give him more time to plan, and second, it would get the bandits out of the bank and onto neutral ground more suitable for their apprehension.

"Two cars are out," Baker said, knowing two vehicles would be more difficult to control. "It's against F.B.I. regulations to permit two government vehicles for such purposes." Baker made that up merely to squelch the idea.

"Then how about one of those airport limos?" John interjected, as another possibility. "You get me a car and I'll let one of the girls go just to show you we want to play ball." The two men bargained, and SAC Baker tried to convince John to let one person go free immediately.

"When you guys leave I'll think about it," John said.

Baker agreed to see what he could do about getting the limo and an airplane, but again said he couldn't promise anything.

Chief Cottell and Agent Baker left the bank and returned to the barber shop to plot their next move. When they were safely inside the shop, Jim Cummings phoned his boss, Jerry VanDorn, and reported the progress, mentioning the possibility that Chase

Wojtowicz and Sal Naturile sit in an airport limousine, surounded by hostages, moments before being driven to Kennedy International Airport.

might have to authorize an airplane for the escape. It was now close to 9:00 p.m.

For the next hour Baker, Fehl and Chief Cottell evaluated the situation and calculated their next moves carefully. They knew now that John Wojtowicz was the leader of the two. They knew also that he could be bargained with and that he might make some concessions. Earlier he had released Calvin Jones, and now he talked of letting one of the tellers go. But the men also had their fears, especially concerning Sal. He was nervous, high strung and volatile, and he had a weapon. The longer the incident was drawn out, the more fatigued, frightened and unbalanced the robbers would become.

It was nearly dark when the chief ordered searchlights brought in to illuminate the entire building, front and back, and the surrounding area. To make matters more difficult for the culprits, he ordered the air conditioning and lights turned off inside the bank.

By 10:00 p.m. everyone knew it was going to be a long night. The lights on the 22nd floor of Chase Manhattan's Wall Street headquarters were still burning, and Jerry VanDorn was busy making calls trying to locate a suitable airplane for a possible flight to an unknown destination. He was successful in contracting for a Hansa Jet Corporation 12-passenger model that was then berthed at Newark Airport about 20 miles west of Manhattan.

In the bank John quizzed some of his captors as to where they wanted to go. He jokingly asked Shirley Ball, "How about Moscow? You wanta go to Russia? Maybe Hawaii or Tel Aviv?" Actually no destination was ever determined.

During the evening hours police brought in a report that earlier, soon after the holdup had begun, several officers had seen an unidentified man get out of a parked car near the bank and disappear on foot. It was later determined that the man was Bobby Westenberg. Officers then checked the registration on the new Mustang and found it had been rented to John Wojtowicz, who had used his real name on the rental contract.

By midnight the barber shop command post was bustling with other people in addition to the police. John's mother came there to talk with her son, hoping to persuade him to surrender. Ernest Aron was there, too. At one point Mrs. Wojtowicz threw her arms around Aron and consoled him, "Don't worry, Ernest, they'll get John out all right. Maybe they'll even put you both in the same room at Kings County Hospital."

Also at the command post was Mrs. Clyde Saunders, mother of Joan Saunders, one of the tellers. Harry Ball, Shirley Ball's husband, had been there for hours. He had heard the news on his Manhattan office radio and had taken the subway to Flatbush late in the afternoon.

John was upset that police officials could not convince Aron to meet him on the street, so he asked to see Patrick Coppola, John's "Boystown" roommate. When Coppola was finally located and brought to Brooklyn, Baker agreed to allow the 22-year-old man to go across the street to see his friend. The F.B.I. called the bank again and told John that Patrick was on his way over. An agent accompanied him, holding onto his belt to make sure Patrick didn't try to break away and enter the bank or that John didn't force him in. They certainly didn't want an additional hostage. The meeting on the street, outside the front door, was brief, but it brought catcalls and jeers when Patrick threw his arms around his good friend and kissed him.

The hours passed into Wednesday morning with reporters still reporting, police still negotiating, and anxious relatives still waiting for something to break. Of several contingency plans devised by the

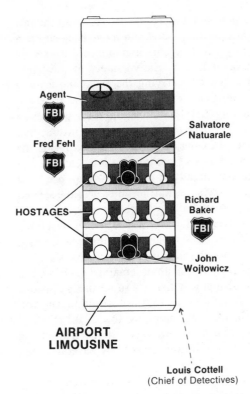

Agent
FBI

Salvatore
Natuarale

Fred Fehl
FBI

Richard
Baker
FBI

HOSTAGES

John
Wojtowicz

**AIRPORT
LIMOUSINE**

Louis Cottell
(Chief of Detectives)

*Diagram shows location of
limousine, FBI agents and
police officers at airport.*

lawmen, F.B.I. agents agreed that a limousine ride to Kennedy International Airport held the best possibilities for a bloodless apprehension.

At 3:50 a.m. Wednesday, August 23, a green 14-passenger airport limo drove through police blockades and parked in the street about 20 yards from the bank. John gathered $37,950 in cash and more than $175,000 in traveller's checks and handed the bundle to Robert Barrett for "safekeeping." Then he came out of the bank, his rifle slung over his shoulder, and approached the car. Dick Baker and other F.B.I. agents, including a volunteer known only as "Murphy," waited for John to make his next move.

"Who's gonna drive?" John asked.

Agent Baker stepped forward and introduced Murphy, who was actually a special agent. While the others stood back, Wojtowicz frisked Murphy from top to bottom and inspected the limousine, looking for a concealed weapon.

"Okay, you get in," he said, pointing to the driver. "And the rest of you Feds drop your guns on the ground and move back so I can see everybody." Reluctantly F.B.I. agents and police did as they were told, and John retreated to the relative safety of the bank. In a few minutes he reappeared, carrying the 30.06 and leading Manager Barrett to the waiting car. Then six of the tellers appeared in the doorway, surrounding Sal like a wagon train protecting settlers from the Indians. The last teller, Josephine Tuttino, had been freed by John moments earlier, and she remained inside the bank. Then the robbers and hostages got into the long car one at a time. Agent Murphy, who was already in the driver's seat, occupied the front seat alone. John made sure that no one sat in the second row and positioned Sal, Shirley Ball and another hostage in the third row. He ordered three more tellers to the fourth row, reserving the fifth and last row for himself and the remaining two women.

At 4:10 a.m. a caravan of police and F.B.I. vehicles slowly snaked their way through the heavy crowds that remained, and wound down darkened streets to the highway that led to Kennedy Airport. There were more than 20 vehicles in the motorcade, each with flashing lights revolving in the early morning fog. F.B.I. Special Agent Joe Corliss and several associates were at the rear of the official entourage, which was followed closely by several dozen civilian cars.

By 4:45 the motorcade reached the long entryway to Kennedy. By pre-arrangement, F.B.I. agents were waiting at a chain link gate that led to a little-used taxi strip and runway. As the cars approached, agents checked the occupants in each vehicle to make certain that they were authorized to enter. The hostage-filled limousine was one of the first to reach the concrete maintenance pad, and slowly the other official cars filed through. Joe Corliss and his associates were the last to enter, and when they were inside, Corliss locked the gate and instructed all civilian vehicles and onlookers to leave.

Out on the taxi strip it was dark, and the only illumination came from police cruiser and F.B.I. car headlight beams criss-crossing the concrete and fading away in the grass.

Murphy parked the limousine on the strip a short distance from the other cars in order to keep it isolated and unable to be used as possible cover for the bandits. During the ride to the airport, Murphy had carried on a light conversation with the subjects and hostages in an effort to keep them relaxed. Several tellers later described the 35-minute drive as very comforting, saying that Murphy had reduced the tension considerably. They spoke highly of his ability to negotiate with the two robbers in a very tense situation.

As soon as the limo was parked, John wanted to know where the airplane was. It had been flown in at 2:40 a.m., but officials had instructed the pilot to remain out of sight until they gave the word to move in. Then John wanted to go into the terminal to get some hamburgers for the group. Murphy balked at this demand, saying he would have to talk to his superiors. He said he felt it was too dangerous to parade all the hostages through a public place, and if food was wanted it would be better if the police brought it to the airplane.

John agreed to let Murphy out of the limo to confer with Agent Baker. This was the break the F.B.I. had been looking for. Murphy got out of the car and walked over to where Baker, Fehl and Chief Cottel were standing. The three lawmen pondered the fact that the critical point had now been reached in their efforts to separate the gunmen from their hostages.

"The lives of seven bank employees are still in imminent jeopardy," Baker said. "If we let John and Sal board that plane, they'll have the crew of the plane to add to their hostages. We've got to stop them *here and now,* but we've got to do it at absolutely minimal risk to the bank employees in that limousine."

At this point, Special Agent Murphy spoke up. "I'm confident I can take Sal. And the success that John had in negotiating for this trip to the airport has gone to his head. He's *real* satisfied with himself—confident that their escape plan is working. I'm sure he's dropped his guard enough to allow me to make a direct move on him.

"There's a gun hidden in the front seat of the limousine. John missed it when he checked the car. I have no doubt that I can handle Sal by myself—even shoot him if it should be necessary—without endangering the hostages on either side of him. But that still leaves John. He'll have to be neutralized the very instant I start my move."

The agents immediately set up an action code related to the food John wanted. It was agreed that when Murphy got back into the car, Fred Fehl would position himself on the driver's side of the limo next to the open window closest to Sal, who was between two hostages in the third seat. Dick Baker said he'd take up a position on the right side of the car closest to John, who was still in the rear seat. Chief Cottell, whom John had never trusted during the long hours of negotiations, stayed about 15 feet away from the rear of the limo.

When everyone was in position, the Hansa Jet rolled into view. The two robbers relaxed a little, visibly exhilarated because they were so close to making a successful escape. As the jet rolled to a halt, Baker asked Murphy whether the group wanted any food brought on board for the long flight. Murphy took the opportunity to turn around in his seat and assess the situation. If conditions weren't just right, Murphy would follow the plan and so indicate by saying he didn't think so.

Without hesitating Murphy said, "Yes." With his left hand, he grabbed his .38, brought his arm up over the back of the seat and yelled, "Freeze." At the same time his right hand grappled with the barrel of Sal's shotgun, knocking it up toward the ceiling. Sal made an effort to level his weapon at Murphy, and as the two engaged in a life-and-death struggle, Murphy fired one shot that hit Sal in the chest. Fred Fehl was now half inside the limo, wrenching the shotgun from Sal's limp hand and pulling it out of the window. Sal slumped in the seat, mortally wounded.

The moment Murphy had made his move toward Sal, Dick Baker had reached into the limousine, lifted the barrel of John's 30.06 to the ceiling and pointed his service revolver at John's head. At the same time, Chief Cottell ran up to the limo so that he could assist Agent Baker in subduing John and removing the automatic from John's belt. In less than a minute, it was all over. The time was 5:28 a.m.

An ambulance that had been standing by rushed Sal to the hospital, but he was pronounced dead on arrival. This eighteen-year-old, who had vowed he would never go back to prison, had his wish come true. John Wojtowicz, the bank robber who "only wanted a better shake in life" was glad it was over. He admitted to Agent Baker that he had been prepared to give it all up earlier in the evening back at the bank, but that Sal hadn't let him. Robert Westenberg the third member of the gang who had fled on foot after the robbery began, gave himself up to police custody at 3:15 p.m. Thursday, August 24, 48 hours after the holdup began.

The bank employees received a great deal of admiration. Each of them had held up well. They had stayed together as a unit during the ordeal and afterwards praised one another, especially Robert Barrett for shepherding the group during their 14½-hour nightmare.

It was finally over. The sun rose over the Kennedy marshes, and Joe Corliss and his Bureau friends, tired and unshaven, chatted as they headed back to Manhattan to start preparing their reports. "Looks like another scorcher," Joe said to the others, keeping his weary eyes on the road. His friends didn't answer.

10
BANK BOMBERS

"Never in bank robbery history has there been anything to equal the escapades of John and James Pardue."

Thurl Stalnaker
Former Special Agent F.B.I.

It was hazy and muggy that August morning in 1959, and the reflection of the sun in the waters of Long Island Sound looked like a huge bouncing orange ball. Few people were on the city beach adjacent to Sherwood Island State Park in Westport, Connecticut— it was too early except for a few fishermen, or an occasional jogger who plodded along the hard sand while trying to dodge the eddies of the incoming tide.

It would be hot that day, maybe it would even reach the 90's. But for two young boys it was a perfect day. John and James Pardue were spending the last few days of summer vacation as they always did—together. John was 16 and his brother was 12.

The boys spent many hours at the beach doing things kids do at that age, playing, rough-housing and letting the sun bronze their well-formed bodies. John's blond curly hair was bleached to a pale yellow, and his younger brother's wavy locks almost matched the pebbly sand. Both boys were perfect physical specimens.

Shuffling along the beach in well-worn sneakers and cut-off jeans, John led his brother over to a rocky breakwater at the far end of the city-owned park.

"Right here is good," he said, sitting down on a large weathered rock that was being licked by the rising water. James found a place next to his brother and sat quietly, pretending he was unconcerned about the .22 rifle John had brought from home.

"I'll go first," John announced, loading the single-action gun from a bulging pocketful of bullets. Taking aim at a bright red danger buoy 100 yards away in the water, John squeezed the trigger. Pop. The small discharge could barely be heard 10 feet away.

"Lemme try it now," James cried excitedly, tugging at the barrel. Just then a seagull glided in for a landing on the bobbing marker.

"Hold it, Jimmy!" John cried. "I'm gonna try and get that old Mother Goose."

Loading quickly, John again took careful aim and squeezed off another round. The seagull flapped its wings a few times trying to get airborne, but the small missile critically punctured the midsection of the bird, and it fell bleeding in the water.

For the next hour, the two brothers practiced their marksmanship on other gulls, and only when the beach began to fill with bathers did they leave, driving home in John's 1950 Ford.

At mid-afternoon, a Westport police cruiser pulled up in front of the Pardue's middle class home, situated on a quiet street just off the Connecticut Turnpike. An officer got out, walked up to the house and knocked on the front door. Mrs. Dorothy Pardue answered.

"Mrs. Pardue?" the officer asked in a polite but official manner.

The woman nodded.

"We have a registered complaint that your sons, John and James, have been shooting at seagulls down at the beach. There's an ordinance forbidding such acts against birds and animals within the city limits, and I'd like to talk to the boys."

Mrs. Pardue was shaken by the policeman's accusations—charges that would soon appear trivial compared to the unbelievable reign of terror her sons were to become involved in for the next 15 years.

John Russell Pardue Sr. had been an intelligent, hard worker from his earliest days. He was an electrical engineer by training. On February 26, 1941, John married Dorothy Eileen Welch in DeSoto, Missouri, and the couple moved to St. Louis, where John was employed by the McDonnell Douglas Corporation. Soon after they were settled, the couple's first son, John Russell Jr. was born, on November 11, 1942. Four years later, the Pardue's second son, James Peter, was born on April 19, 1946.

The elder Pardue continued his successful engineering career, and in 1957 he moved his family to Westport, where he became an employee of the Shell Oil Company, working on a project to develop that organization's revolving overhead signs used in gas stations.

Before the move, however, he had purchased 120 acres of wooded ground near Union, Missouri, a place he thought would be ideal for his retirement years. On many occasions John Sr. took the boys out to his new property, which was located about 50 miles southwest of St. Louis. Here he built a small cabin for the family. It was a fine place for young John and James to play and to grow, and townspeople often noticed them together on weekends.

The Pardue family bought a home in the Green Farms section of Westport, an affluent bedroom community within easy commuting distance of John Sr.'s New York office.

But from the time they moved east, and in the few years that followed, the Pardues experienced a number of domestic problems which ended in the couple's separation. Guns had always been part of the home, and encounters with the law became commonplace. The seagull incident was not atypical of these encounters. On one occasion police were called to the Pardue home after John had fired several shots at his father, and the investigating officer later described the house in his report as "looking like a shooting gallery."

In another incident, John Sr. took a shot at his wife during a domestic quarrel. Family tensions contined to mount, and although neighbors described the Pardues as friendly and quiet, they also noted that they were a family who kept to themselves.

John Jr. and James had every benefit while growing up in their upper-middle-class environment. Both attended Staples High School in Westport, one of Fairfield County's finest public schools with teachers and staff among the best in the country. The beautiful school grounds resembled a small eastern college campus. John graduated in 1960. His I.Q. was far above average, and his pleasing smile, blond hair, good looks and immaculate dress caught the eye of many coeds. Despite these obvious advantages, he was an enigma. His high school yearbook, "The Stapleite," stated in the class will that he was leaving his *red* hair to a junior student. Was this a mistake? Blond hair, red hair—there was an air of mystery about John Pardue. He was unpredictable, like a chameleon, always changing moods, ideas, and perhaps even his appearance.

It was a certainty that John could go on to college if he wanted to. The family was able to afford it, but for some reason he wished to join the marines. After graduation he enlisted, and spent three years before being honorably discharged in 1963.

James Pardue was different from his older brother. While he inherited the same handsome profile, he was more outgoing, willing to help a friend and "was always there in a pinch." That's what the 1964 Staples High School yearbook recorded about this casually dressed, easy-going graduate. Like his older brother, James also entered military service, spending three years with the Army Corps of Engineers and received an honorable discharge in 1967.

After his release from the army, James married a girl from Maryland whom he had known while stationed at Fort Belvoir, Virginia. Not much is known about James during this period except that he and his bride lived in the Chesapeake Bay area in the small town of Lusby, Maryland. It is known, however, that James stole a car while in Maryland, drove it back to Westport and, to disguise it, he painted it a different color. It was one of the few times that either brother was actually arrested on any charge.

On later occasions, John and James together committed some petty acts of breaking and entering, and on at least one job, John forged a $3,000 note. Once, in a fit of anger and desperate for cash, John blasted open a telephone coin box for the money inside.

During these years it is believed that the boys' father, fed up with their brushes with the law, told local police "to do whatever they had to do," that he was through making excuses and trying to cover up their activities. The brothers' dislike for their father grew stronger, as did his feeling for the boys. Their mutual dislike eventually turned to hate.

When John returned from the marines, he was hired as a repairman-installer for Southern New England Telephone Company. His obvious penchant for mechanics and electronics enabled him to learn quickly, and in the five years he worked for the telephone company, according to his fellow employees and supervisors he was unusually neat, courteous, quiet. He was an excellent representative of the company. One co-worker said John hated to get dirty; he would start work in the morning crisp and creased and would go home in the evening still spotless. But his greatest asset was his glib, articulate tongue.

In February 1966 John quit his job, telling the boss he wanted to go back to Missouri to get a job with the telephone company there. But he was not gone long. In May of the same year, he returned to ask for his old job back. He was immediately rehired and transferred to the Stamford office only a few miles away. There he met a frail immigrant girl, Brenda McKeown, who had come to this country from her home near Belfast, Ireland, to escape the poverty she had known as a child.

The couple was soon married and shortly afterward Brenda bore John a son. But the marriage did not last. By December 1966 John had had it. He moved out of the apartment and took all of their belongings, leaving his wife and son destitute. Early the following year, John filed for divorce, and almost immediately Brenda counter-sued, adding adultery to the charge of intolerable cruelty, a contest that was to stretch into 1969.

John continued his work at the phone company throughout that year and into 1968, when he was promoted to PBX repairman, one of the company's highest technical jobs.

Brother James was now out of the army and living down in Lusby, Maryland with his bride. During these months the boys often got together, sometimes brushing with the law on petty counts but probably to plan bigger things. It is here that the real story of John and James Pardue begins.

Nine years to the day after John and James were reprimanded about the seagull affair, the two brothers embarked on one of the most macabre robbery sprees in modern criminal history. The events that followed led to five murders, six bank robberies, two bombings, a rape, multiple prison escape attempts and finally the mortal wounding of John Pardue.

The date was August 17, 1968, the same hazy, muggy type of day the boys had spent at the Westport beach years before.

Right over the state line from Ridgefield, Connecticut, nestles the tiny, quiet village of Lewisboro, New York, barely an intersection in the Berkshire mountain foothills, Mostly it serves as a gas stop for commuters travelling to and from the Katonah, New York, Penn Central station six miles down State Route 35. Just off the road and practically hidden by a rural shopping center stands an isolated bank building. A small sign in front reads "Vista Branch, Northern Westchester National Bank." August 17 was a Saturday, and the Liliputian branch was open for business.

About 9:00 a.m. the phone rang at Somers Barracks of the New York State Police. The voice at the other end sounded crisp and concise to the communications officer, as the yet-unidentified man reported an automobile accident on a side road south of Lewisboro in Pound Ridge, New York.

"Anyone hurt?" asked the officer, as he began jotting down the standard information in his log.

"No sir, I don't believe so. There's only the driver, and when I stopped and spoke to him he said he was okay. It must have happened shortly before I got there. The car's pretty well banged up, and I'm sure this guy'll need some assistance. Can you send someone over right away?"

"May I have your name, sir?"

John Pardue hesitated. He hadn't counted on that question. "Er...I really don't want to get involved, officer; I'd just like to help this guy out, that's all. I'm on my way fishing and I don't want to be delayed. It'll take your man ten minutes to get here and then another half hour of questions before I'd be able to get on my way." John was getting nervous. There was a lot at stake here, and for the first time on the verge of a big score, he was unsure.

The officer interrupted.

"I can't dispatch a car unless I have your name, sir. We get so many crank calls and go on so many wild goose chases, we've got to make sure there's a problem. Now, can I have your name?"

John took the moment the officer was talking to pull himself together.

"Okay," he answered, "but be sure to tell the policeman I'm in a hurry and I don't want to wait around."

"Your name?" came the question again.

"Richard Fishman."

There was a pause as the officer considered the name of the fisherman.

"And your address, Mr. Fishman?" he pressed, now alert to a possible hoax.

"4368 Applecreek Road, Brookfield, Connecticut."

"Thank you, Mr. Fishman," the trooper acknowledged. "If you'll stay with the accident victim for a few minutes, we'll send an officer right away."

John cradled the pay telephone receiver and breathed a nervous sigh of relief. He was sure the cop thought it was a phony call, but maybe everything would work out. The name and address he had given were, of course, false, but not entirely. Fishman was the name of an acquaintance, and the address was part of a telephone number and address of his new girlfriend's mother. He almost dismissed it, but he had a feeling it might get him in trouble later. As it turned out, it did.

Trooper William Hilliard was immediately dispatched to the scene to investigate. When he slowed his cruiser at the place Mr. Fishman had described, a black man emerged by the side of the road and flagged down the car. As the trooper stepped out, John Pardue, his identity concealed by a ski mask, emerged from the bushes, poked a sub-machine gun at the trooper and ordered him into the cruiser's trunk. Pardue and the young Negro, whom the brothers knew as Lee Polk—but whose true name they never learned—got into the cruiser and drove off in the direction of Lewisboro. James, who had been hiding in the fictitious-accident car, pulled out of the brush where he had parked and followed the state police car at a discreet distance.

John and Lee Polk gave their captive trooper a short ride, which included several turns in an attempt to throw him off the direction of their final destination. The car stopped once, Trooper Hilliard later recalled, probably to let Polk out and permit James to enter. Polk stayed with the original getaway car, while the brothers used the cruiser to pull their first major bank robbery.

Moments later, the hijacked state police car pulled up to the Vista Branch office and parked. Both John and James drew ski masks on, picked up their weapons and nonchalantly sauntered into the small bank office. Only two tellers and the manager were there.

"This is a stick-up," one of the boys announced. And with that single warning, John triggered his sub-machine gun from the hip and sprayed the ceiling with a short burst. There was no question about who was in command. Within seconds, the boys filled a bag with tellers' cash and retreated through the front door, dropping a packet as they left which contained violet-colored dye marker. In an instant the bank was billowing a bright reddish-blue. The whole incident took less than three minutes, and before the bank employees could get their bearings, the police cruiser was on its way back to pick up their accomplice.

As the boys passed their parked getaway car, they gave Polk the all-clear signal. Immediately Polk started up and followed them back into Connecticut, where they abandoned the cruiser near an out-of-the-way housing development in New Caanan that John knew from his work as a telephone installer.

Shortly after that the bandits abandoned the cruiser, and when Trooper Hilliard felt it was safe, he activated a trunk release placed there for such emergencies and quickly freed himself.

By noon the trio had separated, each with his share of the loot. John returned to work on Monday as usual, and James presumably drove back to Lusby and his wife.

The total take on that hot August morning was $22,268.

With enough cash to live comfortably for a while, John decided to quit his job. He didn't want to draw suspicion so soon after the Vista job however, so he waited a month, and on September 16 gave his notice, saying he was going back to Missouri again. But he didn't leave the state; instead he rented a small cabin in Redding, Connecticut, about 10 miles from Lewisboro. There he holed up to plan for his and James' next job.

John loved to read. He especially liked stories about cops and robbers, and when he was finally apprehended in March 1970, police and F.B.I. agents found a library of paperbacks and other books in his house. He wanted, more than anything, to develop a reputation that exceeded in notoriety the villains of the 1930's like Alvin Karpis, John Dillinger and Clyde Barrow. During the next 18 months, he and his brother vied for leadership headlines with Jesse and Frank James, who had preceded the Pardues by exactly 100 years.

For hit number two, the Pardues selected another rural branch bank. Again, James travelled back and forth from Maryland to help his older brother mastermind the job at Fairfield County Trust Company's Georgetown branch. It, too, was a bank in an obscure shopping center, within the town of Redding. But this time they changed their modus operandi and again enlisted the aid not only of Lee Polk but also his friend, known as Dick Gregory (not to be confused with the comedian), a mechanic and part-time entertainer in nearby Stamford. These two men would actually do the job, thus, they hoped, throwing police off guard and not linking them with the men who had pulled the recent Vista job. The boys even changed weapons for the heist. Polk and Gregory were given a shotgun and a revolver instead of a machine gun and an automatic.

About 8:30 a.m. Tuesday, October 22, 1968, the Pardues headed out to commandeer their second vehicle, but what immediately followed transformed the brothers from notorious bank robbers to brutal murder suspects. While it is still not entirely clear whether it was Polk and Gregory or John and James Pardue, one of the pairs pulled their car off to the side of a lonely road and waited.

Young William Artman, 19, was on his way to work from his Bridgeport home, jubilant over the recent birth of his son. As in the Lewisboro job, someone flagged down the driver on the pretext that he was in trouble. When Artman pulled over, one of them drew out a gun and announced they were hijacking his car. Bill Artman resisted. His was a new car and he wasn't about to let anyone steal it. The argument lasted only seconds before he was shot dead and his body stuffed into the trunk.

Whoever did the shooting then drove to a designated waiting area, where the four men plotted the final step of their holdup. It was agreed that Polk and Gregory would do the job.

Artman's new car, with his body stuffed in the trunk, pulled up to the Georgetown branch shortly before 9:30 a.m. Instead of ski masks, the men wore surgical masks that exposed much of their brown skin—another trick thought up by the Pardues. Six employees were there that morning, but there was no shooting at the ceiling as in the August robbery. That, too, led police at first to suspect a different gang.

Again, the robbery took only a few short minutes, and when the bandits left, they were $39,752 richer. Later that same day, Bill Artman's body was discovered, still in the trunk of his own car; cigars with "It's a boy" printed on the wrappers were in his pocket. In a little over two months, the gang had taken more than $62,000, cleanly, successfully, and with hardly a clue left behind. The Pardues were well on their way to becoming infamous robbers, and their crimes now included murder.

During the next several weeks a rift developed between the Pardue boys and their black friends, they bitterly complaining that they didn't like an even split of the money. After all, weren't they the ones who had actually pulled off the job? John and James were adamant on the equal-split plan, but this didn't seem to satisfy Polk and Gregory. One day at the cabin, about a month or so after the Georgetown robbery, the Pardues decided to settle the argument then and there. They shot and killed their accomplices and temporarily buried them near the shack.

About the same time, John had a yearning to see his son, John Michael, and went to visit Brenda, who had taken various jobs as a waitress and domestic in the Norwalk and Wilton, Connecticut area. He played up to her as only he could do, saying he wanted a reconciliation. With plenty of money, and as a show of good faith, he offered his wife a vacation trip back to Ireland to visit her parents and to show off the boy. He bought two tickets and sent them off just before Christmas, 1968, telling Brenda he would follow shortly.

But John had something else on his mind before planning another robbery or going to Ireland; he wondered if Polk and Gregory were really safe from discovery in their shallow grave. He contacted his brother in Maryland and told him to drive up and meet him at the cabin. When James arrived, the brothers thought it best to dispose of their erstwhile friends in a more permanent fashion, so they hitched up an old trailer they had, threw the bodies in and covered them with brush and some small Christmas trees.

From Redding, Connecticut, they drove up-country to a wooded area on the Housatonic River near Kent, a place where John had done some hunting. There, in a secluded stand of trees, heavy with undergrowth, they poured oil over the bodies and lit a match to the pyre. It wasn't until the following April that hikers discovered the grave, and when police were called to investigate, it appeared that the badly decomposed and burned bodies would never be identified. Sometime during the late fall of 1968, John Pardue rented a modest house at 13 Crane Street in Danbury, Connecticut, a few miles north of Redding and northeast of Lewisboro. Those three towns formed an almost perfect triangle of death and destruction that culminated on February 13, 1970, with the last robbery the boys ever pulled together. In the meantime John lived in Danbury with his girlfriend Nancy, a woman who later bore him a child before she herself became involved in an escape plot that resulted in a fatal shootout and her imprisonment.

From November through the spring of 1969, John remained at home in seclusion, except for two airplane trips to Ireland. He rarely ventured out except to walk his newly acquired attack dog, a German shepherd he had purchased "to protect vital business property" in the house. Neighbors, and the real estate man who had rented the house to him, were never permitted inside because of "manufacturing equipment and secrets" he wanted to "keep under wraps." In later interviews, they told the press that John was a loner who had always maintained a courteous but standoffish manner, talking with few people except to say hello or to answer a question.

At about this time, since the boys no longer lived at home, the senior Pardues moved out of their Westport residence and bought a smaller house in nearby Southport, Connecticut. It is believed that their relationship was deteriorating further and that Mr. Pardue was preparing to leave his wife altogether.

Right after the Christmas holidays, John, still not working, fulfilled his pledge to Brenda and bought a ticket to Ireland. Landing in Shannon, he rented a car, drove up to Belfast and was reunited with his son, John Michael. Brenda's family was poor, and it was apparent that they could ill afford to support a second family. But John appeared happy and did everything possible to treat his in-laws and Brenda with kindness, even offering them a small sum of money.

After only a week in Ireland, John told his wife he had to return to Connecticut on business. Although this seemed strange, because Brenda knew John had been out of work and had fallen behind in child-support payments, she didn't question the mysterious "business" motive.

Then on March 12, 1969, John unexpectedly returned to Belfast. From his first trip earlier in the year, he had learned everything he needed to know about child kidnapping, passports, the lay of the land, escape routes and airline schedules. It had taken the U.S. State Department about six weeks to get a new passport for him with his son's picture included. When that document arrived, the rest was easily achieved.

He planned a round trip flight to Belfast, arriving there, as most transcontinental flights do, in early morning. When he knocked on the door, Brenda and her parents were surprised to see him. John seemed excited about seeing his son again, saying he didn't even want to sleep before taking young John out for the day, perhaps even to see a parade.

Brenda, somewhat bewildered, said that would be nice, and prepared the boy for a day's outing. But while she dressed her son, John carefully stole Brenda's return airplane ticket and the small amount of money he could find in the small house. As father and son departed, John told Brenda he would be gone all day and not to delay supper; that, he figured, would give the pair enough time to board a return flight during the afternoon.

By late evening on March 13, John Pardue and his son were again on U.S. soil, 24 hours after the kidnap plan had started.

Brenda waited patiently all afternoon and evening for her husband and son to return, and when they hadn't shown up by morning, she became frantic. She phoned police and the U.S. Embassy, but no one seemed able to help.

It took more than a month for her poor family to borrow enough money to send Brenda back to the United States—a country to which she had journeyed five years earlier to escape her poverty.

When Brenda returned to Norwalk, Connecticut, she went directly to the police and told them the bizarre story of her son's abduction. But authorities were unable to assist, on the grounds that the incident hadn't taken place within this country and that, in fact, she was still legally married. There was no kidnap law preventing one legal parent taking the offspring of another.

Brenda did file one complaint, however, that was, at least in part, responsible for locating the whereabouts and making the identification that led to the apprehension of John Pardue and his brother. The charge was "stealing of common property"—the furniture John had taken when he moved out of the couple's apartment in 1966.

Still, no one knew the whereabouts of John Pardue, although actually he was only a stone's throw from Norwalk. He had taken his son back to 13 Crane Street in Danbury where Nancy Brown, soon to become his second wife, waited to greet them and care for the boy.

About this time the situation at the elder Pardues had become intolerable, and John Sr. made plans to leave his wife, Dorothy. The year before, 1968, the elder Pardue had contracted to have a house built on his 120 acres back in Missouri. During the latter part of that year, the Pardues had occasionally traveled back to Union to check on the project's progress. They expected that the stylish home would be finished soon, although they did not yet know that they would never share it.

Mr. Pardue seldom saw his sons, but they were on his mind. At one point, surmising the boys were involved in bank robbery, he threatened to contact the F.B.I. and tell them of his suspicions. Unfortunately, he never followed through with this threat, and that mistake might have been responsible for his own murder less than a year later.

On May 5, 1969, John and Nancy, with young John Michael, travelled to Alexandria, Virginia, to get married. Nancy was 24 and John 27. Strangely enough, if Brenda had known of the ceremony that day, she could have added bigamy to the pending charges against her husband, for their divorce did not become final until early fall.

The couple's new partnership was the opposite of John's first marital experience. Nancy truly loved her husband, and as the months passed, her devotion deepened to a fanatical ardor that unwittingly caused her to lose her husband to a deputy marshal's bullet.

One day after their Virginia marriage, John left his bride and son in nearby Lusby, Maryland, with James' wife, and the two brothers headed west to set up their next caper, a bank in Pacific, Missouri.

John and James drove straight through from Lusby to Union, Missouri, arriving there on May 7. They used their father's proposed retirement house, not yet finished, as a hideout. It was a natural. No one would suspect the boys should they be seen, and furthermore it was located in a remote wooded area no more than five miles from Union and 15 miles from Pacific, where their next robbery would take place.

Once again the ill-fated bank was well chosen. It was in a small town, and there were excellent roads leading away from the scene. As before, in the Lewisboro and Georgetown robberies, the boys needed a getaway car. But this time there was no violence, no kidnaps or commandeered police cruisers. Instead, they selected a car parked in a local lot and drove off to Pacific to stage robbery number three.

The mark was the Citizens Bank, situated in the heart of town. On May 9, 1969, without warning, two men burst into the lobby and immediately sprayed the ceiling with their machine gun. Some tellers and patrons hit the floor without being told. Others, too frightened to move, froze and didn't budge until long after the boys had cleaned out the cash drawers and the vault and taken an estimated $83,000. This robbery, like the two before, lasted less than three minutes, and before anyone could collect his thoughts the two masked bandits had made their getaway, disposing of the stolen car along the road where their own car was hidden.

In less than an hour, the boys were safely back at their Union retreat, counting the day's take and congratulating each other on another successful job. After a short rest, the brothers became anxious to return east. But before they did so, John began laying plans for still another Missouri bank robbery. This time it was to be practically in their own back yard, right in town. The bank was the United Bank of Union.

During the long ride back to James' home in Lusby, John became pensive, the wheels of his mind spinning in a thousand directions as he tried to focus on a new, untested method of attack that would be even more vicious and spectacular than their previous jobs. What he had in mind for the United Bank included a bomb, in addition to their now standard trademark of machine gun warfare, stolen getaway cars and masks.

They had all of the ingredients to pull it off. Brother James had graduated from the Army Engineers in 1967 and was a demolition expert. John had purchased some wilderness land in northwestern Idaho where some day he hoped to hunt, and it would provide natural cover and serve as an excellent experimental station for building bombs and practicing demolition techniques.

Serious planning for the Union bank job began in late August, 1969. John packed some things and threw them in the back of his red International Scout, and he and his attack dog, Duke, headed west for the long drive to Coeur d'Alene, Idaho. They arrived there about September 1, setting up camp at his mountainside retreat near Cataldo and Hayden Lake. The next day John drove into town where he stopped at Amex, Inc., an explosives distributor for the Pacific Northwest, and inquired about several types of ordnance that he needed for clearing land. He told Albert Langston, the owner and manager, that before he could start building on the property, there were numerous trees, stumps and rocks that had to be removed, and blasting was the only way he knew of doing the job. According to Langston, Pardue spent close to an hour talking about various devices and explosive items, and then bought a galvanometer, used for checking electrical circuits, 250 feet of lead wire to make remote connections, and 100 pounds of nitrate explosives. To activate the explosives he also purchased two types of blasting caps—those with instant detonation and others with short delays. During their conversation he also told the Amex manager that his brother, who had just been discharged from the Army Engineers, would assist him in the operation, and he was glad because he still wasn't too sure about handling all those high explosives.

John Pardue Jr. paid for that first order by check, using his real name.

Two days later, he came back to pick up a blasting machine, a small hand-held device containing the electric power source that was connected at one end of the lead wire. Mr. Langston later recalled being afraid of the vicious dog in the cab, and asked John to move him out of the way before loading the Scout.

The September 4th purchase was paid for in cash.

It is known that John remained in Idaho for at least another week, because on September 9, he returned once more and ordered 25 more blasting caps, another 100 feet of wire, some dynamite and 25 safety fuses.

It isn't clear whether John actually did any testing back at his property or even whether his brother had come along on the trip to Idaho. But it really didn't matter. The boys had enough explosives and equipment to mount a small war and could blow up almost anything they wanted to—including a bank or a police station.

The stage was now set for robbery number four. At this point events began to deteriorate for the brothers. First, John Pardue Sr. left his wife to fend for herself in Southport, Connecticut, and he moved into the almost completed retirement home in Union, Missouri, with his mother, 80-year-old Mrs. Daisy Pardue. Pardue had quit his job with Shell and was being considered for a consulting job with a Dallas-based engineering firm. In early November, he was to go to the home office in Texas to receive instructions for his new midwest assignment.

Unfortunately he never got the opportunity to have that interview, because on November 11, 1969, John and James arrived at the house, planning to use it once more as their command post and hideout for the United Bank job.

Not knowing their father had left his wife, they were as surprised to see him at the doorstep as he was to see his sons. John Sr. was furious, and the boys were equally unnerved, because now their cover had been exposed. It is believed that during an argument which followed the heated greeting, the elder Pardue pieced together the Connecticut robberies and the recent Pacific, Missouri, job and threatened again to turn his sons in to the police.

According to a later confession, John Pardue Jr. told F.B.I. authorities that James solved the problem of his father and grandmother by shooting them both on the spot while they stood defenseless, arguing in the kitchen. These were the fourth and fifth murders in which the brothers were involved in little more than a year.

Vividly remembering the Polk and Gregory murders, John didn't feel safe leaving his father and grandmother near the sprawling homestead, so the boys wrapped the riddled bodies in heavy black plastic sheets that the builders had used to cover lumber and other building materials stored near the house. Again, as in the Redding murders, they stuffed the two corpses into a small utility van their father had and rolled it into the garage out of sight. There the two bodies remained undetected until after the robbery which was scheduled for November 13th.

During the remainder of the day, and again on November 12th, the phone rang in the Pardue home, but no one answered. The brothers couldn't afford to let anyone know they were in town and had to remain silent. But the phone kept ringing. The elder Pardue's Dallas company was trying to reach him concerning the job assignment, and two of Mr. Pardue's sisters who lived in nearby St. Louis wanted to tell their brother that a relative had passed away.

The sun rose cold over the Pardue House on the 13th. It was bright and crisp that morning, and the leaves had all but disappeared from the trees. The boys made last minute preparations for their most spectacular appearance yet, James putting the final touches on a bomb he had built and John loading his machine gun and automatic.

Shortly after 1:00 p.m. they left their dead father's house and drove down the winding dirt road to the highway, and then cruised through the busy little town looking for a getaway car to steal. It took only minutes to find one they wanted—a nondescript 1965 Ford. From there the boys, James in the stolen car and John driving his own, headed west on U.S. Route 50 for about three miles. Then they made a U-turn and parked on the eastbound shoulder. In less than an hour, they came back, switched cars and leisurely drove to the house a short distance away.

By 2:00 p.m. they were back in town, and James dropped his brother off in front of the Franklin County Courthouse. It was an older building, formidable looking, with marble columns and heavy brickwork. John entered and immediately climbed a flight of stairs to the second floor, where he casually walked down the hall to the sheriff's department. There he sprawled out on a long wooden bench and nonchalantly placed a brown leather briefcase down next to him. Almost smiling, and in defiance of being caught, John remained in the anteroom for a few minutes in full view of a small group of citizens, and then, without a word, got up and strolled away, leaving the briefcase on the floor. The time was 2:15 p.m.

Exactly two minutes later, a thundering explosion ripped through the entire second floor, bringing screams of pain and shock from the visitors' room and sheriff's office. The explosion was so intense it blew doors clear off their hinges, crumbled interior walls, and shattered 97 windows, many of them cascading to the street below, frames and all. The concussion was terrific, dazing for minutes many of the people closest to the blast, including Sheriff Bill Miller's wife, who was working as a county employee on the same floor. When part of the ceiling collapsed, several people in the hall were badly hurt.

Sheriff Miller was not in the building at the time of the explosion, but even if he had been, he couldn't have called for help, because the communications system had been destroyed. Miraculously no one was killed by the bomb.

By the time those in the courthouse could collect themselves and care for their wounds, John Pardue had reached the United Bank one block down the street, and he and James, masks in place, entered the lobby. At that point, people in the bank were rushing out to find out what had happened down the street, and few even noticed the bandits.

Amid the confusion, John fired a short burst from his machine gun, and the stunned customers and tellers became immobile, some thinking an invasion had started. They were told to lie on the floor, and the patrons—about 20—did so without additional prodding. As John watched the door, James vaulted over the teller counter and began ransacking one cash drawer after another. Being experienced at his profession, he went down the line, quickly extracting bundled and loose cash. Then he backed out of the lobby, holding customers and bank officials at bay.

A moment later, their stolen car was speeding west down the highway to the place where their own car was parked. There they switched cars and calmly drove back to their hideout unnoticed.

Back in town, the sheriff's deputies used their car radios to call for a road-block up and down Route 50 at both five and ten miles from town.

Troopers waited impatiently for the getaway car, but none came. How could they have possibly escaped the dragnet, which soon included helicopter surveillance?

Sheriff Bill Miller, who immediately drove to the scene when he heard the radio report, took command, but he soon felt the elusive robbers had somehow slipped through his fingers. By late afternoon, he called in his patrol and instructed a house-by-house search of the rural area.

When a patrol car pulled up at the Pardue home, investigating officers noticed nothing unusual. There was mail in the mailbox but that was not unusual, since police knew the Pardues often travelled back and forth from Missouri to Connecticut while the house was being built.

The boys watched from inside the house, their arsenal of weapons and bombs ready for any contingency. When the police left, and they felt it was safe, the brothers loaded their own car with $18,300 from the bank, hitched up the small trailer containing the two plastic-wrapped bodies and drove away, heading east to Lusby, Maryland.

Two days later the first break in the case came, although the clues were not of any value for almost four more months. First, Sheriff Miller went out to the house to serve Pardue with the divorce papers that his office had received from the Connecticut courts. The sheriff too noticed the growing pile of mail, but didn't think anything of it at the time.

Then Mr. Pardue's sisters called police to report they had not been able to reach their brother anywhere, and they wanted to tell him of a death in the family. Also, the president of Texlite, the Dallas company, phoned Sheriff Miller indicating concern for an employee who could not be reached.

Aware of these problems, Sheriff Miller and several deputies drove back to the house, and this time they went inside. Still on the stove was a coffee pot, and there was food spilled on the floor, which was unlike the usual meticulous housekeeping of Daisy Pardue. There were also two dining room chairs out of place, positioned next to a kitchen window, an excellent vantage point overlooking the long driveway that wound through the woods from the road.

Sheriff Miller then ordered a search of the entire 120 acres, but it revealed nothing. Now concerned by the disappearance of Pardue Sr. and his mother, Miller issued a missing-persons bulletin to police in surrounding areas, as well as to Southport, Connecticut, authorities and to the F.B.I.

It was almost 1000 miles from Union to Lusby and the boys, tired from the long trip, at last pulled up to a dirt road that led onto property James had bought previously. Here the brothers dug a huge hole with a back-hoe, eased in the trailer containing their father and grandmother and then back-filled the grave. To conceal the excavation permanently, they then poured a 6-inch slab of concrete on top and later built a tool shed on the base. The bodies remained there until John's deathbed confession in April, 1971.

Thurl Stalnaker sat in the New Haven F.B.I. office, shuffling through a mound of official documents and case bulletins received that day from F.B.I. headquarters in Washington. The Union, Missouri bank job immediately caught his eye, and then he remembered the wire service story on the incident he had just finished reading. He picked it up again and read it intently. Somehow this case rang a bell; he connected it with others he had worked on as a veteran criminal investigator and coordinator of bank robbery cases in the F.B.I.'s Connecticut field division. For over an hour he compared notes on the Union job with those on the Vista, New York robbery the year before. Ski masks, machine gun fire, two men—these facts certainly were the same. But he was puzzled. The two small town banks were far from each other, and a state police car had been commandeered. It didn't fit. And what about the Georgetown robbery where two blacks were involved? Certainly they couldn't be part of the same gang—or could they? Thurl tried to file away his ideas, but somehow they persisted; there had to be a rationale for these similar robberies.

Exactly three months to the day after the Union job, Thurl Stalnaker revived his ideas and, as F.B.I. case agent-in-charge, mounted one of the most intensive and professional bank robbery investigations in recent history—an investigation that led law enforcement officers to the apprehension of John Russell Pardue Jr. and James Peter Pardue.

For some people Friday the 13th means bad news. For others, particularly the townspeople of Danbury, Connecticut, Friday,

February 13, 1970 was to take on a special meaning—absolute disaster and destruction.

Dawn broke cold and gray over the hills that surrounded this industrial city of 50,000. The temperature would reach a chilly 31 degrees and then fade to the upper 20's by nightfall. It was a day people would want to forget, not only because of the mid-winter cold, but because of what John and James Pardue were about to do to their average American town.

By 10:30 a.m. Main Street was bustling with traffic, and commerce was going into high gear. Off-duty cops filtered in and out of police headquarters to pick up their paychecks, while two prisoners, picked up on vagrancy and drunk charges the night before, were nursing hangovers, waiting to be arraigned later in the day at circuit court down the street. At 10:41 a.m. a foot patrolman was writing a ticket for an illegally parked car outside the 70-year-old, three-story police station that had, several years before, been converted from a schoolhouse.

One second later a horrible explosion in headquarters ripped out windows and sent glass shards flying out onto the street, the force of the blast throwing the ticket-writing patrolman on top of the hood of the car. The heavy front doors of the building flew off their hinges and landed on the ground out near the sidewalk about 20 feet away. On the third floor, a woman who was working in the board of education office stood dazed and sobbing at an empty window that had been blown away.

Inside, on the first level, Sgt. Nelson Macedo was literally lifted out of his chair and knocked unconscious. When he came to, still stunned, he yelled to his partner, Sgt. Edward Keating.

"The furnace just blew up, let's get out of this Goddamn place."

Keating didn't respond at first. His desk was on top of him and he was bleeding badly.

In the basement, the two drunks thought they would drown. Water from a ruptured main was cascading down on them.

All three floors of the police station were a shambles. One secretary on the second floor tried to escape, and was temporarily halted when she saw the stairs had collapsed. She slid down the bannister and ran out of the building screaming.

Moments after the blast a state police cruiser passed headquarters, and the sergeant who was driving stared in disbelief at the smoke and dust hanging over the building in the wintry air. He immediately radioed Ridgefield State Police Barracks for help and then rushed inside to assist the injured.

The police station in Danbury, Connecticut, as it appeared shortly after the bomb blast detonated by the Pardues.

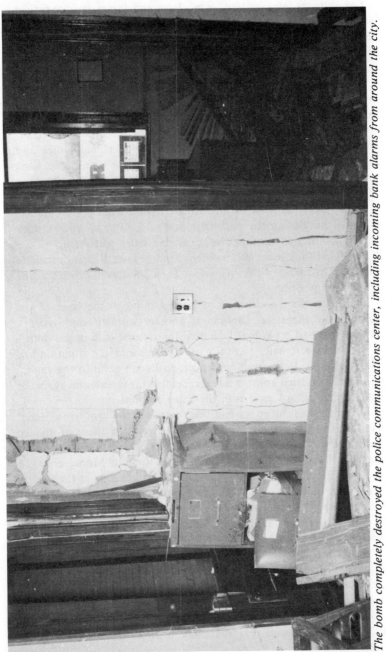

The bomb completely destroyed the police communications center, including incoming bank alarms from around the city.

Two minutes later, at 10:43 a.m., John and James Pardue rushed into the lobby of the Union Savings Bank three blocks away. Both boys were unmasked. John carried his sub-machine gun and James held a shotgun, pointing it at the 18 employees and customers as he entered.

"Everybody down on the floor," James commanded as he nervously pranced around the open lobby, jabbing his weapon forward in an effort to get attention quickly.

As the frightened patrons instantly obeyed the order, one teller, unnoticed, activated a silent holdup device to signal police and summon help. But the signal never reached the communications center. The center had been blown away by the explosion, along with police headquarters itself.

John quickly approached one teller from the front of the counter, pounded his fist on the deal plate and said, "Put all your money here," pointing to the open space in the teller wicket.

The teller took loose and banded cash from her drawer, but made sure the "bait money" was included. Then John went down the line repeating the order.

James, in the meantime, had gone around to the back of the counter and thrust his shotgun at another woman employee.

"You want to get killed? I want all the secured cash in the vault."

The woman remained as calm as anyone could in a situation like that and replied, "I'm not an officer, so I can't get into the vault."

James then tried another teller, repeating his threat, and again the quick-thinking girl gave him the same response.

When the cash drawers had been emptied, the brothers ordered everyone to a back room, demanding they stay there or chance getting hurt. As they were being herded out of the lobby, Mrs. Barbara Dratch and Assistant Manager Richard Moore emerged from the employees' lounge. Mrs. Dratch caught sight of the holdup scene and quickly turned to Moore, putting her finger to her lips.

"Shh. Don't move—freeze," she murmured.

The assistant manager obeyed immediately, understanding the whispered command.

Both retreated back to the lounge in time to hear another explosion rip open the bank lobby and blow window glass onto the street. The bomb intensity was so fierce that the lounge window also was shattered, small pieces striking Moore on the back. The concussion, and the vacuum created, threw the pair against a lunch table, and it was several moments before they could get their bearings.

The Union Savings Bank on Main Street, only three blocks from the Danbury Police Station, as it appeared the day after the Pardue robbery.

Seconds before the explosion, John and James had fled through the front door and rounded an alley next to the bank, heading for a rear parking lot and their getaway car. Richard Moore pulled himself together in time to see the brothers get into a white car, and he immediately wrote down the license number before it sped away. He thought it was an orange and black tag, similar to New York plates, although he couldn't be sure.

Inside the bank lobby, dust and smoke began to filter out the broken windows, disclosing extensive damage to the interior. Parts of the ceiling had crashed to the floor, exposing heating ducts and

The lobby of the Union Savings Bank after the second bomb exploded and the Pardue brothers escaped with $55,365.

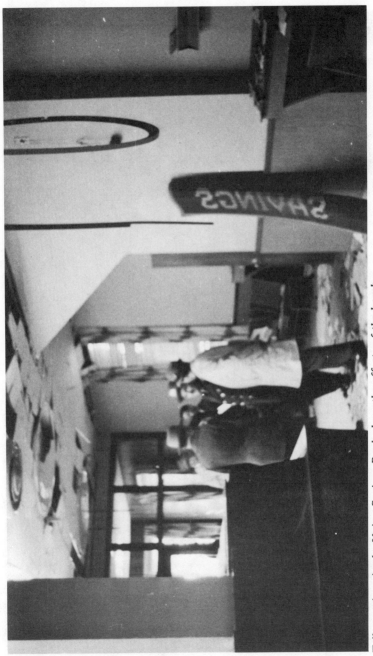

Teller stations in the Union Savings Bank show the effects of the bomb.

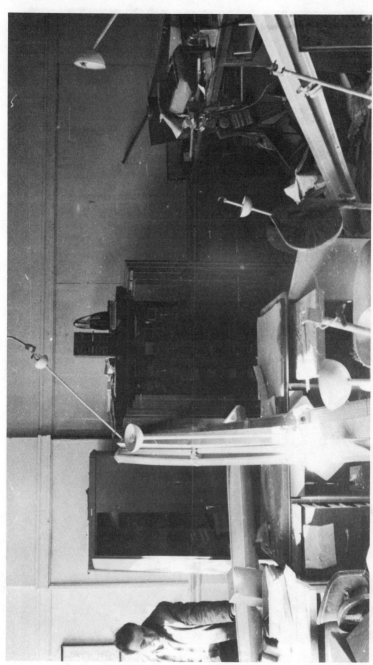

The teller's work area following the bomb blast.

lighting fixtures that had been reduced to twisted junk. Miraculously no one had been severely injured.

Offices on the second floor were only slightly damaged, but immediately after the blast someone phoning police could get no answer.

The Pardues had their escape plan worked out well in advance. Two blocks from the bank and five blocks from the ravaged police station there was a huge parking lot that bordered a discount store and covered mall. Apparently unnoticed, the men drove into the lot, abandoned their white Chrysler station wagon, and taking the bag full of loot and their weapons, transferred to a 1964 Corvair and headed north, away from the town's business center. Before leaving, however, James planted another time-delay bomb in the station wagon, and within seconds it, too, exploded, spewing fenders, hood, radiator hose and even the car's hood high into the air. It wasn't until much later that detectives found the car hood on top of the Grandway store more than 100 feet away.

The Danbury bombings had taken just 19 minutes to execute, but the damage and pain caused were enormous: nearly 50 citizens and police had been injured, property damage was conservatively placed at $250,000, and actual money stolen was audited at $55,365— $26,365 in cash and $29,000 in traveler's checks and securities.

The Pardue boys had done their work well, and it was unlikely that their acts of violence and destruction would soon be forgotten by the residents of Danbury, Connecticut. Friday the 13th ended as it started, cold and damp, the sun setting over the mountains to the west. The temperature was 28 degrees.

Thurl Stalnaker had just set down the telephone receiver, having finished a long conversation with Sheriff Bill Miller out in Union, Missouri, when Special Agent in Charge of the F.B.I.'s New Haven field office, Charles Weeks, walked over to the bank robbery section.

"Thurl, I've got a job for you. I want you to handle the Danbury case, and I want this thing solved now. Whatever you need, you've got. Just tell me how many men you want and they're yours."

Stalnaker was pleased to get the assignment, and after he had talked to Sheriff Miller, he was doubly certain that his suspicions of the past fall would bear fruit. Little did he realize at the time that he alone would hear the dying confession of John Pardue a little over a year later which told, mostly by sign language, of the brutal slayings of the five victims and the detailed execution of the brothers' five bank robberies.

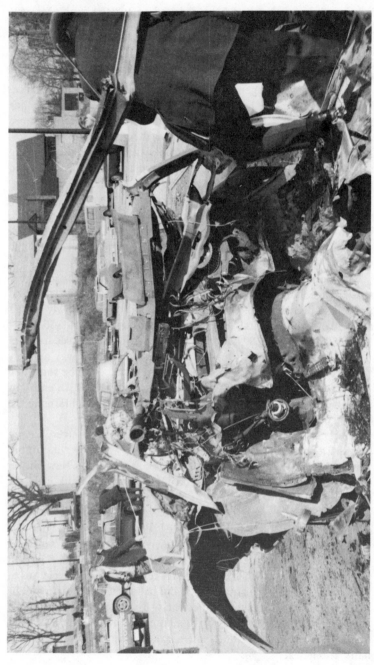

The initial getaway car used by the Pardue brothers was a white Chrysler station wagon. This is what remained.

The hood of this wreck was found on the roof of a nearby shopping center.

Immediately Stalnaker and nearly the entire Connecticut F.B.I. bank robbery team converged on Danbury.

When they arrived there was an army of law enforcement personnel on the scene, including Danbury Police Chief William Tobin, who had been at home sick with flu and had not been in his office when the first bomb had exploded. Temporary headquarters were soon set up at the town's War Memorial Building two blocks away on Main Street, where phones were installed by the Southern New England Telephone Company, John's previous employer. By noon all the injured had been given first aid or taken to Danbury Hospital, and the investigation was in full swing.

During the next three days scores of witnesses helped police and F.B.I. piece together descriptions of the two bandits, who for some reason had made this attack without their traditional ski masks: two men, both in their mid-twenties, one with blond hair, the other with brown hair and mustache, of medium height and both very good-looking. Everyone agreed on the descriptions. One woman in the bank commented on the big blue eyes of the blond "All-American boy" robber. This clue sparked the recall of Sgt. Edward Keating, who said he had noticed a blue-eyed blond young man in the police station about ten minutes prior to the bombings.

Five days after the incident a local woman called police with a tip, one of hundreds that poured in to the War Memorial command post. She related that a man living up the block at 13 Crane Street had been experimenting with some small explosives the past July 4. It didn't appear to be much, but Detective Keating went over to see her and check it out. The woman said the man's name was Pardue. It was the first time Keating had heard the name.

Thurl Stalnaker, with his fellow agents, acted as a clearing house for all information, and when he saw the Pardue name he recognized it as the same name Sheriff Miller had given him earlier as a possible missing person. The Connecticut-Missouri tie-in was more than a coincidence. Next day Thurl sent an F.B.I. agent over to the Pardue house. He was interested in finding out whether John knew where his father was and whether the elder Pardue was capable of pulling off the similar robberies. John answered the door in the presence of his wife, Nancy, and their newborn daughter. Questions put to the as-yet-unsuspected bank robber were short and quick. No, he didn't feel his father could do such a thing and no, he didn't know where he was. That was about all the polite, articulate young man had to say. The F.B.I. agent thanked him for the information and left.

But police were not completely satisfied with John's story. A bulletin was dispatched to surrounding communities, especially to the nearby towns of Norwalk, Westport and Southport, where Sheriff Miller knew the elder Pardues had lived. That decision proved to be a turning point in the case.

Norwalk police called and said they had a warrant out for John, Jr., that he was wanted on a larceny charge for stealing furniture back in 1966 and also for possible child abduction. That was on February 24, 11 days after the Danbury bombings. Two Norwalk police officers went to Danbury with the old warrant and, in a stroke of luck, they stopped to pick up a Danbury detective to do the actual serving of the papers. That officer was Sgt. Keating. Again police knocked on the door at the Crane Street address, and it was answered by the blue-eyed young man Keating had seen in the police station only minutes before the robbery.

"Are you John Pardue?" Sgt. Keating asked in an official tone.

"Yes," came the simple reply.

Then John turned and walked to the back of the house, out to the back yard where he had caged his police dog Duke. The trio of detectives followed. After the warrant had been served, John asked Keating whether that was the only charge against him. The answer was affirmative. As the officers prepared to take John away, he called up to Nancy, who was now watching from the back porch.

"It's only larceny," he shouted, and the four men left.

From his Danbury home, John was taken back to the War Memorial Headquarters, where he was booked and fingerprinted. He later posted $1000 bond and was released.

Everything was beginning to fall into place, although John didn't seem to be aware of it. Maybe he knew authorities were closing in and didn't want to fight it, or maybe he thought he could really beat it. Either way he planned to appear in Bridgeport Municipal Court on March 5 to answer contempt charges for child non-support and stealing common property. The appearance was set for 2:00 p.m., and it was here that still another drama took place.

Brenda McKeown Pardue sat anxiously on a bench up front near the judge's stand. She and her lawyer, Abraham Gordon, had arrived an hour earlier. Brenda had not seen her husband or her son for over a year, and she could barely keep back the tears in the anticipation of seeing her little boy and having him returned. She couldn't sit still during that long hour. She paced up and down the courtroom aisle, then sat down again. Would her estranged husband really bring the boy along, she asked Mr. Gordon repeatedly.

On the stroke of 2:00 p.m., John Pardue, Jr. was led into the chambers dressed in a blue shirt and suit, a red tie and black polished shoes. Holding his hand was a handsome four-year-old boy, as well dressed as his father.

Brenda couldn't hold herself back. She broke from the visitors' rail, rushed to the child and picked him up, pressing him close to her. The boy instantly recognized his mother crying, "Mommy, Mommy, where have you been?"

Also in the courtroom, sitting far back and partially hidden by two policemen, was another important woman in the case, the woman who had told authorities that she remembered the blond, blue-eyed "All-American" at the Danbury bank. Her name was Mrs. Wilma Anderson. F.B.I. agents had shown her an old black-and-white print of John Pardue. She thought he was one of the men who had robbed the Union Savings Bank in February. However, to make sure, she had agreed to attend the hearing, and when John was brought forward to the bench she turned to her escorts and nodded.

"Yes," she said, "that's the boy with the blue eyes."

The next day, federal complaints were filed and warrants issued for the arrests of the Pardue brothers. When officers picked up John on the morning of March 7 he was getting in his car. He offered no resistance, although he did have a .38 revolver in his belt. Some baby's diapers were scattered around the floor of the car, and under them police found several thousand dollars in cash. In addition, on John's person they found some $20 bills whose serial numbers matched those of the bait money from the February 13 bank heist.

One of the arresting officers recalled that John, very close to tears, said, "Don't let them shoot my dog, Duke."

It was over for John Russell Pardue, Jr.

Brother James was picked up in Lusby, Maryland, that same day and extradited to Connecticut where, during the next 13 months, a trial was scheduled and the fate of the boys was settled.

John and James Pardue were finally locked up, John at the Connecticut Correctional Center in Bridgeport, and James, flown in from Baltimore, at the New Haven Correctional Center. Bond for each of the boys was set at $250,000.

Later that month, on March 30, the Pardue brothers were led into U.S. District Court in New Haven to answer charges for the February 13 bombings and bank robbery. In the courtroom were Nancy Pardue and James' wife from Lusby, Maryland. The boys were handcuffed together. John, looking more like a bank executive than a bank robber, wore a gray suit, white button-down collar shirt and gray tie. As usual his black shoes were polished. He looked down at the floor, not speaking as the manacled pair waited for the call to order.

Unlike his brother, James looked like a high school athlete—Levi's, maroon pull-over sweater and badly scuffed suede shoes. He too, stood silently with his head bowed. The brothers made no attempt to look at their wives, who sat without acknowledging their presence or speaking.

Judge Robert Zampano presided and asked the clerk to read aloud the six-count indictment.

"John Russell Pardue, Jr. you are charged with a violation of section 2113, Paragraph A, Sections 2 and 3 of U.S. Code 18. To this charge, how do you plead—guilty or not guilty?"

"Not guilty," John replied, clearing his throat.

The clerk continued, slowly reading the remaining five counts. After each he asked the defendant, "Guilty or not guilty?"

John's reply was the same each time.

"Not guilty."

A court officer led John back to his seat and then summoned James to the stand. Head still bowed, James listened to the same six charges read by the clerk in a monotone. To each, his barely audible reply was the same, "Not guilty."

The proceedings ended 15 minutes later, much as they had started. The boys, handcuffed together, filed out of the chambers without even a smile to reporters or family.

The trial was first set to begin April 20, but a series of legal moves, psychological tests and the first of four escape attempts delayed the actual start until almost one year later.

James was given several psychiatric examinations to determine his stability and capability of standing trial. He was sent to the U.S. Medical Center in Springfield, Missouri, for further testing and then was returned to Connecticut. After six months of psychological examinations by state and federal doctors, a decision was handed down stating that James was schizophrenic and had periods of non-communication and depression. He was remanded to the custody of federal hospital authorities in Missouri, where he remained, except for one short period in a Connecticut prison.

John was not so fortunate. Legal moves cleared the way for him to stand trial, but battles between defense and prosecution delayed the proceeding even further. Taking advantage of these delaying tactics, John plotted the first of his three prison breaks. Wife Nancy, by pre-arrangement, planned to smuggle a .45 caliber Browning automatic pistol and three clips of ammunition into jail. Somehow an unknown intermediary tipped off F.B.I agents, and Nancy was intercepted with the weapon. For her part in the attempt, she was arrested and held in lieu of $50,000 bond.

Months later, John, still determined to cheat the law, offered a $5,000 bribe for his release. That attempt failed, so he raised the ante to $10,000 and again got no takers.

The climax was yet to come, and for John Pardue, it would be his last futile attempt at freedom.

The F.B.I. was still on the case, despite the fact that the Pardues were in custody, and it appeared likely that charges against the brothers for the Danbury job would hold up in court. What the government was after was conviction on all previous counts—the Vista, the Georgetown, the Pacific and the Union, Missouri, bank jobs. Sifting through mounds of evidence, testimony and witness depositions, Thurl Stalnaker and his fellow agents uncovered incriminating links to the multiple robberies that later supported their excellent investigative work.

Thurl called his friend, Sheriff Bill Miller, in Union and asked to have ballistics tests made on the machine gun bullets fired into the Citizens Bank ceiling on May 9, 1969 and the United Bank on November 13. He compared those slugs with several removed from the Vista, New York bank. They matched.

Next, by piecing together the information jotted down by the communications officer at the New York State Police barracks at Somers who had taken the call from "Mr. Fishman" on the August morning in 1968 when Trooper Hilliard had been kidnapped, the agents found several links—bits of the telephone number, the address and the name Fishman. All related to Pardue friends.

Still missing, however, was any hard evidence linking the Pardues to the Georgetown robbery, carried out by the two blacks. Thurl felt strongly that this, too, was a Pardue-related job. The burned bodies of Gregory and Polk had been discovered in April 1969, but positive identification could not be made because they were so badly decomposed. State police took the corpses to Hartford for analysis at their forensic laboratory. Finally, in mid-1971, the identities of the two men were positively established through small pieces of finger and palm prints. The man John Pardue had known as Lee Polk was identified as an army deserter from Tennessee. Dick Gregory was among the names that had been used by a young auto mechanic and part-time entertainer whose family had moved to Connecticut from the south.

Perhaps the toughest job the F.B.I. and Connecticut authorities faced was trying to piece together the ownership of the unidentified white Chrysler station wagon that had been blown to bits in the Danbury shopping mall. All motor serial numbers and other identifying marks had been obliterated, making positive identification nearly impossible. The Union Savings Bank assistant manager Richard Moore had jotted down the license number of the vehicle as it had sped away from the bank's rear parking lot, and he recalled to police the numbers 3825BC, ostensibly New York plates. Investigation disclosed that the tags had been stolen at Kennedy International Airport about a week before the robbery. From illegible bumper stickers and other items from the Chrysler that were sent to the F.B.I. laboratory, the investigators learned a great deal more about the robbery vehicle. The bumper stickers, three well-worn decals overlaid on one another, revealed university markings. One of them bore a number which enabled F.B.I. agents not only to identify it as a University of Maryland parking permit, but also to learn the identity of the student to whom it had been issued.

From this information, F.B.I. agents set about the task of tracing the ownership of the Chrysler station wagon. The University of Maryland student to whom it had belonged had sold it early in 1969. The vehicle had then passed through a series of owners before being purchased by a man who lived in College Park, Maryland. During the first week of February, 1970, this man had sold it to an individual, name unknown, who had responded to a classified ad in a Washington, D.C., newspaper offering the station wagon for sale. The purchaser had paid for it in cash. Although the vehicle had never been registered in his or any other name subsequent to its purchase, investigation strongly pointed to James Pardue as the new owner.

It was now April, 1971, one year, one month, and one day after John and James Pardue had been brought into custody. The scene was U.S. District Court, Bridgeport, Connecticut, and Judge Robert Zampano was preparing to continue the case against John Pardue and his father-and-son defense team, Theodore and Michael Koskoff, and the prosecutors, U.S. attorneys Leslie Byelas and Mac Buckley. These men, along with reporters and a packed gallery, awaited the arrival of the defendant at the fourth floor chambers. It was 10:00 a.m.

Nancy Pardue had left John's jail cell on the third floor moments earlier, a daily visitor's routine she had established after being freed on bond for a previous escape plot a year before.

Waiting in the U.S. Marshal's office outside the block of cells were Danbury Police Chief William Tobin and newly-promoted Detective Lt. Nelson Macedo. They chatted, relaxed, with a couple of deputies.

At 10:12 a.m. U.S. Marshal Anthony Diorenzo, Jr. and his son Anthony III, acting deputy marshal, opened the door that led into the cell block. They were accompanied by federal guard Adolph Scarpa.

As Scarpa unlocked the door to Pardue's cell, John uncovered a sawed off .38 Winchester semi-automatic rifle and leveled it at the elder Diorenzo's belly.

"Turn around slowly, Tony, I'm not kidding."

Young Anthony Diorenzo, partially hidden behind Scarpa and the adjacent cell, acted quickly.

Knowing that John would blow his father away at the slightest provocation, Anthony unsheathed a service revolver from his belt, took quick aim and squeezed off five fast rounds at the prisoner. Two bullets ricocheted off the cell wall, piercing Pardue in the abdomen and chest. Another struck him directly in the left arm. The remaining two shots missed altogether.

John was rocked against the rear wall before he fell to the floor, dropping his rifle without returning fire.

Chief Tobin and Lt. Macedo, along with Thurl Stalnaker, who was also down the hall, rushed to the scene when they heard the muffled popping sound of Diorenzo's .38. As the trio appeared at the open cell, John Pardue was writhing in pain, clutching his chest and calling, "Water, water."

"How the hell did he get that gun?" one of the men yelled, stooping over to retrieve the weapon.

The answer was simple. Nancy Pardue had smuggled it in that morning on her routine visit. She had not been searched, and the 26½-inch rifle, sawed off to the exact dimensions of John's overhead toilet-articles shelf, had sat there for nearly an hour concealed by a towel.

One of the marshals raced back to the office to phone for an ambulance while Stalnaker ran to the elevators. His first thought was of Nancy Pardue, whom he thought would be waiting somewhere nearby—waiting for her husband as he escaped from the downtown jail.

Within minutes Thurl had dispatched all available personnel to search the courthouse, the surrounding parking lots and the alleys within a two-block area. On a hunch, one F.B.I. agent went directly to the local Holiday Inn, a block away, and there, sitting in the couple's 1964 white Corvair, was Nancy Pardue and her 13-month-old daughter. The motor was running and in the car were packed suitcases, a pressed business suit still in the cleaner's plastic bag, rifle ammunition, a passport and a large amount of cash. The agent arrested the young mother and brought her and the child back to the court building.

As they arrived, an ambulance from Park City Hospital screeched to a halt at the court's main entrance and two aides, accompanied by two police officers, unfolded a collapsible stretcher and vanished into the crowd now gathered on the main floor of the building.

Upstairs, still on the floor of his cell, John lay motionless, left arm limp and bleeding, right arm tightly folded over his chest. His face was ashen, eyes gray and blood smears covering his pale cheeks. He looked up at Anthony Diorenzo, who was still with his prisoner, and said, "You know I wouldn't shoot you, Tony."

But those present didn't believe him.

Upstairs in the courtroom, Judge Zampano, who had only minutes before heard of the shooting incident, informed the court of the event and then dismissed the jurors. John Pardue never saw that courtroom again.

At Park City Hospital doctors did what they could to repair John's badly damaged insides. His kidneys, liver and stomach were mangled by bullet splinters. His lungs were filling with fluid, and it was a miracle the young man was still alive. John's athletic body had been well toned by daily calisthenics as he had waited for the trial to begin. He had had a whole year to condition himself.

During the next two weeks, John did little but fight for survival. He was placed on a dialysis machine to keep his kidneys functioning. He couldn't speak because of the lung problem. John, the doctors and Thurl Stalnaker all knew he wouldn't last much longer.

But during those painful, feverish weeks, John wanted to talk about his crime spree—something he hadn't done since being apprehended. He had no one to talk to, no friend to confide in. No one except, ironically, Thurl Stalnaker, the very person who had devoted a major part of his time and talents over a period of months to the capture of John and James Pardue.

At John's request, Thurl visited the hospital on April 21 and by sign language, pencil taps and simple yes and no nods, the older

Pardue brother began recounting the crime spree on which he had embarked in the summer of 1968. The interview continued sporadically over a period of days. John knew he was dying and that police planned to send him back to the Missouri Federal Medical Center for continued treatment and to be with his brother, James.

Each day when Thurl made his hospital visit he had questions ready for the accused bandit. And each day John made his marked answers by scratching on a pad.

Yes, he related, it was he and James who had pulled the Vista, New York bank robbery and who had planned the Georgetown, Connecticut bank heist.

Yes, it was the Pardues who had shot and blown up the Pacific Bank and the Union Courthouse.

And, yes, it was the boys who had killed Polk and Gregory.

Near the end of his interrogation Thurl asked the final question. What had happened to the boys' father and grandmother? John's answer to this was as terse and matter-of-fact as to the other questions. The boys had killed them in Missouri, transported their bodies to Maryland in a utility trailer, and buried them out back, under a shed, on James' rural property.

On April 22, 1971, F.B.I. agents went directly to the spot, broke through the heavy slab of concrete that covered the small utility van, and unearthed the bodies of John Pardue, Sr. and Mrs. Daisy Pardue, the boys' grandmother.

All of the questions now had answers.

On April 28, John was taken to the airport, to be flown in a U.S. Army medical airplane to Springfield, Missouri, and the federal medical center there. Thurl Stalnaker was at his side as the mortally wounded Pardue was lifted into the plane. His was the last friendly face John would see.

During the flight west, he developed severe internal bleeding and further kidney failure. When the plane landed he was rushed to Cox Medical Center near the federal medical prison. There, at 11:40 p.m., John Pardue died, in the state where he had been born. He was only 28 years old.

In June, 1971, Nancy Pardue pleaded guilty to five counts stemming from the April 8 prison break attempt by her late husband. Her sentences totalled 40 years, but the concurrent terms made her eligible for parole in 1974. She served her time at the Federal Reformatory for Women in Alderson, West Virginia.

In September, 1971, James Pardue made an unsuccessful attempt to escape from the correctional center in Connecticut where he was confined for examination to determine his competency to stand trial. Eventually the Federal charges against him were dismissed, and he remained in the custody of Connecticut and Missouri authorities until he was released from a state hospital at Fulton, Missouri, in the spring of 1976.

But by mid-August James Pardue was heard from once again. He and a friend, an ex-convict from California, picked up a woman at a bar near Kansas City and took her to an apartment near the Kansas City International Airport. There the two men reportedly raped her and committed acts of sodomy while intermittently keeping her confined in a coffin-like wooden box.

On September 30, 1976, F.B.I. agents located James and his new compatriot in a suburb of Denver. In addition to the sexual assault charges already placed against them, the pair had also been sought on charges of attempting to rob the First Westland National Bank at Lakewood, Colorado, on September 7. In the latter case, two men dressed in business suits and carrying brief cases had entered the bank and identified themselves as agents of the Colorado Department of Revenue. They had asked to see the bank president and had been led into a lobby conference room. Once inside, one of the men had opened his brief case, displaying a gun. Immediately the president had leaped from his chair and bolted from the room yelling, "Help, call the police." He had raced across the lobby and up a flight of stairs which led to his second floor office.

Just as he disappeared around the corner, the two "revenue agents" had fled toward the front door, firing one shot as they escaped.

As a result of this crime, James Pardue was tried and convicted in the federal court at Denver, and in July, 1977 he was received at the U.S. Penitentiary at Leavenworth, Kansas, to begin serving a 25-year sentence. His accomplice was convicted on state charges and sentenced to the penitentiary at Canon City, Colorado. Thus, for now, James is doing his time, quietly, undisturbed and out of newspaper headlines, while seagulls fly silently over the beaches at Westport.

EPILOGUE

"No matter what you've got and how well you've got it protected, if I want it, I'll get it."

Robert Earl Barnes
professional burglar

Robert Earl Barnes, author of *Are You Safe from Burglars?* (Doubleday, 1971) proved that the above statement is true—his claim to fame is that he has burglarized more than 3,000 victims.

Amil Dinsio, and his compatriots almost succeeded in their elaborate plot because of their training and experience in the use of electronics and explosives. They failed because they made five ludicrous errors.

Joel Singer's plot was so unique that he and his associates probably succeeded due to sheer guts and unnerving perseverance. It is doubtful that such folly could be successfully duplicated.

Harmon Hansen had no particular skills. His dedication to crime was, and may still be, his chosen way of life. He thrived on intrigue, danger and the exhilaration achieved by a good hit.

Only the Pardues were different in their lust for wealth. Their motives and methods were unpredictable. Their meticulously planned and ruthlessly executed operations evolved from daring daylight robberies to the near-terrorist acts of bombings, killings and commando-like tactics of deployment and surprise.

Could these attacks have been avoided? Probably not under the conditions which existed then.

For the most part then, the games thieves play can be categorized as reckoned, premeditated events. Crimes are often shrewdly planned and are usually enacted with cunning. But from the victim's point of view, they are always unforeseen. It is here, in the area of the unpredictable, that bankers and businessmen are most often ill-prepared. It is here too that logical precaution and preparation can best be achieved. It is no longer a matter of if it will happen, but when. Being adequately prepared is simply a matter of survival in an era when crime against person and property is epidemic.

Security practitioners are not so naive as to believe that crime can or will be eliminated or even reduced in the foreseeable future. But if crime levels can be stabilized and kept from escalating any further, then law enforcement agencies, insurance companies, security manufacturers and criminal justice teachers will have time to regroup and organize a unified program of crime prevention and risk management designed for protection of business and citizen alike.

Despite national concern for run-away inflation and a frightening international situation, overall crime ranks third as our nation's most critical problem. In *federal bank* crimes alone, robbery has soared from 257 incidents in 1957 to 6,148 in 1979—an incredible 2292% increase in just 22 years. *Bank burglary,* a more skilled art, increased from 142 to 552 during the same period. The U.S Chamber of Commerce has estimated that burglary and robbery-related crimes in all categories, including financial institutions, industry and the private sector, cost the American taxpayer nearly 40 billion dollars in 1976. The Government Accounting Office issued a statement in April, 1979, estimating that theft-related crimes cost almost $200 billion—nearly $1,000 for every U.S. citizen during 1978. (This estimate includes items stolen, cost of investigation, trial and prosecution, and incarceration of prisoners.)

Whichever figures you choose to believe one fact remains certain; as the security industry's technology and understanding increased over the past 20 years, so did the burglar's. As for alarm systems—of those devices listed by the Underwriters Laboratory and installed in banks, over 95% can be defeated with less than $15 worth of standard hardware store equipment. As fast as electronics devices in alarm systems improve, new underworld techniques are devised to defeat them. This may sound like an indictment against the security industry and, in a way, it is. Not for producing inadequate systems, but for its failure to properly inform and educate users in peripheral safeguards and proper implementation.

Also, it's a tribute to the many military and trade schools in which highly technical subjects are taught so well. On the inside cover of a matchbook, there might appear a message like this: "Get your high school diploma—learn a technical trade at home. Make extra

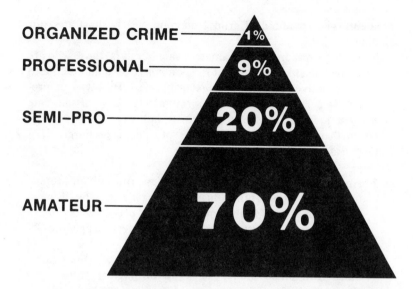

ORGANIZED CRIME ——— 1%

PROFESSIONAL ——— 9%

SEMI–PRO ——— 20%

AMATEUR —— 70%

money in your spare time." These home-study programs frequently offer courses in T.V. repair, electronics and computer programming. All you need to do is mail in the coupon and the school will send you a trial lesson free of charge. In that first lesson, there is often enough basic electronics information (such as Ohms law and how to read resistor values) to defeat most alarm systems currently in service. This is not to suggest that these institutions teach burglary, but that the information they impart could very easily be put to underworld use.

Figures show that the vast majority of free-standing-safe burglaries are accomplished by amateurs and semi-pros, not the so-called professionals. Based on a broad sampling of successful attacks known to have occurred in small businesses, large commercial establishments and all types of financial institutions, the following estimates have been made:

- about 70% of all safe burglaries are perpetrated by amateurs.
- about 20% are by semi-pros.
- about 9% are by professionals.
- about 1% by organized crime.

There is an interesting corollary to the above statistics. The percentage of safe jobs attempted by each category of safe cracker roughly equals the number or volume of jobs they pulled. In other words, nearly 70% of all safe·burglaries are attempted by the amateur. The "pyramid of crime" diagram clearly illustrates this finding.

It stands to reason that the amateur safe burglars, those who are short on technical know-how but long on muscle, would attempt to crack the relatively easy-to-open records safes. This type of fire-resistant safe also represents approximately 70% of all safe equipment manufactured by the security industry.

To further understand the profile of each safe burglar the following description is offered:

1. Amateur—A novice burglar who relies primarily on brute force. One who confines his work to records safes using conventional hand tools to punch, pry or peel the safe door open. Victims are usually small store owners, drug stores, home safes, gas stations, dry cleaners, etc.
2. Semi-Pro—Skilled in the use of power tools. Attempts the more formidable money safes by drilling or torching. Generally works with a partner. May have some knowledge of basic alarms. Marks include supermarkets, jewelry stores, warehouses, racetracks.
3. Professional—Expert in all methods of entry to safes and vaults. Capable of defeating most alarm systems. Tools used may include explosives, core drill, burning bar. Victims are generally the highest risk business establishments: banks, jewelry manufacturers, armored car companies.
4. Organized Crime—Those who plan and organize a selected mark and then hire either a key professional or a trusted gang to do the job. Seldom does the organization gang member ever participate in the actual job.

To graduate from one category to another requires field experience and a degree of education—other than the matchbook variety. Much of this basic training is learned by word of mouth from present or former prison inmates.

There are even underground newspapers and technical publications. One such booklet is called "Guide to Successful Safe Cracking." It contains full scale diagrams of burglary resistive money safe doors, boltwork and locking mechanisms from most major safe manufacturers. The dimensions are surprisingly accurate, and the text provides details for successful penetration. Although there is no price on the jacket, it is known that these photocopy volumes have been sold inside prisons for as much as

$100 each. Another is titled "Lockpickers' Manual." The detail in this volume is also quite accurate. It even includes methods of opening doors with a plastic credit card—a common and widely-used technique. And it's great for a burglar, because a plastic credit card is not usually considered incriminating evidence if it should be found on a suspect.

What can be done to cope with this escalating crime wave? Most important is to create an awareness that the problem exists. If executives can be made to realize that solutions are possible, and that professional security personnel are essential—complete with high level reporting responsibilities—then, and only then can solutions be found. It is a matter of record that less than 20% of all financial institutions—banks, savings and loans, and credit unions, employ a full-time professional security officer. Fewer still have top management reporting accountability.

Only after management fully realizes the seriousness of the problem will it mandate the implementation of controls and training. And training of security personnel as well as all those involved—police, insurance underwriters and security manufacturers, is essential to the development of a coordinated risk management program.

Over the past 20 years the Mosler Anti-Crime Bureau has developed a unique series of training programs designed to teach security practitioners, including police agencies, the vulnerabilities of safes, vaults and alarm systems.

By actual demonstration these nationally conducted seminars show defeat techniques used by the criminal. The demonstrations themselves, performed by extremely knowledgeable but "legal" burglars, are revealing and sometimes even shocking to the uninitiated. For instance, a "punch job," probably the most basic technique used by an amateur, is completed by the technician with a few simple tools in an average of 18 seconds.

The "rip-and-peel" job is also demonstrated in the sessions. It is another kind of amateur entry that became popular during the early days of the so-called "fireproof" safes. Burglars quickly learned that, although the thick walls made the safe look impregnable, once the metal skin was peeled back, access to the contents was a simple matter of chopping through 3 to 6 inches of concrete fill, a material which, when subjected to extreme heat, released moisture to preserve the documents inside.

The purpose of these simple demonstrations is to dramatize the effectiveness (or lack of) of storing cash and valuables in a records safe which was designed specifically for fire protection. By properly keeping cash in a solid steel money safe that is appropriately rated by the Underwriters Laboratory, it is estimated that millions of dollars would be saved. In fact, it might be helpful if owners left their records safes closed, but unlocked, unless there were proprietary documents stored inside. It is the same idea as leaving the cash register open at night to show the burglar that there is nothing of value inside.

Everyone is aware of the fact that burglars use explosives—plastic charges, nitroglycerine, dynamite. Fortunately, the use of these materials has become limited in recent years, probably because of the physical danger involved. But there are far more complicated methods of attack. The core drill, which is sometimes referred to as the ultimate burglar tool because it's safe, quick and sure. Another sophisticated weapon for entry is the burning bar, or oxygen lance. When there is evidence of that kind of equipment, security personnel know that they are dealing with hard-core professionals.

There are two schools of thought on alarm systems. One favors an audible alarm (bell) to scare off the burglars. The other prefers a silent signal that is transmitted to police headquarters or a central station monitor such as ADT (American District Telegraph). Law enforcement people prefer the latter, because it provides an opportunity to apprehend the criminals. In certain high-risk areas, however, both systems may be employed.

There are many kinds of alarm signal transmission systems— open circuit, closed circuit, balanced circuit, supervised line, coded signal, line reversal and the newest and most sophisticated system known as, random digitally coded, interrogate-response alarm. The only materials required to defeat most of them are thin wire, alligator clips, a battery and a few small black boxes—a total expenditure of about $15. A certain amount of risk is involved in attempting to defeat an alarm particularly if the attacker is not sure what type of transmission is being used. In that case he uses the trial and error method, just as Billy Howe did in the "J.J.'s Goldmine" story. Patience is often as necessary as guts in pulling these jobs.

Once clients and the public become aware of the true situation in the field of protection, it is to be hoped that they will take all precautions possible. Companies will create industrial security departments or strengthen already existing ones. Businessmen, especially top executives, will be more careful about what they say and to whom, and make sure that meeting rooms and telephones are "de-bugged." Perhaps most important, firms and private individuals alike will make sure they're as invulnerable to crime as possible. Vulnerability is an engraved invitation to the criminal, whether he is an employee or a professional burglar. Unless it is clear to a potential attacker that all steps necessary for protection have been taken, there is an open invitation to attack.

Our business is to make the attack as difficult for the criminal, as unrewarding, and as costly in time, effort, and fear of exposure as is humanly possible. To consider anything less could prove costly.

It's a matter of survival.